The Mental Health Act 1983

with annotations by

RICHARD M. JONES M.A.
C.Q.S.W., *Solicitor,*
Lecturer in Social Work,
University College, Cardiff

LONDON

SWEET & MAXWELL

1982

Published in 1983 by
Sweet & Maxwell Limited of
11 New Fetter Lane, London,
and printed in Great Britain
by The Eastern Press Limited
of London and Reading

Reprinted 1984

ISBN 0 421 318309

MENTAL HEALTH ACT 1983*

(1983 c.20)

ARRANGEMENT OF SECTIONS

PART I

APPLICATION OF ACT

SECT.

PART II

COMPULSORY ADMISSION TO HOSPITAL AND GUARDIANSHIP

Procedure for hospital admission

Guardianship

General provisions as to applications and recommendations

Position of patients subject to detention or guardianship

Duration of detention or guardianship and discharge

Functions of relatives of patients

* Annotations by Richard M. Jones M.A., C.Q.S.W., Solicitor, Lecturer in the Department of Social Administration and School of Social Work, University College, Cardiff.

PART X

MISCELLANEOUS AND SUPPLEMENTARY

Miscellaneous provisions

Supplemental

An Act to consolidate the law relating to mentally disordered persons.
[9th May 1983]

TABLE OF DERIVATIONS

MENTAL HEALTH ACT 1959

1959	1983	1959	1983	1959	1983
s.1	s.1(1)	s.31(3A)	s.66(1)(*a*),	s.41	s.69
3(1)–(4)	65		(2)(*a*)	(1)–(4)	19
4	1(2)	(4)	66(1)(*b*),	(5)	66(1)(*e*),
(5)	1(3)		(2)(*b*)		(2)(*e*)
5	131	32	15	42	10
10(1)	116	33(2), (3)	7	43	20
20(4)	29	33(4)	ss.7, 11(2)	(6)	66(1)(*f*),
22	115	(5)	11(1),		(2)(*f*)
25	2		(4)–(7), 12	45	21
26(1)–(3)	3	34(1)–(4)	s.8	46	22
(4)	11(6)	(5)	66(1)(*c*),	47	23
27(1)	11(1), (2)		(2)(*c*)	48(2), (3)	25
(1A)	11(3)	(6)	8	(3)	66(1)(*g*),
(2)	11(4)	35	9		(2)(*d*)
(3)	ss.11(5), 12	37	24	49	26
(4)	s.11(7)	(1)	76	50	27
29	4	38	16	51	28
30	5	39	17	52(1)–(5)	29
31(1)	ss.6, 7	(3)	72	(6)	66(1)(*h*),
(2)	s.6	40	18		(2)(*g*)
(3), (5)	6	(4)	145	53	30

MENTAL HEALTH ACT 1959—*continued*

1959	1983	1959	1983	1959	1983
s.54	s.13	s.99	s.123	s.149(3)	s.144
55	31	100(1)–(4)	93	(4)	29
56	32	101	94	(5)	30
57	67	102	95	150	146
(5)	29	103	96	154(2)	149
58	33	103A	97	Sch. 1,	
(3)	29	104	98	para.	
59	34	105	99	1	Sch. 2, para. 1
(1)	145	106	100	2	Sch. 2, para. 2
(2)	79(6)	107	101	3	Sch. 2, para. 3
60	37	108	102	4	Sch. 2, para. 4
(1)	54(1)	109	103	5	Sch. 2, para. 5
62(1)	54(1)	110	104	6	Sch. 2, para. 6
63(1)–(3)	40	111	105	Sch. 3,	
(3A)	69	112	106	columns 1	
(4)	69	113	107	and 2	Sch. 1, Pt. 1
(5)	40	114	108	columns 1	
64	37	115(1)	93	and 3	Sch. 1, Pt. II
65	41	116	109	para. 4	s.72
66(1)–(5)	42	117	110	para. 5	29
67	43	118	111	7	37
68	44	119	112	16	50
70(1), (3)	45	121	113	22	72
71(2)–(4)	46	122	77	69	29
72(1)–(3),		s.123	72	72	40
(5), (6)	47	124	78	Sch. 4,	
(4)	54(1)	125	126	para.	
73	48	129	128	95	145
(3)	54(1)	130	129	Sch. 5	Sch. 3
74	49	131	130	Sch. 6,	
75	50	132	140	para.	
76	51	133	122	9, 10	s.31
(3)	54(1)	135	135	11	33
80	55	136	136	12	34
(5)	79(6)	137	141	13	35
(7)	47	138	142	14	36
81	80	139	137	15	37
85	81	140	138	16(1)	38
87	82	141	139	17	39
89	84	142	124	19	40
90	86	143	125	22	41
92	87	144(1)(*b*)	141	23	42(1),
93	88	145	143		(2), (3)
94	90	147	145	25	43
95	91	147(2)	33	27	45
96	92	148(2)	42(4)	26	44

MENTAL HEALTH SCOTLAND ACT 1960

1960	1983
s.74	s.80
Sch. 4	ss.88, 90, 92, 116, 135

MENTAL HEALTH ACT (NORTHERN IRELAND) 1961

1961	1983
Sch. 5,	
para.	
1	s.81
2	82
3	87
4	88

CRIMINAL PROCEDURE (INSANITY) ACT 1964

1964	1983
s.4(7)	s.51

ADMINISTRATION OF JUSTICE ACT 1965

1965	1983
Sch. 1	s.96

COURTS—MARTIAL APPEALS ACT 1968

1968	1983
Sch. 4	s.46

SOCIAL WORK SCOTLAND ACT 1968

1968	1983
Sch. 8,	
para.	
48	s.116
49	27

FAMILY LAW REFORM ACT 1969

1969	1983
Sch. 1, Pt. 1 ..	ss.26, 28

CHILDREN AND YOUNG PERSONS ACT 1969

1969	1983
Sch. 5,	
para.	
40	s.37

ADMINISTRATION OF JUSTICE ACT 1969

1969	1983
s.17	s.96
18	97
19(1)	101
(2)	110
(3)	112

COURTS ACT 1971

1971	1983
Sch. 8,	
para.	
38	ss.37, 41, 43, 44, 45, 51

IMMIGRATION ACT 1971

1971	1983
s.30	s.86

NATIONAL HEALTH SERVICE SCOTLAND ACT 1972

1972	1983
Sch. 6,	
para.	
102	s.80

LOCAL GOVERNMENT ACT 1972

1972	1983
s.11(3)–(5) ...	s.18
272(2)	125
Sch. 3,	
para.	
67	18
Sch. 23,	
para.	
9	34
(1)	ss.9, 32

1972	1983
Sch. 23,	
para.	
9(2)	ss.7, 8, 10, 11(2), (4), 16, 18, 19, 20, 23, 29, 30, 37, 115, 116, 124, 130, 140
(5)	s.135
(6)	145

GUARDIANSHIP ACT 1973

1973	1983
s.1(8)	s.26

NATIONAL HEALTH SERVICE REORGANISATION ACT 1973

1973	1983
Sch. 4,	
para.	
83	s.65
86	12
87	24
88	23
89	32
90	145
91	ss.47, 54(1)
93	s.140

NORTHERN IRELAND CONSTITUTION ACT 1973

1973	1983
Sch. 5,	
para.	
1	s.28
8	82

NORTHERN IRELAND ACT 1974

1974	1983
Sch. 1	
para.	
1(7)	s.28

NURSING HOMES ACT 1975

1975	1983
Sch. 1	
para.	
1	s.24
2	23
3(a)	145
(b)	34
4	145

NATIONAL HEALTH SERVICE ACT 1977

1977	1983
Sch. 15	
para.	
23	s.65
26	12
27	19
28	145
30	122
31	135
32	124
33	145
34	149

CRIMINAL LAW ACT 1977

1977	1983
s.31(1)	s.129
32	ss.126, 128
Sch. 6	s.129

CHILD CARE ACT 1980

1980	1983
Sch. 5	
para.	
13	s.116
14	27

HEALTH SERVICES ACT 1980

MAGISTRATES COURTS ACT 1980

FORGERY AND COUNTERFEITING ACT 1981

SUPREME COURT ACT 1981

BRITISH NATIONALITY ACT 1981

CRIMINAL JUSTICE ACT 1982

MENTAL HEALTH (AMENDMENT) ACT 1982

MENTAL HEALTH ACT (AMENDMENT) 1982—*continued*

1982	1983
s.39(4)	s.72
(5)	78
(6) ....,	78
(7)	ss.78, 86
40(1)–(6) ...	s.68
41	66(1)(b), (d), (f), 2(b), (d), (f)
42(1)	56
(2), (3) ...	64
43	57
44	58
45	59
46	60
47	61
48	62
49	62
50	56
51	117
52	134
53	118
54	119
55	120
56	121
(1)	Sch. 5, para. 5
57(1)–(4) ...	s.132
58(1), (2) ...	133
59(1)	93
60	139
61(1)	Sch. 5, para. 4
(2), (3) ...	s.114
(4)	Sch. 5, para. 4
63	s.145
64(1)	129
(2)	141
(5)	Sch. 5, para. 4
(6)	ss.128, 145
66	s.143
68(2)	ss.32, 34, 55, 90, 91, 92
(3)(a)	s.1(2), (3)
(b)	77
(c)	126
(d)	128
(e)	129

1982	1983
s.68(3)(f)	s.135
(g)	137
(i)	ss.124, 144
(j)	s.125
69	149
(3)	Sch. 5, para. 5
(4)	ss.89, 118, Sch. 5, para. 4
70(2)	ss.105, 147
(3)	s.149
Sch. 1 para.	
1	79(1), (2), (6)
2	70
3	71
5	73
6	74
7(1)	75
(2)	75
(3)	77
(4)	75
8(1)	78
(2)	Sch. 2, para. 6
9(1)	s.79(1)
(3), (4) .	79(3), (4)
(5), (6) .	71
(7)	79(5)
Sch. 3 para.	
1	ss.4, 5, 11(1), 15
2(a)	s.7
(b)	ss.11(1), (4), (5), (6), (7), 12
3	s.19
4	10
5	23
6	34
8	41
9	42
10	43
11	44
12	46
13	47

1982	1983
Sch. 3—*cont.* para.	
14	48
15	49
17	51
19	80
20	81
21	82
23	138
25	Sch. 1, Pt. I, Pt. II
26(a)	s.34
(b)	37
(c)	39
63	115
64	11(1), (3), (4)
65	4
66	8
68	10
70	30
71	13
72	ss.87, 88, 135, 136
73	s.138
paras.	
75, 76	Sch. 5 para. 4
Sch. 5 para.	
1	Sch. 5 para. 6
2	7
paras.	
3, 4	8
para.	
5	9
6	10
8	14
7	11
9(1), (2) .	15
(3)	20
10	16
11	s.17
12	para. 13
13	s.18
14	19
15	para. 12

Derivations for Statutory Instruments

HEALTH AND PERSONAL SOCIAL SERVICES (NORTHERN IRELAND) ORDER 1972

1972	1983
1972 S.I. No. 1265...	s.86

SUPREME COURT (OFFICERS) (No. 2) ORDER 1982

1972	1983
S.I. 1982 No. 1755 Art. 4(a)...	s.94

GENERAL NOTE

The origins of modern mental health legislation lie with the Mental Health Act 1959 which repealed all existing legislation dealing with mental illness and mental deficiency. It was based on the Report of the Royal Commission on the Law Relating to Mental Illness (Cmnd. 169) and incorporated the principles that no one should be admitted to hospital if care in the community would be more appropriate, and that where admission to hospital was required compulsion which was to be a medical instead of a judicial matter, should if possible be avoided. In January 1975 the Labour Government announced its intention to review the 1959 Act in the light of the many changes which had taken place in treatment and care, in the patterns of services for the mentally disordered, and in public attitudes. An Interdepartmental Committee of civil servants was set up to undertake the review and it considered a number of suggestions for amending the Act including comprehensive reviews which had been carried out by the Royal College of Psychiatrists and by MIND in Vol. 1 of its publication, "A Human Condition." It also considered that part of the "Report of the Committee on Mentally Abnormal Offenders," Cmnd. 6244 (The Butler Report) which reviewed Pt. V of the 1959 Act which was concerned with offenders.

The Committee's suggestions were set out in a consultative document, "A Review of the Mental Health Act 1959" (HMSO, 1976) and comments were invited from interested bodies and individuals. Following the publication of the consultative document two more major contributions to the debate came in the form of the second volume of MIND's, "A Human Condition," on offender patients and the British Association of Social Worker's document, "Mental Health Crisis Services—A New Philosophy."

In 1976 the Government published its response to this consultative exercise in a White Paper, "The Review of the Mental Health Act 1959" (Cmnd. 7320). Some of the proposals in this White Paper were set out in a tentative form because they were either not put forward in the consultative document or were not fully developed at that time. Comments on these proposals were invited but before the Government could translate its proposals into an amending Bill a change of government took place. Further consultations then took place and the Conservative Government's conclusions were embodied in a Bill which was published in November 1981, together with an accompanying White Paper, "Reform of Mental Health Legislation" (Cmnd. 8405). This Bill, which was scrutinised by a Special Standing Committee of the House of Commons, was enacted in October 1982 as the Mental Health (Amendment) Act 1982. It made substantial amendments to the 1959 Act as well as introducing new powers relating to the treatment and discharge of mentally disordered patients. In Cmnd. 8405 the Government announced its intention to introduce a consolidation measure soon after the Royal Assent had been given to the 1982 Act. A Consolidation Bill was introduced in the House of Lords on January 20, 1983. It was referred to the Joint Committee on Consolidation Bills which reported on February 9, 1983 (H.L. 81, H.C. 193). The Bill received the Royal Assent on May 9, 1983.

Although this Act conveniently brings together the law relating to mentally disordered persons the fact that certain provisions of the 1959 Act are not repealed might cause confusion. In particular ss.8 and 9 which deal with the welfare and child care functions of local authorities, and s.128 which is concerned with sexual offences relating to mentally disordered patients will remain in the 1959 Act until consolidated elsewhere. These provisions are to be interpreted by the use of the definitions contained in ss.1 and 145(1) of this Act (Sched. 5 para. 2).

Commencement
Apart from ss.35, 36, 38 and 40(3) this Act will come into force on September 30, 1983 (s.149).

Transitional Provisions
Detailed transitional provisions are set out in Sched. 5. General continuity between the repealed legislation and this Act is provided for in paras. 1 and 3 which specify that periods of time which began under the repealed legislation are to be re-calculated under the corresponding provision of this Act (para. 1) and that anything done under the repealed legislation, *e.g.* detention for treatment under the 1959 Act, does not cease to have effect because of the repeal of that legislation.

Approved Social Workers
Until October 28, 1984 this Act shall have effect as if s.114 were omitted and for any reference to an "approved social worker" there were substituted a reference to a "mental welfare officer" (Sched. 5, para. 4).

Extent
This Act applies to Scotland and Northern Ireland only to the extent provided for in ss.146 and 147, respectively.

ABBREVIATIONS
    In the annotations the following abbreviations are used:
    Butler Committee: Report of the Committee on Mentally Abnormal Offenders (Cmnd.
6244).
    Royal Commission: Report of the Royal Commission on the Law Relating to Mental
Illness and Mental Deficiency 1954–1957, Chairman—Lord Percy (Cmnd. 169).
    The 1959 Act: The Mental Health Act 1959.
    The 1982 Act: The Mental Health (Amendment) Act 1982.
    Consultative Document: A Review of the Mental Health Act 1959 (HMSO, 1976).
    Cmnd. 7320: Review of the Mental Health Act 1959.
    Cmnd. 8405: Reform of Mental Health Legislation.
    Special Standing Committee: The special Standing Committee which considered the
Mental Health (Amendment) Bill.

PARLIAMENTARY DEBATES
    Hansard, H.L. Vol. 437, col. 1533; Vol. 438, col. 519; Vol. 440, cols. 616, 833; Vol. 441,
col. 1049; Vol. 442, col. 342; H.C. Vol. 40, col. 642; Vol. 41, col. 260.

PART I

APPLICATION OF ACT

Application of Act: "mental disorder"

1.—(1) The provisions of this Act shall have effect with respect to the
reception, care and treatment of mentally disordered patients, the management of their property and other related matters.
    (2) In this Act—
        "mental disorder" means mental illness, arrested or incomplete
            development of mind, psychopathic disorder and any other
            disorder or disability of mind and "mentally disordered" shall
            be construed accordingly;
        "severe mental impairment" means a state of arrested or incomplete
            development of mind which includes severe impairment of
            intelligence and social functioning and is associated with abnor-
            mally aggressive or seriously irresponsible conduct on the part
            of the person concerned and "severely mentally impaired" shall
            be construed accordingly;
        "mental impairment" means a state of arrested or incomplete devel-
            opment of mind (not amounting to severe mental impairment)
            which includes significant impairment of intelligence and social
            functioning and is associated with abnormally aggressive or
            seriously irresponsible conduct on the part of the person
            concerned and "mentally impaired" shall be construed
            accordingly;
        "psychopathic disorder" means a persistent disorder or disability of
            mind (whether or not including significant impairment of intel-
            ligence) which results in abnormally aggressive or seriously
            irresponsible conduct on the part of the person concerned;
and other expressions shall have the meanings assigned to them in section
145 below.
    (3) Nothing in subsection (2) above shall be construed as implying that
a person may be dealt with under this Act as suffering from mental
disorder, or from any form of mental disorder described in this section,
by reason only of promiscuity or other immoral conduct, sexual deviancy
or dependence on alcohol or drugs.

DEFINITION
    "Patient": s.145(1)

GENERAL NOTE

Apart from indicating the extent of this Act this section defines the generic term "mental disorder" and sets out three of the four specific categories of mental disorder. The definitions of "severe mental impairment," "mental impairment," and "psychopathic disorder" are remarkably similar in their scope in that all three definitions refer to "abnormally aggressive or seriously irresponsible conduct" and can also include "impairment of intelligence." As Larry Gostin has pointed out, these three definitions "appear to be tautological in that they infer a disease from anti-social behaviour, while purporting to explain that behaviour by a disease" ("A Review of the Mental Health (Amendment) Act" N.L.J., Dec. 2, 1982, p.1127).

Subs. (2)

Mental disorder: More than one of the conditions set out in this definition may affect the patient at any one time. For many of the purposes of this Act a general diagnosis of "mental disorder" is not sufficient and a diagnosis of one of the four specific categories of mental disorder—mental illness, mental impairment, severe mental impairment or psychopathic disorder—is required.

Mental Illness: This category of mental disorder, which accounts for the majority of persons detained in hospital (Cmnd. 8405, para. 11), is not defined in this Act and the question of whether a person is to be placed in this category is therefore entirely a matter for clinical judgment.

The Royal Commission felt that "the term 'mental illness' would be used in the same sense as at present, including the mental infirmity of old age" (Cmnd. 169, para. 17(*a*)). This "lay view" of mental illness has received judicial blessing from Lawton L.J. who, in *W.* v. *L.* [1974] Q.B. 711, 719, C.A., said that the words "mental illness," are, "ordinary words of the English language. They have no particular medical significance. They have no particular legal significance. How should the court construe them? The answer in my judgment is to be found in the evidence which Lord Reid recently gave in *Cozens* v. *Brutus* [1973] A.C. 854, 861, namely, that ordinary words of the English language should be construed in the way that ordinary sensible people would construe them. That being, in my judgment the right test, then I ask myself, what would the ordinary sensible person have said about the patients condition in this case if he had been informed of his behaviour . . .? In my judgment such a person would have said: 'Well, the fellow is obviously mentally ill'. . . . It is that application of the sensible person's assessment of the condition, plus the medical indication [of an E.E.G. test], which in my judgment brought the case within the classification of mental illness." This approach has been described as "the man-must-be-mad" test (Brenda Hoggett *Mental Health* 1976 p.43). The Butler Committee considered that the expression mental illness "denotes a disorder which has not always existed in the patient but has developed as a condition overlying the sufferer's usual personality" (*Butler Report* para. 1.13).

The following attempt by the D.H.S.S. to define mental illness provides a useful guide to the symptoms that are associated with the legal category of "mental illness":

"*Mental illness* means an illness having one or more of the following characteristics:—

(i)   More than temporary impairment of intellectual functions shown by a failure of memory, orientation, comprehension and learning capacity;

(ii) More than temporary alteration of mood of such degree as to give rise to the patient having a delusional appraisal of his situation, his past or his future, or that of others or to the lack of any appraisal;

(iii) Delusional beliefs, persecutory, jealous or grandiose;

(iv) Abnormal perceptions associated with delusional misinterpretation of events;

(v)   Thinking so disordered as to prevent the patient making a reasonable appraisal of his situation or having reasonable communication with others.

The mental illness should be of a nature or degree which warrants the detention of the patient in the interest of his health or safety for the protection of others" (Consultative Document, Appendix II).

Any other disorder or disability of mind: The conditions that will come within this residual category will, to a certain extent, depend upon how broad a view is taken of "mental illness." The Minister of Health, speaking on the Committee stage of the 1959 Act said that the phrase would cover "disabilities arising from head injuries or encephalitis or mental enfeeblement as the aftermath of mental illness." (Standing Committee, February 12, 1959).

Severe mental impairment: The intention behind the definitions of "mental impairment" and "severe mental impairment" is to limit the effect of this Act "on mentally handicapped people to those very few people for whom detention in hospital is essential so that treatment can be provided and for whom detention in prison should be avoided," *per* Lord Elton,

H.L., Vol. 426, col. 533. However, as the definition of "mental disorder" includes those who are suffering from "arrested or incomplete development of mind" which need not necessarily be "associated with abnormally aggressive or seriously irresponsible conduct" most mentally handicapped persons will be liable to be detained under the short term provisions of this Act which do not require a specific diagnosis, *e.g.* admissions for assessment under ss.2 and 4, below.

Includes: What follows is not an exclusive list of attributes associated with this disorder.

Impairment: This term is used by the World Health Organisation in its *International Classification of Impairments, Disabilities and Handicaps* (1979) to describe any loss or abnormality of psychological, physiological or anatomical structure or function. It was criticised by some of the professional bodies which gave evidence to the Special Standing Committee on the ground that it implied a reduction from a higher level of function which does not apply to the majority of cases of mental handicap. MIND expressed its concern that the term mental impairment "brings with it the dangers of prejudice, alienation and rejection."

Social functioning: This phrase appears to cover all aspects of a person's social behaviour.

Is associated with: An amendment by Mr. Christopher Price to insert "recent" after this phrase was defeated by the Special Standing Committee. He was concerned that "is associated with," could be construed as "has been associated with," and that an event of seriously irresponsible or abnormally aggressive conduct that has occurred in the patient's past could be used to satisfy the test of association. The Minister for Health responded to this concern by stating that the definition had the effect of "asking people to determine the current state of the patient when deciding whether to detain him. They should not be asking whether he is being violent at that moment but whether his state of mind makes him liable to be violent or seriously irresponsible unless a detention order is made . . . A patient's past conduct may be highly relevant as evidence . . . for those who must appraise his conduct and state of mind" (sitting of May 11, 1982).

Abnormally aggressive or seriously irresponsible: The use of this phrase which was taken from the definition of psychopathy in the 1959 Act was criticised by a number of witnesses to the Special Standing Committee on the ground that it may result in mentally impaired patients being confused with patients who are suffering from psychopathic disorder. What is "abnormal" or "serious" must, to a certain extent, depend upon the cultural context within which the behaviour occurs.

Mental impairment: The distinction between "severe mental impairment" and "mental impairment" is one of degree in that while the former includes a "*severe* impairment of intelligence and social functioning", the latter includes a "*significant* impairment of intelligence and social functioning." A slight impairment would not be sufficient for either definition. Whether an impairment is considered to be slight, significant or severe is a matter for clinical judgment.

Psychopathic disorder: "Since its introduction more than 90 years ago the term 'psychopathic disorder' has been subject to a variety of different practical usages: it has been taken to cover a narrow or broad group of mental disorders, and to indicate differences either of causation or of clinical manifestation from other mental disorders. In consequence there is now a multiplicity of opinions as to the aetiology, symptoms and treatment of 'psychopathy', which is only to be understood by reference to the particular sense in which the term is being employed by the psychiatrist in question" (*Butler Report*, para. 5.2). Their analysis of the term "psychopathic disorder" led the Butler Committee to conclude that, "it is no longer a useful or meaningful concept" (para. 5.23). The definition used here enables a patient to be diagnosed as a psychopath largely on the basis of the adequacy of his social functioning. Although the definition does not refer to the treatability of the condition the effect of ss.3, 37 and 47 are that psychopathic (and mentally impaired) patients cannot be compulsorily admitted to hospital for treatment unless it can be shown that the medical treatment is likely to alleviate or prevent a deterioration of their condition. It is possible for a patient to be diagnosed as suffering from both mental illness and psychopathic disorder (*W.* v. *L. ibid.*).

Persistent: The disorder must have existed for some time prior to the patient being diagnosed as psychopathic under this Act.

Subs. (3)

Sexual deviancy: "Where a mentally disordered person commits a sexual offence it will of course remain open to the court to consider making a hospital order under [s.37] instead of a penal disposition" (Cmnd. 7320, para. 1.32).

Dependence on alcohol or drugs: This exclusion does not rule out the possibility of a person being detained on the ground of a mental disorder arising from, or suspected to arise from, alcohol or drug dependence or from the withdrawal of alcohol or a drug.

PART II

COMPULSORY ADMISSION TO HOSPITAL AND GUARDIANSHIP

Procedure for hospital admission

Admission for assessment

2.—(1) A patient may be admitted to a hospital and detained there for the period allowed by subsection (4) below in pursuance of an application (in this Act referred to as "an application for admission for assessment") made in accordance with subsections (2) and (3) below.

(2) An application for admission for assessment may be made in respect of a patient on the grounds that—

(*a*) he is suffering from mental disorder of a nature or degree which warrants the detention of the patient in a hospital for assessment (or for assessment followed by medical treatment) for at least a limited period; and

(*b*) he ought to be so detained in the interests of his own health or safety or with a view to the protection of other persons.

(3) An application for admission for assessment shall be founded on the written recommendations in the prescribed form of two registered medical practitioners, including in each case a statement that in the opinion of the practitioner the conditions set out in subsection (2) above are complied with.

(4) Subject to the provisions of section 29(4) below, a patient admitted to hospital in pursuance of an application for admission for assessment may be detained for a period not exceeding 28 days beginning with the day on which he is admitted, but shall not be detained after the expiration of that period unless before it has expired he has become liable to be detained by virtue of a subsequent application, order or direction under the following provisions of this Act.

DEFINITIONS
"Patient": s.145(1)
"Hospital": ss.34(2), 145(1)
"Mental disorder": ss.1, 145(1)
"Medical treatment": s.145(1)

GENERAL NOTE
This section authorises compulsory admission to hospital for assessment (or for assessment followed by treatment), and for detention for this purpose for up to 28 days. If, after the 28 days have elapsed, the patient is to remain in hospital, he must do so either as an informal patient or be detained for treatment under s.3, below, if the conditions of that section are satisfied. There is some evidence that applications have been renewed at the expiration of the 28 day period (*see*, Cmnd. 7320, para. 2.18); this practice is illegal as this section does not provide for renewal.

An order for the patient's discharge can be made at any time prior to the expiration of the 28 day period by his responsible medical officer, the hospital managers or, subject to s.25, below, his nearest relative (s.23(2)(*a*)). The patient can seek to obtain his own discharge by making an application to a Mental Health Review Tribunal within 14 days of his admission (s.66(1)(*a*), 2(*a*)).

Subs. (1)
Application: An application under this section can be made by either the patient's nearest relative or by an approved social worker (s.11(1)). If the applicant is an approved social worker he must inform the nearest relative that the application is to be or has been made (s.11(3)). The patient's nearest relative cannot prevent an approved social worker making an application. The applicant must have seen the patient within the previous 14 days (s.11(5)) and the patient must be admitted to hospital within 14 days of the time when he was last medically examined prior to the recommendations required by subs. (3) being made

(s.6(1)(*a*)). It is possible to make an application in respect of a person who is already receiving hospital treatment as an in-patient on an informal basis (s.5). An application for the admission of a ward of court cannot be made without the leave of the High Court (s.33(1)).

For applications for admission for assessment in cases of emergency, see s.4, below.

Subs. (2)

Mental Disorder: A specific diagnosis is not required.

Warrants the detention of the patient: It is not possible to detain a patient under this section merely because he is seen to need assessment as the conditions of para. (*b*) must also be satisfied.

Assessment followed by medical treatment: Treatment under this section need not be confined to treatment which is an inherent part of the assessment process. Patients detained under this section are subject to the consent to treatment provisions contained in Pt. IV of this Act.

Protection of other persons: It is submitted that "protection" is not limited to protection from physical harm, but could include protection from emotional strain.

Subs. (3)

Written recommendations: Made either separately or jointly (s.11(7)).

Two registered medical practitioners: Complying with the provisions of s.12, below.

Subs. (4)

Not exceeding 28 days: The patient can cease to be liable to be detained before the 28 days expire if an order for his discharge is made under s.23, below.

Beginning with: Including the day on which the patient was admitted (*Hare* v. *Gocher* [1962] 2 Q.B. 641).

Admission for treatment

3.—(1) A patient may be admitted to a hospital and detained there for the period allowed by the following provisions of this Act in pursuance of an application (in this Act referred to as "an application for admission for treatment") made in accordance with this section.

(2) An application for admission for treatment may be made in respect of a patient on the grounds that—

    (*a*) he is suffering from mental illness, severe mental impairment, psychopathic disorder or mental impairment and his mental disorder is of a nature or degree which makes it appropriate for him to receive medical treatment in a hospital; and

    (*b*) in the case of psychopathic disorder or mental impairment, such treatment is likely to alleviate or prevent a deterioration of his condition; and

    (*c*) it is necessary for the health or safety of the patient or for the protection of other persons that he should receive such treatment and it cannot be provided unless he is detained under this section.

(3) An application for admission for treatment shall be founded on the written recommendations in the prescribed form of two registered medical practitioners, including in each case a statement that in the opinion of the practitioner the conditions set out in subsection (2) above are complied with; and each such recommendation shall include—

    (*a*) such particulars as may be prescribed of the grounds for that opinion so far as it relates to the conditions set out in paragraphs (*a*) and (*b*) of that subsection; and

    (*b*) a statement of the reasons for that opinion so far as it relates to the conditions set out in paragraph (*c*) of that subsection, specifying whether other methods of dealing with the patient are available and, if so, why they are not appropriate.

DEFINITIONS

    "Patient": s.145(1).

    "Hospital": ss.34(2), 145(1).

"Severe mental impairment": ss.1, 145(1).
"Psychopathic disorder": ss.1, 145(1).
"Mental impairment": ss.1, 145(1).
"Mental disorder": ss.1, 145(1).
"Medical treatment": s.145(1).

GENERAL NOTE

This section provides for the compulsory admission of a patient to hospital for treatment and for his subsequent detention, which can last for an initial period of up to six months (s.20(1)). Patients admitted under this section are subject to the consent to treatment provisions contained in Pt. IV of this Act.

An order for the patient's discharge can be made by his responsible medical officer, the hospital managers or, subject to s.25, below, his nearest relative (s.23(2)(*a*)). A patient can seek to obtain his own discharge by making an application to a Mental Health Review Tribunal (s.66(1)(*a*), (2)(*b*)) and in certain circumstances the patient will have his case automatically referred to a Tribunal (s.68). The authority to detain a patient under this section can be renewed (s.20(2)).

If a patient who has been detained under this section ceases to be so detained and leaves hospital, he has to be provided with after-care services (s.117).

Subs. (1)

The period allowed: An initial period of six months renewable for a further six months and thereafter renewable at yearly intervals (s.20(1)(2)). It is possible for the patient to be granted leave of absence from hospital under s.17, below.

Application: An application can be made by either the patient's nearest relative or by an approved social worker (s.11(1)). If an approved social worker makes the application he must consult with the patient's nearest relative if this is practicable and he cannot proceed with the application if the nearest relative objects (s.11(4)). The applicant must have seen the patient within the previous 14 days (s.11(5)) and the patient must be admitted to hospital within 14 days of the time when he was last medically examined prior to the recommendations required by subs. (3) being made (s.6(1)(*a*)). It is possible to make an application in respect of a person who is already receiving hospital treatment as an in-patient on an informal basis (s.5). An application for the admission of a ward of court cannot be made without the leave of the High Court (s.33(1)).

Subs. (2)

Suffering from: A patient who is suffering from "any other disorder or disability of mind" (see the definition of mental disorder in s.1(2), above) cannot be detained under this section.

Para. (a): Appropriate for him to receive medical treatment in a hospital: And not in the community or under guardianship. Note that this requirement can be satisfied even though it is considered that the patient might not obtain any benefit from the treatment. "Medical treatment" is given a very wide definition by s.145(1), below.

Para. (b): The suggestion in the Consultative Document that the "treatability test" set out in this para. might apply to all four categories of mental disorder was rejected because "there is a possibility that such a requirement would preclude the compulsory admission of some severely [mentally impaired] people or of mentally ill persons suffering from illnesses who are unlikely to benefit from treatment in the sense that their condition may not improve; these people might nevertheless need to be admitted on occasions, for example, to tide them over a crisis" (Cmnd. 7320, para. 2.40).

Although a patient who is suffering from mental illness or severe mental impairment does not have to satisfy the "treatability test" on admission, the authority to detain such a patient can only be renewed if his responsible medical officer certifies either: (a), that treatment is likely to alleviate or prevent a deterioration of his condition, or, (b), that if discharged he would be unlikely to be able to cope for himself, to obtain the care which he needs or to guard himself against serious exploitation (s.20(3)(4)). If a patient who is suffering from mental illness or severe mental impairment is reclassified to the effect that he is suffering from psychopathic disorder or mental impairment the authority to detain the patient ceases unless his responsible medical officer certifies that the "treatability test" is satisfied (s.16(2)).

Alleviate: But not necessarily cure the patient's disorder.

Para. (c): *Necessary:* A stronger term than "ought" in s.2(2)(*b*), above.

Protection: See the note on s.2(2)(*b*), above.

And that it cannot be provided: By, for example, a voluntary admission.

Subs. (3)

Written recommendations: Made either separately or jointly (s.11(7)).

Two registered medical practitioners: Complying with the provisions of s.12, below.

Admission for assessment in cases of emergency

4.—(1) In any case of urgent necessity, an application for admission for assessment may be made in respect of a patient in accordance with the following provisions of this section, and any application so made is in this Act referred to as "an emergency application".

(2) An emergency application may be made either by an approved social worker or by the nearest relative of the patient; and every such application shall include a statement that it is of urgent necessity for the patient to be admitted and detained under section 2 above, and that compliance with the provisions of this Part of this Act relating to applications under that section would involve undesirable delay.

(3) An emergency application shall be sufficient in the first instance if founded on one of the medical recommendations required by section 2 above, given, if practicable, by a practitioner who has previous acquaintance with the patient and otherwise complying with the requirements of section 12 below so far as applicable to a single recommendation, and verifying the statement referred to in subsection (2) above.

(4) An emergency application shall cease to have effect on the expiration of a period of 72 hours from the time when the patient is admitted to the hospital unless—

(*a*) the second medical recommendation required by section 2 above is given and received by the managers within that period; and

(*b*) that recommendation and the recommendation referred to in subsection (3) above together comply with all the requirements of section 12 below (other than the requirement as to the time of signature of the second recommendation).

(5) In relation to an emergency application, section 11 below shall have effect as if in subsection (5) of that section for the words "the period of 14 days ending with the date of the application" there were substituted the words "the previous 24 hours".

DEFINITIONS

"Application for admission for assessment": ss.2, 145(1).

"Patient": s.145(1).

"Approved social worker": s.145(1).

"Nearest relative": ss.26(3), 145(1).

"Hospital": ss.34(2), 145(1).

GENERAL NOTE

This section provides, in a case of urgent necessity, for the compulsory admission of a person to hospital for assessment for a period of up to 72 hours. The Royal Commission expected this procedure to be used only in exceptional circumstances: "It is important that the emergency procedure should not be used except in real emergencies when action to remove the patient must be taken before there is time to obtain the two medical recommendations required under the normal procedure [*i.e.* admission under s.2]" (Cmnd. 169, para. 409). The emergency procedure has been used far more frequently than the Royal Commission envisaged, and it has become the most widely used form of compulsory admission. This situation has caused concern and as long ago as 1966, the Ministry of Health instituted an inquiry to try and establish why the procedure was being used so frequently. That enquiry found, *inter alia*, that, (1) many medical and social work professionals were largely ignorant of the relevant legislative provisions; (2) those involved in compulsory admissions considered that the emergency procedure, being quicker, easier and of shorter duration than the normal procedure was a more humane method of admitting formally; and (3) the emergency procedure was more administratively convenient than the normal procedure. In 1974 the Hospital Advisory Service added its voice to the disquiet that was being expressed about the emergency procedure, and in 1976 the Royal College of

Psychiatrists said that the advantages of the emergency procedure had "led to misuse and abuse in some areas" (see further, Consultative Document, para. 2.7 *et seq.*).

Most of the criticism of the emergency procedure has been based upon the frequency of its use but, as Philip Bean has pointed out, one cannot say that the emergency procedure is being misused because there is a high percentage of admissions under this procedure because "it may be that the high percentage of admissions reflects a psychiatric reality, *i.e.* that there are a large number of emergencies which required short-term admissions," *Compulsory Admissions to Mental Hospitals* 1980, p.69. However, the fact that there have been large regional variations in the use that has been made of the emergency procedure does suggest that the procedure has been used inappropriately on many occasions.

An application under this section cannot be renewed at the end of the 72 hour period. If compulsory detention is to be continued the application must either be "converted" into a s.2 application under the provisions of subs. (4), in which case the patient can be detained for 28 days beginning with the date of his admission, or an application for treatment should be made under s.3, above.

Patients admitted under this section are *not* subject to the consent to treatment provisions contained in Pt. IV of this Act.

Subs. (1)

Application: The applicant must have seen the patient within the previous 24 hours (s.11(5) and subs. (5), below) and the patient must be admitted to hospital within 24 hours beginning from the time when he was medically examined or when the application was made, whichever is the earlier (s.6(1)(*b*). These time limits were introduced by the 1982 Act to help "to prevent [this section] being used for cases other than those of real emergency" (Cmnd. 7320, para. 2.6). An application for the admission of a ward of court cannot be made without the leave of the High Court (s.33(1)).

Subs. (2)

Urgent necessity . . . undesirable delay: These terms, which are not defined, are linked, in that the urgency of the situation must be such that the delay in obtaining the second medical recommendation required by s.2 would be undesirable bearing in mind the patient's condition. The delay involved in obtaining a second medical recommendation could depend, *inter alia*, on local geography, the administrative procedures adopted locally to respond to crises, or on the hour at which the crisis occurs. If an approved social worker is unable to persuade an "approved" medical practitioner to visit the patient with a view to making an application under s.2, above, an application under this section should not automatically follow as the social worker would need to be satisfied that it is "necessary or proper" for the application to be made (see, s.13(1), below). If approved social workers consider that they are being forced to make inappropriate use of this section because of difficulties in obtaining the second medical recommendation required by s.2, it is submitted that they should try to resolve the difficulty at local level or, if this turns out to be unproductive, inform the Mental Health Act Commission which is required to keep this Act under review (see s.121(2)(*b*), below).

N.B. It is difficult to envisage a nearest relative applicant being aware of the distinction between an application made under this section and an application made under s.2, above.

If practicable: If the recommending doctor has not had previous acquaintance with the patient, it is suggested that he should attempt to consult with the patient's general practitioner before he signs the recommendation.

Subs. (4)

Period of 72 hours: If the application is "converted" into a s.2 application under this subsection, the 28 day period provided for in s.2 will run from the time of the patient's admission to hospital under this section.

Hospital: Local social services authorities must be informed of those hospitals where arrangements are in force for the reception, in cases of special urgency, of patients requiring treatment for mental disorder (s.140).

Application in respect of patient already in hospital

5.—(1) An application for the admission of a patient to a hospital may be made under this Part of this Act notwithstanding that the patient is already an in-patient in that hospital or, in the case of an application for admission for treatment that the patient is for the time being liable to be detained in the hospital in pursuance of an application for admission for assessment; and where an application is so made the patient shall be treated for the purposes of this Part of this Act as if he had been admitted to the hospital at the time when that application was received by the managers.

(2) If, in the case of a patient who is an in-patient in a hospital, it appears to the registered medical practitioner in charge of the treatment of the patient that an application ought to be made under this Part of this Act for the admission of the patient to hospital, he may furnish to the managers a report in writing to that effect; and in any such case the patient may be detained in the hospital for a period of 72 hours from the time when the report is so furnished.

(3) The registered medical practitioner in charge of the treatment of a patient in a hospital may nominate one (but not more than one) other registered medical practitioner on the staff of that hospital to act for him under subsection (2) above in his absence.

(4) If, in the case of a patient who is receiving treatment for mental disorder as an in-patient in a hospital, it appears to a nurse of the prescribed class—

(*a*) that the patient is suffering from mental disorder to such a degree that it is necessary for his health or safety or for the protection of others for him to be immediately restrained from leaving the hospital; and

(*b*) that it is not practicable to secure the immediate attendance of a practitioner for the purpose of furnishing a report under subsection (2) above,

the nurse may record that fact in writing; and in that event the patient may be detained in the hospital for a period of six hours from the time when that fact is so recorded or until the earlier arrival at the place where the patient is detained of a practitioner having power to furnish a report under that subsection.

(5) A record made under subsection (4) above shall be delivered by the nurse (or by a person authorised by the nurse in that behalf) to the managers of the hospital as soon as possible after it is made; and where a record is made under that subsection the period mentioned in subsection (2) above shall begin at the time when it is made.

(6) The reference in subsection (1) above to an in-patient does not include an in-patient who is liable to be detained in pursuance of an application under this Part of this Act and the references in subsections (2) and (4) above do not include an in-patient who is liable to be detained in a hospital under this Part of this Act.

(7) In subsection (4) above "prescribed" means prescribed by an order made by the Secretary of State.

DEFINITIONS
　"Patient": s.145(1).
　"Hospital": ss.34(2), 145(1).
　"Application for admission for treatment": ss.3, 145(1).
　"Application for admission for assessment": ss.2, 145(1).
　"The managers": s.145(1).
　"Mental disorder": s.145(1).

GENERAL NOTE
　This section provides for applications for compulsory detention under ss.2 or 3 of this Act to be made in respect of mentally disordered patients who are already receiving treatment in hospital. It also sets out the procedures that can be used if it is considered that a patient might leave the hospital before there is time to complete an application under ss.2 or 3.

Subs. (1)

In-patient: Apart from the power to make an application for treatment in respect of a patient who is already compulsorily detained for assessment, this subsection does not provide authority for applications to be made in respect of patients who are already in hospital under compulsory powers (subs. (6)).

Subs. (2)

This subsection enables an informal patient to be detained for up to 72 hours if the doctor in charge of his treatment reports that an application for "admission" ought to be made. This power cannot be used in respect of a patient who is liable to be detained in a hospital under this Part (subs. (6)).

In-patient in a hospital: The patient could be receiving treatment in a general hospital for a physical condition.

Medical practitioner in charge: In most cases this will be the consultant psychiatrist on the staff of the hospital under whose care the patient has been admitted. However, determining the "medical practitioner in charge" is a question of fact, and he need not necessarily have consultant status or even be a psychiatrist. Subject to subs. (3), below, the power to furnish a report under this subsection cannot be delegated.

An application ought to be made: There is no requirement for the medical practitioner to certify *why* he considers an application ought to be made.

72 hours: This is the maximum period during which a patient can be detained under this subsection.

Subs. (3)

This subsection was introduced by the 1982 Act to lessen the pressures on medical practitioners to contravene the provisions of subs. (2) by, for example, allowing persons other than the "medical practitioner in charge", such as a night duty doctor, to sign the relevant form or by the consultant signing a number of blank forms for use when emergencies occurred. Only the "medical practitioner in charge" or his nominated deputy have authority to detain a patient under subs. (2).

To act for him: The nominated doctor should exercise his own judgment when exercising his powers under subs. (2).

Subs. (4)

This subsection provides for nurses of a prescribed class to invoke a "holding power" in respect of a patient for a period of not more than six hours. During this period the "medical practitioner in charge" or his nominated deputy would consider whether a report under subs. (2) should be made. This power should end the uncertainty that nursing staff have felt about their legal position when restraining informal patients. Action to prevent a patient from causing injury to others is allowed for by s.3(1) of the Criminal Law Act 1967 which permits reasonable force to be used in the prevention of crime. There is also a common law defence available to staff who act to prevent violence, to save life or in self-defence. However, there may be occasions where violence has not yet arisen, but staff have good reason to believe that it is likely to do so or where the behaviour of an informal patient requires physical control and he clearly should not be allowed to leave hospital. This subsection empowers nursing staff to detain a patient in these circumstances.

Receiving treatment for mental disorder: This power can only be used against patients who have already been receiving hospital treatment for mental disorder on a voluntary basis (subs. (6)).

Prescribed class: See subs. (7).

Record: Regulations under s.32 below, will prescribe the form in which the record should be made.

Six hours: This is the maximum, and non-renewable, period during which a patient can be detained.

From the time when that fact is so recorded: The record should be made immediately after the nurse has decided to exercise his "holding power." The power will end six hours later or on the earlier arrival of one of the two doctors entitled to make a report under subs. (2). If that doctor decides not to exercise his powers under subs. (2), the patient can either leave the hospital or remain as a voluntary patient.

Subs. (5)

This subsection provides that where the "holding power" provided for in subs. (4) is followed by a report made under subs. (2), the period of 72 hours provided for in that subsection runs from the time when the record required by subs. (4) is made.

Effect of application for admission

6.—(1) An application for the admission of a patient to a hospital under this Part of this Act, duly completed in accordance with the provisions of this Part of this Act, shall be sufficient authority for the applicant, or any person authorised by the applicant, to take the patient and convey him to the hospital at any time within the following period, that is to say—

(*a*) in the case of an application other than an emergency application, the period of 14 days beginning with the date on which the patient was last examined by a registered medical practitioner before giving a medical recommendation for the purposes of the application;

(*b*) in the case of an emergency application, the period of 24 hours beginning at the time when the patient was examined by the practitioner giving the medical recommendation which is referred to in section 4(3) above, or at the time when the application is made, whichever is the earlier.

(2) Where a patient is admitted within the said period to the hospital specified in such an application as is mentioned in subsection (1) above, or, being within that hospital, is treated by virtue of section 5 above as if he had been so admitted, the application shall be sufficient authority for the managers to detain the patient in the hospital in accordance with the provisions of this Act.

(3) Any application for the admission of a patient under this Part of this Act which appears to be duly made and to be founded on the necessary medical recommendations may be acted upon without further proof of the signature or qualification of the person by whom the application or any such medical recommendation is made or given or of any matter of fact or opinion stated in it.

(4) Where a patient is admitted to a hospital in pursuance of an application for admission for treatment, any previous application under this Part of this Act by virtue of which he was liable to be detained in a hospital or subject to guardianship shall cease to have effect.

DEFINITIONS
"Patient": s.145(1).
"Hospital": ss.34(2), 145(1).
"The managers": s.145(1).
"Application for admission for treatment": ss.3, 145(1).

GENERAL NOTE
This section authorises the applicant or anyone authorised by him to take the patient and convey him to hospital within specified periods, and authorises the hospital managers to detain the patient once he has been admitted. Health authorities, who have a duty to provide an ambulance service, must transport the patient to hospital if this proves to be necessary.

Subs. (1)
Duly completed: Note that by virtue of section 15, below, it is possible to amend incorrect or defective applications and medical recommendations.
Applicant: Who will be the patient's nearest relative or an approved social worker (ss.4(2), 11(1)).
Any person authorised by the applicant: Such as a member of the ambulance service.
To take the patient: If an application is not duly completed there is no authority, for an approved social worker, medical practitioner or other authorised person to enter a person's home for the purpose of taking him and conveying him to hospital. Such persons would be trespassers and the householder would be entitled to use reasonable force in ejecting them; see *Townley* v. *Rushworth,* 62 L.G.R. 95, D.C. where an attempt was made to detain a patient on an emergency application before the medical recommendation had been completed. A duly completed application does not provide authority for the applicant to force his way into the patient's home. If force is required an approved social worker should apply for a warrant under s.135, below.

Convey him to hospital: An applicant who conveys a patient to hospital has all the powers that a policeman has when taking a person into custody (s.137(2)). A patient who is being conveyed to hospital is deemed to be in legal custody (s.137(1)) and he may be retaken if he escapes (s.138).

Beginning with the date: Including the date on which the patient was last examined (*Hare* v. *Gocher* [1962] 2 Q.B. 641).

Subs. (3)

Appears to be duly made: After reasonable care has been taken to scrutinise the application.

Guardianship

Application for guardianship

7.—(1) A patient who has attained the age of 16 years may be received into guardianship, for the period allowed by the following provisions of this Act, in pursuance of an application (in this Act referred to as "a guardianship application") made in accordance with this section.

(2) A guardianship application may be made in respect of a patient on the grounds that—

(*a*) he is suffering from mental disorder, being mental illness, severe mental impairment, psychopathic disorder or mental impairment and his mental disorder is of a nature or degree which warrants his reception into guardianship under this section; and

(*b*) it is necessary in the interests of the welfare of the patient or for the protection of other persons that the patient should be so received.

(3) A guardianship application shall be founded on the written recommendations in the prescribed form of two registered medical practitioners, including in each case a statement that in the opinion of the practitioner the conditions set out in subsection (2) above are complied with; and each such recommendation shall include—

(*a*) such particulars as may be prescribed of the grounds for that opinion so far as it relates to the conditions set out in paragraph (*a*) of that subsection; and

(*b*) a statement of the reasons for that opinion so far as it relates to the conditions set out in paragraph (*b*) of that subsection.

(4) A guardianship application shall state the age of the patient or, if his exact age is not known to the applicant, shall state (if it be the fact) that the patient is believed to have attained the age of 16 years.

(5) The person named as guardian in a guardianship application may be either a local social services authority or any other person (including the applicant himself); but a guardianship application in which a person other than a local social services authority is named as guardian shall be of no effect unless it is accepted on behalf of that person by the local social services authority for the area in which he resides, and shall be accompanied by a statement in writing by that person that he is willing to act as guardian.

DEFINITIONS

"Patient": s.145(1).
"Mental disorder": ss.1, 145(1).
"Severe mental impairment": ss.1, 145(1).
"Psychopathic disorder": ss.1, 145(1).
"Local social services authority": s.145(1).

GENERAL NOTE

The guardianship powers in this Act are largely based on recommendations made by the Royal Commission (Cmnd. 169, paras, 387, 399, 400, 411). The "Commission argued that care outside hospital should usually be on the basis of persuasion to accept help and advice and take advantage of arrangements for employment and training. However, the Commission recommended that where a person's unwillingness to receive training or social help could not be overcome by persuasion it would be appropriate to place him under guardianship if this offered the prospect of success. The Commission suggested that care under guardianship might be more appropriate for some people, particularly those with mild or chronic forms of mental illness, than compulsory admission to or continued detention in hospital. . . . The use of guardianship powers has declined steadily since their introduction and practice varies considerably between local authorities. The Royal Commission expected that as community psychiatric services developed guardianship would become more frequent, but this hope has not been borne out. Nor has their hope that guardianship would be used for the mentally ill and psychopaths. In practice, guardianship has been used predominantly for the mentally handicapped and the severely mentally handicapped and only very rarely for the mentally ill" (Cmnd. 7320, paras. 4.5, 4.7).

The present Government's view is that guardianship powers are needed for "a very small number of mentally disordered people who do not require treatment in hospital, either formally or informally, [but who] nevertheless need close supervision and some control in the community as a consequence of their mental disorder. These include people who are able to cope provided that they take their medication regularly, but who fail to do so, and those who neglect themselves to the point of seriously endangering their health" (Cmnd. 8405, para. 43).

Although the Royal College of Psychiatrists, MIND and the Butler Committee have all said that more use could be made of guardianship as an alternative to hospital treatment, it is difficult to see how this will be achieved in the absence of additional resources and a substantial professional commitment to view guardianship as a positive means of assisting mentally disordered persons in the community.

As a patient under guardianship is not "liable to be detained" for the purposes of s.56(1), below, he is not subject to the consent to treatment provisions contained in Pt. IV of the Act.

A patient shall cease to be subject to guardianship if an order for his discharge is made by his responsible medical officer, by the responsible local social services authority or by his nearest relative (s.23(2)(*b*)). A patient can attempt to seek his own discharge from guardianship by making an application to a Mental Health Review Tribunal under s.66(1)(*c*), below.

This section specifies the circumstances whereby a patient aged 16 or over may be received into the guardianship of a local social services authority or a person who is acceptable to the authority.

Subs. (1)

Attained the age: At the commencement of his sixteenth birthday (Family Law Reform Act 1969, s.9(1)). Where on September 30, 1983 a person who is not yet 16 years old is subject to guardianship, the authority for his guardianship shall terminate on that day (s.148(1), Sched. 5, para. 8(1)). Note that it might be possible to bring proceedings under s.1 of the Children and Young Persons Act 1969 in respect of a child under 16 who requires supervision and control in the community as a consequence of mental disorder.

Period allowed: Is set out in section 20, below.

An application: An application cannot be made in respect of a ward of court without the consent of the High Court (s.33(3)).

Subs. (2)

A guardianship application may be made: By either the patient's nearest relative or by an approved social worker (s.11(1)). An approved social worker cannot make an application if the nearest relative objects (s.11(4)). The application must either be sent to the local social services authority named as guardian or to the social services authority for the area in which the individual named as guardian resides (s.11(2)).

Interests of the welfare of the patient: All factors which might affect the future well-being of the patient would be relevant.

Subs. (3)

Written recommendations: Made either separately or jointly (s.11(7)).

Two registered medical practitioners: Complying with the provisions of s.12, below.

Subs. (5)

This subsection provides for the guardian to be either a local social services authority or a person who is accepted by the authority to act in that capacity.

Guardian: Note that although the guardian can require the patient to attend for medical treatment (s.8(1)(*b*)), he cannot make him accept the treatment.

Resides: Temporary absences from the place where a person lives does not affect residence, as long as there is an intention to return (*R.* v. *St. Leonard's Shoreditch (Inhabitants),* (1865) L.R. 1 Q.B. 21).

Effect of guardianship application, etc.

8.—(1) Where a guardianship application, duly made under the provisions of this Part of this Act and forwarded to the local social services authority within the period allowed by subsection (2) below is accepted by that authority, the application shall, subject to regulations made by the Secretary of State, confer on the authority or person named in the application as guardian, to the exclusion of any other person—

(*a*) the power to require the patient to reside at a place specified by the authority or person named as guardian;

(*b*) the power to require the patient to attend at places and times so specified for the purpose of medical treatment, occupation, education or training;

(*c*) the power to require access to the patient to be given, at any place where the patient is residing, to any registered medical practitioner, approved social worker or other person so specified.

(2) The period within which a guardianship application is required for the purposes of this section to be forwarded to the local social services authority is the period of 14 days beginning with the date on which the patient was last examined by a registered medical practitioner before giving a medical recommendation for the purposes of the application.

(3) A guardianship application which appears to be duly made and to be founded on the necessary medical recommendations may be acted upon without further proof of the signature or qualification of the person by whom the application or any such medical recommendation is made or given, or of any matter of fact or opinion stated in the application.

(4) If within the period of 14 days beginning with the day on which a guardianship application has been accepted by the local social services authority the application, or any medical recommendation given for the purposes of the application, is found to be in any respect incorrect or defective, the application or recommendation may, within that period and with the consent of that authority, be amended by the person by whom it was signed; and upon such amendment being made the application or recommendation shall have effect and shall be deemed to have had effect as if it had been originally made as so amended.

(5) Where a patient is received into guardianship in pursuance of a guardianship application, any previous application under this Part of this Act by virtue of which he was subject to guardianship or liable to be detained in a hospital shall cease to have effect.

DEFINITIONS
   "Local social services authority": s.145(1).
   "Medical treatment": s.145(1).
   "Patient": s.145(1).
   "Approved social worker": s.145(1).
   "Hospital": s.145(1).

TRANSITIONAL PROVISIONS
   Sched. 5, para. 8(2).

GENERAL NOTE
   This section confers specific powers on the local social services authority or on the person named in the guardianship application as guardian. The 1959 Act gave the guardian the power that a father has over a child of 14. These powers were therefore very wide, as well

as being somewhat ill-defined, and it was felt that they were out of keeping, in their paternalistic approach, with modern attitudes to the care of the mentally disordered. Subs. (1) replaces these general powers with specific powers limited to restricting the liberty of the person under guardianship only to the extent necessary to ensure that various forms of treatment, social support, training, education or occupation are undertaken.

Subs. (1)

Reside at a place: There is no power to require that the patient resides with a particular person. If the patient leaves the place where he is required to live, without his guardian's consent, he can be taken into custody and returned to that place within 28 days of his departure (s.18(3)(4)).

For the purposes of medical treatment: The guardian cannot consent to treatment on the patient's behalf.

Requires access to the patient: A refusal to permit an authorised person to have access to the patient is an offence under s.129, below.

Subs. (2)

Beginning with: Including the date on which the patient was last examined by a medical practitioner (*Hare* v. *Gocher* [1962] 2 Q.B. 641).

Subs. (3)

Appears to be duly made: An incorrect or defective application can be amended under subs. (4).

Subs. (4)

Amended: This provision provides a means of righting genuine mistakes; it is not a device for overcoming breaches of procedure. The amended application must comply with all the requirements for making an application.

By whom it was signed: i.e. the applicant. It is submitted that Brenda Hoggett is correct in her opinion that an unsigned application form cannot be remedied under this provision (*Mental Health*, 1976, p.83).

Regulations as to guardianship

9.—(1) Subject to the provisions of this Part of this Act, the Secretary of State may make regulations—

    (*a*) for regulating the exercise by the guardians of patients received into guardianship under this Part of this Act of their powers as such; and

    (*b*) for imposing on such guardians, and upon local social services authorities in the case of patients under the guardianship of persons other than local social services authorities, such duties as he considers necessary or expedient in the interests of the patients.

(2) Regulations under this section may in particular make provision for requiring the patients to be visited, on such occasions or at such intervals as may be prescribed by the regulations, on behalf of such local social services authorities as may be so prescribed, and shall provide for the appointment, in the case of every patient subject to the guardianship of a person other than a local social services authority, of a registered medical practitioner to act as the nominated medical attendant of the patient.

DEFINITIONS

"Patients": s.145(1).

"Local social services authority": s.145(1).

GENERAL NOTE

This section, which gives power to the Secretary of State to make regulations for regulating guardianship, is applied to patients who have been placed under guardianship by a guardianship order made by a court under s.37, below (Sched. 1, Pt. I, para. 1).

Subs. (1)
   Powers: Are set out in s.8, below.

Subs. (2)
   Visited: A person who refuses to allow an authorised person to visit a patient commits an offence under s.129, below.
   Nominated medical attendant: Is defined in s.34(1), below.

Transfer of guardianship in case of death, incapacity, etc., of guardian

10.—(1) If any person (other than a local social services authority) who is the guardian of a patient received into guardianship under this Part of this Act—

(*a*) dies; or

(*b*) gives notice in writing to the local social services authority that he desires to relinquish the functions of guardian,

the guardianship of the patient shall thereupon vest in the local social services authority, but without prejudice to any power to transfer the patient into the guardianship of another person in pursuance of regulations under section 19 below.

(2) If any such person, not having given notice under subsection (1)(*b*) above, is incapacitated by illness or any other cause from performing the functions of guardian of the patient, those functions may, during his incapacity, be performed on his behalf by the local social services authority or by any other person approved for the purposes by that authority.

(3) If it appears to the county court, upon application made by an approved social worker, that any person other than a local social services authority having the guardianship of a patient received into guardianship under this Part of this Act has performed his functions negligently or in a manner contrary to the interests of the welfare of the patient, the court may order that the guardianship of the patient be transferred to the local social services authority or to any other person approved for the purpose by that authority.

(4) Where the guardianship of a patient is transferred to a local social services authority or other person by or under this section, subsection (2)(*c*) of section 19 below shall apply as if the patient had been transferred into the guardianship of that authority or person in pursuance of regulations under that section.

DEFINITIONS
   "Local social services authority": s.145(1).
   "Patient": s.145(1).
   "Approved social worker": s.145(1).

GENERAL NOTE
   This section provides for the transfer of guardianship in circumstances where the guardian of a patient dies, becomes incapacitated, wishes to relinquish his functions, or is found to be performing his functions negligently. It is applied to patients who have been placed under guardianship by a guardianship order made by a court under s.37, below (Sched. 1, Pt. I, para. 1).

Subs. (1)
   This subsection provides for the automatic transfer of guardianship to a local social services authority.
   Notice in writing to the local social services authority: It is not clear whether this refers to the authority for the area in which the patient resides or the authority for the area in which the guardian resides. It is submitted that the notice should be sent to the first named authority.
   Shall thereupon: The authority cannot resist a notice of relinquishment.

Subs. (2)

This subsection allows the local Social Services Authority, or a person authorised by them, to act temporarily on behalf of a guardian who is ill or incapacitated.

May, during his incapacity, be performed: Note that the local social services authority is not placed under a duty to take over the functions of an incapacitated guardian.

On his behalf: The authority is not empowered to act against any instructions the guardian may have given.

Subs. (3)

This subsection empowers the local social services authority to apply to the county court for an order transferring the guardianship of the patient to itself.

County court: The procedure on an application to the county court is set out in Order 49 of the County Court Rules 1981 (S.I. 1981 No. 1687).

General provisions as to applications and recommendations

General provisions as to applications

11.—(1) Subject to the provisions of this section, an application for admission for assessment, an application for admission for treatment and a guardianship application may be made either by the nearest relative of the patient or by an approved social worker; and every such application shall specify the qualification of the applicant to make the application.

(2) Every application for admission shall be addressed to the managers of the hospital to which admission is sought and every guardianship application shall be forwarded to the local social services authority named in the application as guardian, or, as the case may be, to the local social services authority for the area in which the person so named resides.

(3) Before or within a reasonable time after an application for the admission of a patient for assessment is made by an approved social worker, that social worker shall take such steps as are practicable to inform the person (if any) appearing to be the nearest relative of the patient that the application is to be or has been made and of the power of the nearest relative under section 23(2)(*a*) below.

(4) Neither an application for admission for treatment nor a guardianship application shall be made by an approved social worker if the nearest relative of the patient has notified that social worker, or the local social services authority by whom that social worker is appointed, that he objects to the application being made and, without prejudice to the foregoing provision, no such application shall be made by such a social worker except after consultation with the person (if any) appearing to be the nearest relative of the patient unless it appears to that social worker that in the circumstances such consultation is not reasonably practicable or would involve unreasonable delay.

(5) None of the applications mentioned in subsection (1) above shall be made by any person in respect of a patient unless that person has personally seen the patient within the period of 14 days ending with the date of the application.

(6) An application for admission for treatment or a guardianship application, and any recommendation given for the purposes of such an application, may describe the patient as suffering from more than one of the following forms of mental disorder, namely mental illness, severe mental impairment, psychopathic disorder or mental impairment; but the application shall be of no effect unless the patient is described in each of the recommendations as suffering from the same form of mental disorder, whether or not he is also described in either of those recommendations as suffering from another form.

(7) Each of the applications mentioned in subsection (1) above shall be sufficient if the recommendations on which it is founded are given either

as separate recommendations, each signed by a registered medical practitioner, or as a joint recommendation signed by two such practitioners.

DEFINITIONS
   "Application for admission for assessment": s.145(1).
   "Application for admission for treatment": s.145(1).
   "Nearest relative": ss.26(3), 145(1).
   "Approved social workers": s.145(1).
   "The managers": s.145(1).
   "Hospital": ss.34(2), 145(1).
   "Local social services authority": s.145(1).
   "Patient": s.145(1).
   "Mental disorder": ss.1, 145(1).
   "Severe mental impairment": ss.1, 145(1).
   "Psychopathic disorder": ss.1, 145(1).
   "Mental impairment": ss.1, 145(1).

GENERAL NOTE
   This section contains general provisions relating to applications for admission for assessment, applications for admission for treatment, and guardianship applications. Although primary responsibility for checking that the statutory forms have been completed correctly rests with the applicant, hospital managers and local social services authorities should each designate an officer to scrutinise the documents as soon as they have been completed and to take any necessary action if they have been improperly completed (Cmnd. 7320, para, 3.20).

Subs. (1)
   Application: An application in respect of a ward of court cannot be made without the leave of the High Court (s.33(1)).
   Nearest relative: Or an acting nearest relative appointed by the court under s.29, below.
   Approved social worker: See s.13, below, for the duty of an approved social worker to make an application. At present, the great majority of applications for compulsory admission are made by social workers (Cmnd. 7320, para, 3.16).

Subs. (2)
   The managers: Hospital managers are not obliged to admit patients in respect of whom applications under Pt. II of this Act have been made. In volume 2 of his *A Human Condition,* Larry Gostin refers to the opinion that Sir Geoffrey Howe Q.C., M.P. gave to the North West Thames Regional Health Authority in 1974 on the role of hospital managers in respect of hospital admissions. Sir Geoffrey concluded that a hospital consultant had no right to admit a patient, except with the authority of the hospital managers (*ibid.,* pp. 53, 59).
   Hospital: As the application does not authorise the applicant to take the patient to any other hospital than the hospital specified in the application, it is suggested that the name of the hospital should not be written on the application form until the recommending doctor has confirmed that a hospital bed has been arranged for the patient.
   Local social services authority for the area in which the person so named resides: The guardianship application does not take effect until it is accepted by the authority. If it is accepted the authority will become the "responsible local social services authority" for the purposes of Pt. II (s.34(3)).
   Resides: Temporary absences from the place where a person lives does not affect residence, as long as there is an intention to return (*R.* v. *St. Leonard's Shoreditch* (*Inhabitants*) (1865) L.R. 1 Q.B. 21).

Subs. (3)
   This subsection requires an approved social worker who makes an application for admission for assessment to take such steps as are practicable to inform the patient's nearest relative that the application is about to be or has been made and of his power to discharge the patient.
   Within a reasonable time: As an admission for assessment under s.2 of this Act lasts for a maximum of 28 days it is submitted that the approved social worker should not wait longer than twenty-four hours before taking steps to inform the patient's nearest relative that an application has been made.
   That social worker: The duty to inform is placed upon the approved social worker.

Such steps as are practicable: This could include the sending of a telegram to inform a nearest relative who resides at some distance from the admitting hospital or asking a social worker from the area where the nearest relative resides to inform him of the application.

Inform: The information could be given orally or in writing.

Appearing to be the nearest relative: The approved social worker should take reasonable steps to discover the identity of the nearest relative, using the formula set out in s.26, below.

The power . . . under section 23(2)(a): Of the nearest relative to order the patients discharge from hospital.

Subs. (4)

This subsection provides that an application by an approved social worker for admission for treatment or for guardianship cannot proceed if the patient's nearest relative objects.

Objects: Unreasonable objection by a nearest relative to an application is one of the grounds in s.29(3), below, for a county court to transfer the powers of the nearest relative to an "acting nearest relative".

Consultation with: There is no requirement that the nearest relative has to give him express consent to the application. "Consultation" implies that the nearest relative is informed of the reasons for the application and its effect, and asked for his views on the proposed course of action.

Not reasonably practicable or would involve undesirable delay: Given the circumstances of most guardianship applications and applications for treatment it is unlikely that this situation would often obtain. It might occur if the patient's condition is such that the approved social worker is unable to obtain the information that would enable him to identify the nearest relative or if the patient has no clear recollection of the whereabouts of his relatives.

Subs. (6)

Suffering from the same form of mental disorder: Although the recommending doctors can each state that the patient is suffering from more than one of the forms of mental disorder specified in this subsection, they must both agree on at least one of them. An application would not be invalidated if one of the recommending doctors made a general diagnosis as to the form of mental disorder and the other made a specific diagnosis coming within the same form, *e.g.* if Dr. A. diagnosed mental illness and Dr. B. diagnosed paranoid schizophrenia, a form of mental illness; see the note on s.37(2), below.

General provisions as to medical recommendations

12.—(1) The recommendations required for the purposes of an application for the admission of a patient under this Part of this Act (in this Act referred to as "medical recommendations") shall be signed on or before the date of the application, and shall be given by practitioners who have personally examined the patient either together or separately, but where they have examined the patient separately not more than five days must have elapsed between the days on which the separate examinations took place.

(2) Of the medical recommendations given for the purposes of any such application, one shall be given by a practitioner approved for the purposes of this section by the Secretary of State as having special experience in the diagnosis or treatment of mental disorder; and unless that practitioner has previous acquaintance with the patient, the other such recommendation shall, if practicable, be given by a registered medical practitioner who has such previous acquaintance.

(3) Subject to subsection (4) below, where the application is for the admission of the patient to a hospital which is not a mental nursing home, one (but not more than one) of the medical recommendations may be given by a practitioner on the staff of that hospital, except where the patient is proposed to be accommodated under section 65 or 66 of the National Health Service Act 1977 (which relate to accommodation for private patients).

(4) Subsection (3) above shall not preclude both the medical recommendations being given by practitioners on the staff of the hospital in question if—

(a) compliance with that subsection would result in delay involving serious risk to the health or safety of the patient; and

(b) one of the practitioners giving the recommendations works at the hospital for less than half of the time which he is bound by contract to devote to work in the health service; and

(c) where one of those practitioners is a consultant, the other does not work (whether at the hospital or elsewhere) in a grade in which he is under that consultant's directions.

(5) A medical recommendation for the purposes of an application for the admission of a patient under this Part of this Act shall not be given by—

(a) the applicant;

(b) a partner of the applicant or of a practitioner by whom another medical recommendation is given for the purposes of the same application;

(c) a person employed as an assistant by the applicant or by any such practitioner;

(d) a person who receives or has an interest in the receipt of any payments made on account of the maintenance of the patient; or

(e) except as provided by subsection (3) or (4) above, a practitioner on the staff of the hospital to which the patient is to be admitted,

or by the husband, wife, father, father-in-law, mother, mother-in-law, son, son-in-law, daughter, daughter-in-law, brother, brother-in-law, sister or sister-in-law of the patient, or of any person mentioned in paragraphs (a) to (e) above, or of a practitioner by whom another medical recommendation is given for the purposes of the same application.

(6) A general practitioner who is employed part-time in a hospital shall not for the purposes of this section be regarded as a practitioner on its staff.

(7) Subsections (1), (2) and (5) above shall apply to applications for guardianship as they apply to applications for admission but with the substitution for paragraph (e) of subsection (5) above of the following paragraph—

"(e) the person named as guardian in the application.".

DEFINITIONS
"Patient": s.145(1).
"Mental disorder": ss.1, 145(1).
"Hospital": s.145(1).
"Mental nursing home": s.145(1).

GENERAL NOTE
This section specifies the requirements that apply to medical recommendations. The recommending doctor owes a duty of care to the patient when carrying out functions under this Act (*Harnett* v. *Fisher* [1927] A.C. 573).

Subs. (1)
This subsection provides that where the two recommending doctors examine the patient separately not more than five days must have elapsed between the days on which the separate examinations took place.

Recommendations: Incorrect or defective recommendations can be rectified under section 15, below.

On or before the date of the application: An applicant should not sign an application and then try to obtain the medical recommendation to support it.

Personally examined: Even if the patient is well known to the doctor, a recommendation should not be signed without a prior examination of the patient.

Five days: i.e. five clear days between the days on which the examinations took place.

Subs. (2)

Approved . . . by the Secretary of State: Approval is delegated to District Health Authorities by the National Health Service Functions (Directions to Authorities and Administration
Arrangements) Regulations 1982 (S.I. 1982 No. 287).

If practicable: If the "other" doctor has not had previous acquaintance with the patient it
is suggested that he should attempt to consult with the patient's general practitioner before
he signs a recommendation.

Subs. (3)

This subsection provides that the general rule if a patient is to be admitted to hospital as
a National Health Service patient is that only one of the two medical recommendations may
come from a doctor on the staff of the hospital to which the patient is to be admitted. If the
patient is admitted as a private patient or is admitted to a mental nursing home, neither
recommendation may come from a doctor on the staff of the hospital or nursing home. This
subsection and subs. (4) do not apply to guardianship applications (subs. (7)).

Practitioner on the staff of that hospital: Note subs. (6), below.

Subs. (4)

This subsection specifies when both medical recommendations may come from doctors on
the staff of the admitting hospital.

Delay: A delay which would involve serious risk to the patient is only likely to occur when
an emergency application under s.4 is about to expire and it is considered that the patient
should continue to be detained under either s.2 or 3. If the patient has been admitted for
assessment under s.2 there should be ample time to comply with the provisions of subs. (3)
of this section if an application for treatment under s.3 is to be made.

Under the consultant's directions: A query was raised at the Special Standing Committee
as to the relationship between a doctor's independent clinical judgment and his position of
being under the "direction" of a consultant. The Under-Secretary of State responded by
saying that "it was commonsense to say in this context that 'direction' means that a junior
doctor, a registrar working as part of a consultant's team, finally has to accept the directions,
advice or instructions of the consultant. If the doctor believes that those instructions are
wholly wrong, he must decide whether to obey them" (sitting of May 18, 1982).

Subs. (5)

This subsection is aimed at preventing collusion between the various participants involved
in applications for admission to hospital and guardianship applications.

Duty of approved social workers to make applications for admission or guardianship

13.—(1) It shall be the duty of an approved social worker to make an
application for admission to hospital or a guardianship application in
respect of a patient within the area of the local social services authority by
which that officer is appointed in any case where he is satisfied that such
an application ought to be made and is of the opinion, having regard to
any wishes expressed by relatives of the patient or any other relevant
circumstances, that it is necessary or proper for the application to be made
by him.

(2) Before making an application for the admission of a patient to
hospital an approved social worker shall interview the patient in a suitable
manner and satisfy himself that detention in a hospital is in all the
circumstances of the case the most appropriate way of providing the care
and medical treatment of which the patient stands in need.

(3) An application under this section by an approved social worker may
be made outside the area of the local social services authority by which he
is appointed.

(4) It shall be the duty of a local social services authority, if so required
by the nearest relative of a patient residing in their area, to direct an
approved social worker as soon as practicable to take the patient's case
into consideration under subsection (1) above with a view to making an
application for his admission to hospital; and if in any such case that

approved social worker decides not to make an application he shall inform the nearest relative of his reasons in writing.

(5) Nothing in this section shall be construed as authorising or requiring an application to be made by an approved social worker in contravention of the provisions of section 11(4) above, or as restricting the power of an approved social worker to make any application under this Act.

DEFINITIONS
　"Approved social worker": s.145(1).
　"Hospital": ss.34(2), 145(1).
　"Patient": s.145(1).
　"Local social services authority": s.145(1).
　"Medical treatment": s.145(1).
　"Nearest relative": ss.26(3), 145(1).

GENERAL NOTE
This section places a duty on an approved social worker to make an application for admission to a hospital or a guardianship application if he considers that an application ought to be made and if, after taking into account the views of relatives and any other relevant circumstances, he considers that it is necessary or proper for him to do so.

The House of Lords has held that a medical practitioner who carries out functions under the mental health legislation owes a duty of care to the patient (*Harnett* v. *Fisher* [1927] A.C. 573). It is submitted that an approved social worker owes a similar duty to patients and is therefore bound to take reasonable care to ensure that legislative formalities are complied with.

The British Association of Social Workers has suggested that the role of the approved social worker in compulsory admissions should be:
"(*a*)　to investigate the client's social situation and how that has developed; and to estimate, in consultation with others involved, the extent to which the social and environmental pressures have contributed to the client's observed behaviour;
(*b*)　to apply professional skill to help modify any contributory personal relationship or environmental factors;
(*c*)　to mobilise the resources of the health service, the community service and acknowledge and use the community as a therapeutic resource;
(*d*)　to ensure that any intervention is the least restructive necessary in the circumstances;
(*e*)　to ensure strict compliance with the law." ("Review of the Mental Health Act 1959—Further Evidence", 1980, p.25.)

Some suggestions for a "Code of Practice" which would provide a procedure for resolving disagreements between the applicant and the recommending doctors have been made by Fisher, Newton and Sainsbury in *Mental Welfare Officers: A Code of Practice*, Community Care, July 23, 1981, p.16.

Subs. (1)
Duty of an approved social worker: An approved social worker is personally liable for his actions whilst carrying out functions under this Act. He should therefore exercise his own judgment and not act at the behest of his employers, medical practitioners or other persons who might be involved with the patients' welfare. Speaking of the role of the approved social workers precursor, Devlin L.J., said: "It is the business of the duly authorised officer, rather than that of the doctor, to see that statutory powers are not used for the purpose [of hospital treatment] unless the circumstances warrant it" (*Buxton* v. *Jayne* [1960] 1 W.L.R. 783, 784). The duty placed on the approved social worker by this section does not affect the provisions as to consultation with nearest relatives set out in s.11(4), above (subs. (5)).

Make an application: It is submitted that the approved social worker is obliged, as far as he is able, to ensure that the medical recommendations upon which the application is founded comply with the provisions of s.12, above. He should not make an application and then look for the medical recommendations to support it.

Satisfied: The approved social worker has a duty to make an application if he is satisfied having regard to the provisions of this subsection and, for an application for admission to hospital, subs. (2) that it ought to be made. If the approved social worker is satisfied that an application ought to be made but considers that it would be more appropriate if the patient's nearest relative made the application, he should not refrain from making the application himself if the nearest relative decides not to become the applicant.

Ought to be made: In the case of an application for admission to hospital the approved social worker can only be satisfied that an application ought to be made if the requirements of subs. (2) have been met.

Having regard to: The approved social worker must take the wishes of relatives and other relevant circumstances into account when he considers whether he should proceed to make an application.

Relatives: As defined in s.26(1), below.

Other relevant circumstances: Which could include the provisions that have to be satisfied before an emergency application under s.4 of this Act can be made.

Subs. (2)

Hospital: This subsection does not apply to guardianship applications.

Suitable manner. These words were added to this section as a result of an amendment moved at the Special Standing Committee by Mr. Tom Benyon who stressed the need for those who are involved in the management of deaf psychiatric patients having either the use of an interpreter or a fluency in British Sign Language. He also drew the Committee's attention to a number of cases where patients had to be compulsorily detained under the 1959 Act in circumstances where a lack of speech had been mistakenly attributed to mental disorder. Other members were concerned that approved social workers should be sensitive to the difficulties faced by members of ethnic minorities who might not speak English or who might not speak it well. The words "suitable manner" should direct the approved social worker's attention to the particular needs of all groups who might have difficulties in communicating effectively.

Satisfy himself: The approved social worker would need to consult with others who have been involved with the patient's welfare. Speaking of the role that approved social workers should take in compulsory admissions the Under-Secretary of State said that he would "expect the [approved social worker], the doctor and others to discuss what should be done" (Special Standing Committee, Sitting of May 27, 1982). A doctor who has made a recommendation might refuse to meet with the approved social worker to discuss the case and, if the case is one of sufficient urgency, the social worker might have to make an application without the benefit of a discussion with a medical practitioner. It is submitted that such a procedure would contravene the spirit of this Act and that if an approved social worker considers that he has been forced by these circumstances to make such an "improper" application he should, in the first instance, attempt to resolve the difficulty by involving relevant bodies at the local level. If the difficulty cannot be resolved in this way, the social worker should consider contacting the Mental Health Act Commission which, under s.121(2)(*b*), below, has a duty to keep matters relating to the detention of patients under review.

An approved social worker should not make an application solely because a doctor has made a recommendation; he must exercise his own judgement as to whether the provisions of this section have been satisfied (see *Buxton* v. *Jayne*, above).

All the circumstances of the case: Such as the medical opinion of the patient's condition, the patient's wishes, the relationship between the patient's condition and his social situation, whether the patient has a history of mental disorder and the attitude of relatives. The approved social worker would also need to consider whether suitable alternatives to compulsory hospital treatment exist for the patient. They might include in-patient treatment as an informal patient, out-patient or day hospital treatment, community psychiatric nursing, social work support, accommodation in a hostel and support from relatives and the primary health care team.

If a patient vacillates between consenting and refusing to consent to admission to hospital as an informal patient it is suggested that the patient should be admitted informally if this is possible, with the powers contained in s.5, above, being used where necessary.

The most appropriate way: "My criticism of [this] formulation is that it starts from the supposition that the hospital is the most appropriate place, and then looks outward to see whether it is not. I should like to reverse that to see whether the community could provide the appropriate environment, given the circumstances of the case", *per* Mr. David Ennals, Special Standing Committee, May 27, 1982. A comprehensive knowledge of local resources available for the mentally disordered is essential if an informed judgement is to be made.

Subs. (3)

May: The approved social worker is not placed under a duty to make an application outside the area of his appointing authority.

Subs. (4)

Required: It might not always be clear whether a communication from a nearest relative amounts to a request to a local authority to act under the provisions of this subsection. It is submitted that if a nearest relative indicates his concern about the patient by saying, for example, that the patient "ought to be in hospital" or that "something ought to be done" about the patient, the nearest relative should be informed of his power under this subsection and asked whether he wishes to exercise it. If a local social services authority is repeatedly asked by a particular nearest relative to direct an approved social worker to consider the patient's case, the authority is not required, on each occasion when the request is made, to interview the patient "in a suitable manner" to comply with subs. (1). Although such an interview is a pre-condition to the making of an application, it is not a pre-condition to "taking the case into consideration under subs. (1)".

Nearest relative: Or acting nearest relative appointed by the court under s.29, below.

Direct: Once the direction has been made the approved social worker must exercise his own judgement in considering whether to make an application.

Take the patient's case into consideration: The approved social worker might wish to consult with the patient's general practitioner.

Hospital: The provision does not apply to a nearest relative who wants a guardianship application to be made.

Inform: Note that it is the approved social worker, and not the local authority, who has to inform the nearest relative. If the social worker decides not to make an application the nearest relative could proceed to make an application himself if the required medical recommendation(s) had been made. If the nearest relative's application was made under either s.2 or 3 of this Act a local authority social worker would be required to provide the hospital managers with a social circumstances report under s.14, below.

Subs. (5)

Section 11(4): Which provides, (1) that the approved social worker must consult with the patient's nearest relative before making an application for treatment or guardianship, if this is practicable; and (2) that the social worker cannot proceed if the nearest relative objects.

Social reports

14. Where a patient is admitted to a hospital in pursuance of an application (other than an emergency application) made under this Part of this Act by his nearest relative, the managers of the hospital shall as soon as practicable give notice of that fact to the local social services authority for the area in which the patient resided immediately before his admission; and that authority shall as soon as practicable arrange for a social worker of their social services department to interview the patient and provide the managers with a report on his social circumstances.

DEFINITIONS
   "Patient": s.145(1).
   "Hospital": ss.34(2), 145(1).
   "Nearest relative": ss.26(3), 145(1).
   "The managers": s.145(1).
   "Local social services authority": s.145(1).

GENERAL NOTE

This section places a duty on social services authorities to provide hospital managers with a report on a patient's social circumstances if the patient has been admitted to hospital pursuant to an application made by his nearest relative under s.2 or 3 of this Act.

Nearest relative: Or an acting nearest relative appointed by the County Court under s.29, below. It is presumably assumed that an approved social worker applicant would automatically provide the hospital with the sort of information that would be contained in a social circumstances report.

Area in which the patient resided: This need not necessarily be the place where the patient was staying immediately prior to his admission, as temporary absences from the place where a person lives does not affect residence, as long as there is an intention to return (*R.* v. *St. Leonard's Shoreditch (Inhabitants)*, (1865) L.R. 1 Q.B. 21).

Social worker: Who need not be an approved social worker. The social worker who provides the report could be the hospital social worker who interviews the patient on his admission.

Report on his social circumstances: This could include an account of the patient's family and social relationships, his employment record, his financial situation and his accommodation.

Rectification of applications and recommendations

15.—(1) If within the period of 14 days beginning with the day on which a patient has been admitted to a hospital in pursuance of an application for admission for assessment or for treatment the application, or any medical recommendation given for the purposes of the application, is found to be in any respect incorrect or defective, the application or recommendation may, within that period and with the consent of the managers of the hospital, be amended by the person by whom it was signed; and upon such amendment being made the application or recommendation shall have effect and shall be deemed to have had effect as if it had been originally made as so amended.

(2) Without prejudice to subsection (1) above, if within the period mentioned in that subsection it appears to the managers of the hospital that one of the two medical recommendations on which an application for the admission of a patient is founded is insufficient to warrant the detention of the patient in pursuance of the application, they may, within that period, give notice in writing to that effect to the applicant; and where any such notice is given in respect of a medical recommendation, that recommendation shall be disregarded, but the application shall be, and shall be deemed always to have been, sufficient if—

(a) a fresh medical recommendation complying with the relevant provisions of this Part of this Act (other than the provisions relating to the time of signature and the interval between examinations) is furnished to the managers within that period; and

(b) that recommendation, and the other recommendation on which the application is founded, together comply with those provisions.

(3) Where the medical recommendations upon which an application for admission is founded are, taken together, insufficient to warrant the detention of the patient in pursuance of the application, a notice under subsection (2) above may be given in respect of either of those recommendations; but this subsection shall not apply in a case where the application is of no effect by virtue of section 11(6) above.

(4) Nothing in this section shall be construed as authorising the giving of notice in respect of an application made as an emergency application, or the detention of a patient admitted in pursuance of such an application, after the period of 72 hours referred to in section 4(4) above, unless the conditions set out in paragraphs (a) and (b) of that section are complied with or would be complied with apart from any error or defect to which this section applies.

DEFINITIONS
  "Patient": s.145(1).
  "Hospital": ss.34(2), 145(1).
  "Application for admission for assessment": ss.2, 145(1).
  "Application for admission for treatment": ss.3, 145(1).
  "The managers": s.145(1).

GENERAL NOTE
  This section provides for documents which are found to be incorrect or defective to be rectified after they have been acted upon. It cannot be used to remedy a genuine deficiency which would otherwise invalidate the application, such as a failure by the recommending doctors to specify at least one form of mental disorder in common (see, s.11(6), above). If the application is incapable of rectification under this section and the patient is already in hospital, it might be possible to detain him under s.5, above, to enable a fresh application to be made.

A person who wilfully makes a false entry or statement in an application commits an offence under s.126(4), below.

Subs. (1)

Beginning with: Including the day on which the patient was admitted to hospital (*Hare* v. *Gocher* [1962] 2 Q.B. 641).

Amended: The amended application or medical recommendation must comply with the relevant provisions of this Act. The patient can continue to be detained for the short period required for the rectification to be made.

By whom it was signed: It is submitted that Brenda Hoggett is correct in her opinion that an unsigned application [or medical recommendation] cannot be remedied under this section (*Mental Health,* 1976, p.83). It is further submitted that an application or medical recommendation which is signed by a person who is not empowered to do so under this Act is also incapable of rectification.

Subs. (2)

This subsection provides a remedy if *one* of the medical recommendations required under ss.2 or 3 of this Act is found to be incorrect or defective. This procedure could be used if, for example, spaces on the form have been left blank or the entries relating to the patient's name fail to agree. It cannot be used to remedy breaches of procedure, *e.g.* a failure to observe the provisions of s.12(1), above.

Subs. (3)

Insufficient: If, for example, neither recommending doctor is "approved", under s.12, above.

No effect by virtue of s.11(6): A new recommendation under this subsection cannot be sought where an application under s.3, above, is defective because the doctors do not agree about the form of the mental disorder from which the patient suffers.

Subs. (4)

This subsection provides that this section cannot be used to rectify an emergency application after it has expired unless it has been "converted" into an application for assessment under s.4(4), above.

Position of patients subject to detention or guardianship

Reclassification of patients

16.—(1) If in the case of a patient who is for the time being detained in a hospital in pursuance of an application for admission for treatment, or subject to guardianship in pursuance of a guardianship application, it appears to the appropriate medical officer that the patient is suffering from a form of mental disorder other than the form or forms specified in the application, he may furnish to the managers of the hospital, or to the guardian, as the case may be, a report to that effect; and where a report is so furnished, the application shall have effect as if that other form of mental disorder were specified in it.

(2) Where a report under subsection (1) above in respect of a patient detained in a hospital is to the effect that he is suffering from psychopathic disorder or mental impairment but not from mental illness or severe mental impairment the appropriate medical officer shall include in the report a statement of his opinion whether further medical treatment in hospital is likely to alleviate or prevent a deterioration of the patient's condition; and if he states that in his opinion such treatment is not likely to have that effect the authority of the managers to detain the patient shall cease.

(3) Before furnishing a report under subsection (1) above the appropriate medical officer shall consult one or more other persons who have been professionally concerned with the patient's medical treatment.

(4) Where a report is furnished under this section in respect of a patient, the managers or guardian shall cause the patient and the nearest relative to be informed.

(5) In this section "appropriate medical officer" means—
(*a*) in the case of a patient who is subject to the guardianship of a person other than a local social services authority, the nominated medical attendant of the patient; and
(*b*) in any other case, the responsible medical officer.

DEFINITIONS
"Patient": s.145(1).
"Hospital": ss.34(2), 145(1).
"Application for admission for treatment": ss.3, 145(1).
"Mental disorder": ss.1, 145(1).
"The managers": s.145(1).
"Psychopathic disorder": ss.1, 145(1).
"Mental impairment": ss.1, 145(1).
"Severe mental impairment": ss.1, 145(1).
"Nearest relative": ss.26(3), 145(1).
"The nominated medical attendant": s.34(1).

GENERAL NOTE
This section provides for the reclassification of a patient who is detained for treatment or is subject to guardianship. It is applied, with modifications, to patients who have been placed under hospital or guardianship orders by a court under s.37, below (Sched. 1, Pt. I, para. 2). Either the patient or his nearest relative has a right to appeal to a Mental Health Review Tribunal within 28 days of a report being furnished under this section (s.66(1)(*d*), (2)(*d*)).

Subs. (1)
Appropriate medical officer: Is defined in subs. (5). He is placed under an obligation to consult before furnishing a report (subs. (3)).
He may furnish: If the doctor who makes a report under s.20, above, renewing the authority to detain a patient or keep him subject to guardianship, states in his report that the patient is suffering from a form of mental disorder other than that specified on the original application, this has the effect of automatically reclassifying the patient (s.20(9)).
Shall have effect as if that other form of mental disorder were specified in it: Thus a patient's mental disorder could be reclassified more than once.

Subs. (2)
This subsection provides that where a patient's diagnosis has been changed from either mental illness or severe mental impairment to either psychopathic disorder or mental impairment and a report to that effect has been made under subs. (1), the authority to detain the patient terminates unless the patient's responsible medical officer certifies that further medical treatment in hospital is likely to alleviate or prevent a deterioration of the patient's condition.
Detained in a hospital: This subsection does not apply to patients who are subject to guardianship.

Subs. (3)
Consult: It is submitted that the process of consultation should include the exchange of information and the seeking and giving of advice.
One or more other persons: Although Parliamentarians who spoke on this provision, which derives from the 1982 Act, referred to it in terms of placing a duty on the appropriate medical officer to consult with professionals from *other* disciplines, the wording of this subsection is such that the duty could be discharged by the medical officer consulting with other medical practitioners who have been involved with the patient's treatment.
Professionally concerned: In respect of a patient who is being treated in hospital, it is submitted that it is not sufficient for the person consulted merely to have been involved in working on the same ward as the patient's responsible medical officer: he must have had a particular involvement with the patient's treatment.

Subs. (4)
Nearest relative: Or acting nearest relative appointed by the county court under s.29, below.

Leave of absence from hospital

17.—(1) The responsible medical officer may grant to any patient who is for the time being liable to be detained in a hospital under this Part of this Act leave to be absent from the hospital subject to such conditions (if any) as that officer considers necessary in the interests of the patient or for the protection of other persons.

(2) Leave of absence may be granted to a patient under this section either indefinitely or on specified occasions or for any specified period; and where leave is so granted for a specified period, that period may be extended by further leave granted in the absence of the patient.

(3) Where it appears to the responsible medical officer that it is necessary so to do in the interests of the patient or for the protection of other persons, he may, upon granting leave of absence under this section, direct that the patient remain in custody during his absence; and where leave of absence is so granted the patient may be kept in the custody of any officer on the staff of the hospital, or of any other person authorised in writing by the managers of the hospital or, if the patient is required in accordance with conditions imposed on the grant of leave of absence to reside in another hospital, of any officer on the staff of that other hospital.

(4) In any case where a patient is absent from a hospital in pursuance of leave of absence granted under this section, and it appears to the responsible medical officer that it is necessary so to do in the interests of the patient's health or safety or for the protection of other persons, that officer may, subject to subsection (5) below, by notice in writing given to the patient or to the person for the time being in charge of the patient, revoke the leave of absence and recall the patient to the hospital.

(5) A patient to whom leave of absence is granted under this section shall not be recalled under subsection (4) above after he has ceased to be liable to be detained under this Part of this Act; and without prejudice to any other provision of this Part of this Act any such patient shall cease to be so liable at the expiration of the period of six months beginning with the first day of his absence on leave unless either—

(*a*) he has returned to the hospital, or has been transferred to another hospital under the following provisions of this Act, before the expiration of that period; or

(*b*) he is absent without leave at the expiration of that period.

DEFINITIONS
 "Patient": s.145(1).
 "Hospital": ss.34(2), 145(1).
 "Absent without leave": ss.18(6), 145(1).
 "Responsible medical officer": s.34(1).

GENERAL NOTE
 This section provides for a patient to be granted leave of absence from the hospital in which he is liable to be detained. It is applied, with modifications for restriction order patients, to patients who have been placed under hospital orders, restriction orders or guardianship orders by a court under s.37 or 41, below (Sched. 1, Pt. I, para. 1, Pt. II, para. 2).
 If the discharge of a patient is under consideration, this section can be used to enable the hospital and social services authority to work together towards his rehabilitation in the community by sending him on leave as a trial for discharge.
 Detailed guidelines covering unescorted leave arrangements for special hospital patients being prepared for discharge are contained in, "Review of Leave Arrangements for Special Hospital Patients," D.H.S.S., 1981.
 Under s.128, below, it is an offence to induce or help a patient absent himself without leave or to harbour or prevent a patient being returned to hospital.

Subs. (1)
Liable to be detained: Patients who have been granted leave of absence remain subject to the consent to treatment provisions contained in Pt. IV of this Act.
Conditions: For example, to live with a particular person or at a specified place.

Subs. (2)
Extended: Leave can be extended in the absence of the patient from the hospital.

Subs. (3)
Custody: For provisions relating to the powers of the person having custody of the patient, see s.137, below.
Officer on the staff of the hospital: "Officer" is not defined in this Act and could include a person who is neither a nurse nor a doctor.

Subs. (4)
This subsection provides for the revocation of leave of absence.

Subs. (5)
This subsection provides that a patient cannot be recalled to hospital if either the period for his detention has lapsed or he has had six months' continuous leave, unless he is absent *without* leave at the end of that period.
Beginning with: Including the first day of his absence (*Hare* v. *Gocher* [1962] 2 Q.B. 641).

Return and readmission of patients absent without leave

18.—(1) Where a patient who is for the time being liable to be detained under this Part of this Act in a hospital—

(a) absents himself from the hospital without leave granted under section 17 above; or

(b) fails to return to the hospital on any occasion on which, or at the expiration of any period for which, leave of absence was granted to him under that section, or upon being recalled under that section; or

(c) absents himself without permission from any place where he is required to reside in accordance with conditions imposed on the grant of leave of absence under that section,

he may, subject to the provisions of this section, be taken into custody and returned to the hospital or place by any approved social worker, by any officer on the staff of the hospital, by any constable, or by any person authorised in writing by the managers of the hospital.

(2) Where the place referred to in paragraph (c) of subsection (1) above is a hospital other than the one in which the patient is for the time being liable to be detained, the references in that subsection to an officer on the staff of the hospital and the managers of the hospital shall respectively include references to an officer on the staff of the first-mentioned hospital and the managers of that hospital.

(3) Where a patient who is for the time being subject to guardianship under this Part of this Act absents himself without the leave of the guardian from the place at which he is required by the guardian to reside, he may, subject to the provisions of this section, be taken into custody and returned to that place by any officer on the staff of a local social services authority, by any constable, or by any person authorised in writing by the guardian or a local social services authority.

(4) A patient shall not be taken into custody under this section after the expiration of the period of 28 days beginning with the first day of his absence without leave; and a patient who has not returned or been taken into custody under this section within the said period shall cease to be liable to be detained or subject to guardianship, as the case may be, at the expiration of that period.

(5) A patient shall not be taken into custody under this section if the period for which he is liable to be detained is that specified in section 2(4), 4(4) or 5(2) or (4) above and that period has expired.

(6) In this Act "absent without leave" means absent from any hospital or other place and liable to be taken into custody and returned under this section, and related expressions shall be construed accordingly.

DEFINITIONS
"Patient": s.145(1).
"Hospital": ss.34(2), 145(1).
"Approved social worker": s.145(1).
"The managers": s.145(1).
"Local social services authority": s.145(1).

GENERAL NOTE
This section, which should be read in conjunction with s.21, below, identifies the action that can be taken when a detained patient or a patient subject to guardianship absents himself without leave, and provides that such a patient will cease to be liable to be detained or subject to guardianship if he has remained absent without leave for 28 days. It is applied, with modifications, to patients who have been placed under hospital orders, guardianship orders or restriction orders by a court under s.37 or 41, below (Sched. 1, Pt. I, para. 2, Pt. II, para. 2) and to patients who have been sentenced to imprisonment (s.22(2)(*b*)).
In the opinion of the Butler Committee "absconding often results either from mistaken diagnosis leading to inappropriate disposal to the hospital system or from the patient's inability to accept and co-operate in treatment" (Butler Report, para. 14.14).

Subs. (1)
Taken: The patient may be taken into custody in, and returned to England or Wales from, any other part of the United Kingdom or the Channel Islands or the Isle of Man (s.88).
Custody: Officer on the staff of the hospital: See the notes on s.17(3), above.

Subs. (2)
This subsection provides that if a patient has been granted leave of absence on condition that he resides in a hospital other than the one in which he is formally liable to be detained, he can be taken into custody by an officer on the staff of the hospital where he is on leave, or by a person authorised by the managers of that hospital.

Subs. (3)
Officer on the staff of the local social services authority: Who should, but need not be, a social worker.

Subs. (4)
After the expiration of the period of 28 days: But see subs. (5).
Beginning with: Including the first day of the patient's absence without leave.
At the expiration of that period: If the patient is returned to hospital within the 28 day period he can be detained for up to one week to enable the formalities for renewing the authority to detain to be completed (s.21(1)).

Subs. (5)
This subsection provides that a patient cannot be taken into custody under this section if the period of his detention under one of the following powers has expired: admission for assessment (s.2(4)), emergency admission (s.4(4)), or the detention of an in-patient by a doctor (s.5(2)) or nurse (s.5(4)).

Regulations as to transfer of patients

19.—(1) In such circumstances and subject to such conditions as may be prescribed by regulations made by the Secretary of State—
  (*a*) a patient who is for the time being liable to be detained in a hospital by virtue of an application under this Part of this Act may be transferred to another hospital or into the guardianship of a

local social services authority or of any person approved by such an authority;

(b) a patient who is for the time being subject to the guardianship of a local social services authority or other person by virtue of an application under this Part of this Act may be transferred into the guardianship of another local social services authority or person, or be transferred to a hospital.

(2) Where a patient is transferred in pursuance of regulations under this section, the provisions of this Part of this Act (including this sub-section) shall apply to him as follows, that is to say—

(a) in the case of a patient who is liable to be detained in a hospital by virtue of an application for admission for assessment or for treat-ment and is transferred to another hospital, as if the application were an application for admission to that other hospital and as if the patient had been admitted to that other hospital at the time when he was originally admitted in pursuance of the application;

(b) in the case of a patient who is liable to be detained in a hospital by virtue of such an application and is transferred into guardianship, as if the application were a guardianship application duly accepted at the said time;

(c) in the case of a patient who is subject to guardianship by virtue of a guardianship application and is transferred into the guardianship of another authority or person, as if the application were for his reception into the guardianship of that authority or person and had been accepted at the time when it was originally accepted;

(d) in the case of a patient who is subject to guardianship by virtue of a guardianship application and is transferred to a hospital, as if the guardianship application were an application for admission to that hospital for treatment and as if the patient had been admitted to the hospital at the time when the application was originally accepted.

(3) Without prejudice to subsections (1) and (2) above, any patient, who is for the time being liable to be detained under this Part of this Act in a hospital vested in the Secretary of State for the purposes of his functions under the National Health Service Act 1977 or any accommo-dation used under Part I of that Act by the managers of such a hospital, may at any time be removed to any other such hospital or accommodation for which the managers of the first-mentioned hospital are also the managers; and paragraph (a) of subsection (2) above shall apply in relation to a patient so removed as it applies in relation to a patient transferred in pursuance of regulations made under this section.

(4) Regulations made under this section may make provision for regulating the conveyance to their destination of patients authorised to be transferred or removed in pursuance of the regulations or under subsection (3) above.

DEFINITIONS
"Patient": s.145(1).
"Hospital": ss.34(2), 145(1).
"Local social services authority": s.145(1).
"Application for admission for assessment": ss.2, 145(1).
"Application for admission for treatment": ss.3, 145(1).
"The managers": s.145(1).

GENERAL NOTE
This section empowers the Secretary of State to regulate the circumstances in which detained patients and patients who are subject to guardianship may be transferred between hospitals or guardians or between hospital and guardianship. It is applied, with modifications,

to patients who have been placed under hospital orders, restriction orders or guardianship orders by a court under ss.37 or 41, below (Sched. 1, Pt. I, para. 2, Pt. II, para. 2).

Provisions relating to the transfer of patients to and from special hospitals are contained in s.123, below.

Subs. (1)

Regulations: For general provisions, see s.143, below.

para. (*b*)

Transferred to hospital: If a patient is transferred from guardianship to a hospital in pursuance of regulations made under this section he has a right of appeal to a Mental Health Review Tribunal (s.66(1)(*e*)). If he does not exercise this right within six months of the transfer, the hospital managers will automatically refer the case to the Tribunal (s.68(1)).

Subs. (3)

This subsection enables a patient to be transferred to another hospital managed by the same District Health Authority or special health authority.

Duration of detention or guardianship and discharge

Duration of authority

20.—(1) Subject to the following provisions of this Part of this Act, a patient admitted to hospital in pursuance of an application for admission for treatment, and a patient placed under guardianship in pursuance of a guardianship application, may be detained in a hospital or kept under guardianship for a period not exceeding six months beginning with the day on which he was so admitted, or the day on which the guardianship application was accepted, as the case may be, but shall not be so detained or kept for any longer period unless the authority for his detention or guardianship is renewed under this section.

(2) Authority for the detention or guardianship of a patient may, unless the patient has previously been discharged, be renewed—

(*a*) from the expiration of the period referred to in subsection (1) above, for a further period of six months;

(*b*) from the expiration of any period of renewal under paragraph (*a*) above, for a further period of one year,

and so on for periods of one year at a time.

(3) Within the period of two months ending on the day on which a patient who is liable to be detained in pursuance of an application for admission for treatment would cease under this section to be so liable in default of the renewal of the authority for his detention, it shall be the duty of the responsible medical officer—

(*a*) to examine the patient; and

(*b*) if it appears to him that the conditions set out in subsection (4) below are satisfied, to furnish to the managers of the hospital where the patient is detained a report to that effect in the prescribed form;

and where such a report is furnished in respect of a patient the managers shall, unless they discharge the patient, cause him to be informed.

(4) The conditions referred to in subsection (3) above are that—

(*a*) the patient is suffering from mental illness, severe mental impairment, psychopathic disorder or mental impairment, and his mental disorder is of a nature or degree which makes it appropriate for him to receive medical treatment in a hospital; and

(*b*) such treatment is likely to alleviate or prevent a deterioration of his condition; and

(*c*) it is necessary for the health or safety of the patient or for the protection of other persons that he should receive such treatment and that it cannot be provided unless he continues to be detained;

but, in the case of mental illness or severe mental impairment, it shall be an alternative to the condition specified in paragraph (*b*) above that the patient, if discharged, is unlikely to be able to care for himself, to obtain the care which he needs or to guard himself against serious exploitation.

(5) Before furnishing a report under subsection (3) above the responsible medical officer shall consult one or more other persons who have been professionally concerned with the patient's medical treatment.

(6) Within the period of two months ending with the day on which a patient who is subject to guardianship under this Part of this Act would cease under this section to be so liable in default of the renewal of the authority for his guardianship, it shall be the duty of the appropriate medical officer—

(*a*) to examine the patient; and

(*b*) if it appears to him that the conditions set out in subsection (7) below are satisfied, to furnish to the guardian and, where the guardian is a person other than a local social services authority, to the responsible local social services authority a report to that effect in the prescribed form;

and where such a report is furnished in respect of a patient, the local social services authority shall, unless they discharge the patient, cause him to be informed.

(7) The conditions referred to in subsection (6) above are that—

(*a*) the patient is suffering from mental illness, severe mental impairment, psychopathic disorder or mental impairment and his mental disorder is of a nature or degree which warrants his reception into guardianship; and

(*b*) it is necessary in the interests of the welfare of the patient or for the protection of other persons that the patient should remain under guardianship.

(8) Where a report is duly furnished under subsection (3) or (6) above, the authority for the detention or guardianship of the patient shall be thereby renewed for the period prescribed in that case by subsection (2) above.

(9) Where the form of mental disorder specified in a report furnished under subsection (3) or (6) above is a form of disorder other than that specified in the application for admission for treatment or, as the case may be, in the guardianship application, that application shall have effect as if that other form of mental disorder were specified in it; and where on any occasion a report specifying such a form of mental disorder is furnished under either of those subsections the appropriate medical officer need not on that occasion furnish a report under section 16 above.

(10) In this section "appropriate medical officer" has the same meaning as in section 16(5) above.

DEFINITIONS

"Patient": s.145(1).

"Hospital": ss.34(2), 145(1).

"Application for admission for treatment": ss.3, 145(1).

"The managers": s.145(1).

"Severe mental impairment": ss.1, 145(1).

"Psychopathic disorder": ss.1, 145(1).

"Mental impairment": ss.1, 145(1).

"Mental disorder": ss.1, 145(1).

"Medical treatment": s.145(1).

"Local social services authority": s.145(1).

"Responsible medical officer": s.34(1).

"Responsible local social services authority": s.34(1).

Transitional Provisions
Sched. 5, paras. 9, 33.

General Note
This section provides for patients who have been detained for treatment or placed under guardianship to be detained or kept under guardianship for an initial period of up to six months. It also sets out the criteria that have to be satisfied if the authority to detain a patient or keep him in guardianship is to be renewed. Renewal can be for one further period of six months and subsequently for periods of one year at a time.

This section is applied, with modifications, to patients who have been placed under hospital or guardianship orders by a court under s.37, below (Sched. 1, Pt. I, para. 2).

All patients, except those placed under hospital orders, have a right to appeal to a Mental Health Review Tribunal within six months of the application or guardianship order being made. Further appeals can be made by all patients on every occasion when authority to detain or keep a patient under guardianship is renewed under this section (s.66, as applied by Sched. 1).

Subs. (1)
Subject to the following provisions of this Part of this Act: Note especially the powers of discharge granted by s.23, below.
Beginning with: Including the day on which the patient was admitted to hospital or the day on which the guardianship application was accepted by the local social services authority (*Hare* v. *Gocher* [1962] 2 Q.B. 641).

Subs. (3)
This subsection requires the responsible medical officer to examine a patient detained for treatment during the two months preceding the day on which the authority for his detention is due to expire.
The day on which: The period of detention can be extended by virtue of s.21, below.

Subs. (4)
This subsection specifies the conditions which have to be satisfied if the authority to detain a patient who has been admitted for treatment is to be renewed. The alternative to condition (*b*) for patients who are mentally ill or severely mentally impaired was introduced because "the health and social services authorities have a clear responsibility to care for the mentally and severely mentally [impaired] and, where necessary, to protect the public from their actions. There will be a few cases where continued detention may be necessary but where there can be little expectation of treatment having a beneficial effect" (Cmnd. 7320, para. 2.44).

para. (*b*)
Unlikely to be able to care for himself, to obtain the care that he needs or to guard against serious exploitation: These words are capable of very wide interpretation.

para. (*c*)
This paragraph, which has to be satisfied for all patients to whom this section applies, means that a patient should not continue to be detained if he could be treated either informally or in the community.

Subs. (5)
One or more other persons: See the note on s.16(3), above.

Subs. (6)
This subsection provides for the renewal of the authority for guardianship.
The day on which: The period of guardianship can be extended under section 21, below.
Appropriate medical officer: Is defined in s.16(5), above.

Subs. (7)
This subsection specifies the conditions which have to be satisfied if the authority for guardianship is to be renewed.

Subs. (9)
This subsection states that if the doctor who makes a report under this section states in his report that the patient is suffering from a form of mental disorder other than that specified

in the original application, this has the effect of reclassifying the patient. There is, therefore, no need for the doctor to make a separate report under s.16, above.

Special provisions as to patients absent without leave

21.—(1) If on the day on which, apart from this section, a patient would cease to be liable to be detained or subject to guardianship under this Part of this Act or, within the period of one week ending with that day, the patient is absent without leave, he shall not cease to be so liable or subject—

(a) in any case, until the expiration of the period during which he can be taken into custody under section 18 above or the day on which he is returned or returns himself to the hospital or place where he ought to be, whichever is the earlier; and

(b) if he is so returned or so returns himself within the period first mentioned in paragraph (a) above, until the expiration of the period of one week beginning with the day on which he is so returned or so returns.

(2) Where the period for which a patient is liable to be detained or subject to guardianship is extended by virtue of this section, any examination and report to be made and furnished under section 20(3) or (6) above may be made and furnished within that period as so extended.

(3) Where the authority for the detention or guardianship of a patient is renewed by virtue of this section after the day on which, apart from this section, that authority would have expired under section 20, above, the renewal shall take effect as from that day.

DEFINITIONS
"Patient": s.145(1).
"Absent without leave": ss.18(6), 145(1).
"Hospital": ss.34(2), 145(1).

GENERAL NOTE
This section provides that if on the day on which a patient would otherwise cease to be liable to be detained or subject to guardianship he is absent without leave, he will not then cease to be so liable or subject until the expiration of the period within which he could have been taken into custody under s.18, above, or until he is returned or returns to the hospital or place where he ought to be, whichever is the earlier. If the patient is returned or returns himself within the 28-day period specified in s.18(4), above, he can be detained for a period of one week beginning with the day on which he returned.

This section is applied to patients who have been placed under hospital or guardianship orders by a court under s.37, below (Sched. 1, Pt. I, para. 1), to patients who have been sentenced to imprisonment (s.22(2)(b)) and to patients who have been retaken after having escaped from custody (s.138(6)).

Special provisions as to patients sentenced to imprisonment, etc.

22.—(1) Where a patient who is liable to be detained by virtue of an application for admission for treatment or is subject to guardianship by virtue of a guardianship application is detained in custody in pursuance of any sentence or order passed or made by a court on the United Kingdom (including an order committing or remanding him in custody), and is so detained for a period exceeding, or for successive periods exceeding in the aggregate, six months, the application shall cease to have effect at the expiration of that period.

(2) Where any such patient is so detained in custody but the application does not cease to have effect under subsection (1) above, then—

(a) if apart from this subsection the patient would have ceased to be liable to be so detained or subject to guardianship on or before the day on which he is discharged from custody, he shall not cease and shall be deemed not to have ceased to be so liable or subject until the end of that day; and

(*b*) in any case, sections 18 and 21 above shall apply in relation to the patient as if he had absented himself without leave on that day.

DEFINITIONS.
"Patient": s.145(1).
"Application for admission for treatment": ss.3, 145(1).
"Absent without leave": ss.18(6), 145(1).

GENERAL NOTE
This section provides that if a patient who is the subject of an application for treatment or a guardianship application is sentenced, or committed or remanded to custody, by a court for a period of more than six months, the application will cease to have effect at the expiration of the period spent in custody. If the patient is detained in custody for less than six months and would, in the ordinary course of events, have ceased to be liable to be detained for treatment or subject to guardianship prior to his discharge from custody, he does not cease to be so liable or subject until end of the day on which he is discharged, and for the purposes of ss.18 and 21 of this Act he will be treated as if he had absconded himself without leave on that day, *i.e.* the patient can be taken into custody within 28 days of his release (s.18(3)) and the authority to detain him can be renewed during that period (s.21(1)).
This section is applied, with modifications, to patients who have been placed under hospital, guardianship or restriction orders by a court under ss. 37 or 41, below (Sched. 1, Pt. I, para. 2, Pt. 2, para. 2).

Subs. (1)
United Kingdom: This means Great Britain and Northern Ireland (Interpretation Act 1978, s.5, Sched. 1).

Discharge of patients

23.—(1) Subject to the provisions of this section and section 25 below, a patient who is for the time being liable to be detained or subject to guardianship under this Part of this Act shall cease to be so liable or subject if an order in writing discharging him from detention or guardianship (in this Act referred to as "an order for discharge") is made in accordance with this section.

(2) An order for discharge may be made in respect of a patient—

(*a*) where the patient is liable to be detained in a hospital in pursuance of an application for admission for assessment or for treatment by the responsible medical officer, by the managers or by the nearest relative of the patient;

(*b*) where the patient is subject to guardianship, by the responsible medical officer, by the responsible local social services authority or by the nearest relative of the patient.

(3) Where the patient is liable to be detained in a mental nursing home in pursuance of an application for admission for assessment or for treatment, an order for his discharge may, without prejudice to subsection (2) above, be made by the Secretary of State and, if the patient is maintained under a contract with a Regional Health Authority, District Health Authority or special health authority, by that authority.

(4) The powers conferred by this section on any authority or body of persons may be exercised by any three or more members of that authority or body authorised by them in that behalf or by three or more members of a committee or sub-committee of that authority or body which has been authorised by them in that behalf.

DEFINITIONS
"Patient": s.145(1).
"Hospital": ss.34(2), 145(1).
"Application for admission for assessment": ss.2, 145(1).

"The managers": s.145(1).
"Nearest relative": ss.26(3), 145(1).
"Local social services authority": s.145(1).
"Mental nursing home": s.145(1).
"Application for admission for treatment": ss.3, 145(1).
"Responsible medical officer": s.34(1).

TRANSITIONAL PROVISION
Sched. 5, para. 10.

GENERAL NOTE
This section provides for the discharge of detained patients and patients who are subject to guardianship to be ordered by the responsible medical officer, the hospital managers (or the responsible local social services authority for guardianship patients) or the patient's nearest relative. It is applied, with modifications, to patients who have been placed under hospital, guardianship or restriction orders by a court under s.37 or 41, below (Sched. 1, Pt. 1, para. 2, Pt. 2, para. 2).

Subs. (2).
Order for discharge: There are no criteria governing the exercise of this power.
Responsible medical officer: Note that neither the responsible medical officer nor the hospital managers are placed under a legal obligation to change the status of detained patients or patients subject to guardianship if the grounds for the original application are found to no longer exist.
The managers: It appears that the hospital managers rarely make an independent assessment of the patient's need for continued detention. The managers can delegate their functions under subs. (4).
Nearest relative: Seventy-two hours notice to the hospital managers must be given (s.25(1)). The patient's responsible medical officer can nullify the nearest relative's order for the discharge of a patient detained for treatment or assessment by furnishing a report under s.25, below. In the case of a patient detained for treatment, the nearest relative has a right to apply to a Mental Health Review Tribunal if a report is furnished under s.25 (s.66(1)(g), (2)(d)).
A doctor may visit and examine the patient for the purpose of advising a nearest relative on the exercise of his right of discharge; see section 24(1)(2), below.
Guardianship: The responsible medical officer has no power to prevent a nearest relative obtaining the discharge of a patient who is subject to guardianship.
Responsible local social services authority: Is defined in s.34(3), below.

Subs. (3).
Mental nursing home: For powers relating to patients detained in mental nursing homes, see s.24(3)(4), below.

Subs. (4)
May be: Health authorities have been advised to appoint a small committee or sub-committee to carry out their functions under this section (Cmnd. 7320, para. 3.19).

Visiting and examination of patients

24.—(1) For the purpose of advising as to the exercise by the nearest relative of a patient who is liable to be detained or subject to guardianship under this Part of this Act of any power to order his discharge, any registered medical practitioner authorised by or on behalf of the nearest relative of the patient may, at any reasonable time, visit the patient and examine him in private.

(2) Any registered medical practitioner authorised for the purposes of subsection (1) above to visit and examine a patient may require the production of and inspect any records relating to the detention or treatment of the patient in any hospital.

(3) Where application is made by the Secretary of State or a Regional Health Authority, District Health Authority or special health authority to exercise, in respect of a patient liable to be detained in a mental nursing

home, any power to make an order for his discharge, the following persons, that is to say—

  (*a*) any registered medical practitioner authorised by the Secretary of State or, as the case may be, that authority; and
  (*b*) any other person (whether a registered medical practitioner or not) authorised under the Nursing Homes Act 1975 to inspect the home,

may at any reasonable time visit the patient and interview him in private.

  (4) Any person authorised for the purposes of subsection (3) above to visit a patient may require the production of and inspect any documents constituting or alleged to constitute the authority for the detention of the patient under this Part of this Act; and any person so authorised, who is a registered medical practitioner, may examine the patient in private, and may require the production of and inspect any other records relating to the treatment of the patient in the home.

DEFINITIONS
  "Nearest relative": ss.26(3), 145(1).
  "Patient": s.145(1).
  "Hospital": ss.34(2), 145(1).
  "Mental nursing home": s.145(1).

GENERAL NOTE
  This section provides for the visiting and examination of patients and for the production of documents in connection with the power to order the discharge of a detained patient from a hospital or a mental nursing home. Subss. (3) and (4) are applied to patients who have been placed under hospital, restriction or guardianship orders by a court under s.37 or 41, below (Sched. 1, Pt. I, para. 1, Pt. II, para. 2).
  A person who fails to allow the visiting, interviewing or examination of a patient or who refuses to produce any document for inspection commits an offence under s.129, below.

Subs. (1).
  Nearest relative: Or acting nearest relative appointed by a county court under s.29, below.
  Power to order his discharge: Under s.23(2), above.

Restrictions on discharge by nearest relative

  25.—(1) An order for the discharge of a patient who is liable to be detained in a hospital shall not be made by his nearest relative except after giving not less than 72 hours' notice in writing to the managers of the hospital; and if, within 72 hours after such notice has been given, the responsible medical officer furnishes to the managers a report certifying that in the opinion of that officer the patient, if discharged, would be likely to act in a manner dangerous to other persons or to himself—

  (*a*) any order for the discharge of the patient made by that relative in pursuance of the notice shall be of no effect; and
  (*b*) no further order for the discharge of the patient shall be made by that relative during the period of six months beginning with the date of the report.

  (2) In any case where a report under subsection (1) above is furnished in respect of a patient who is liable to be detained in pursuance of an application for admission for treatment the managers shall cause the nearest relative of the patient to be informed.

DEFINITIONS
  "Patient": s.145(1).
  "Hospital": ss.34(2), 145(1).
  "Nearest relative": ss.26(3), 145(1).
  "The managers": s.145(1).
  "Application for admission for treatment": ss.3, 145(1).
  "Responsible medical officer": s.34(1).

GENERAL NOTE
This section states that a nearest relative must give 72 hours notice to the hospital managers of his intention to order the discharge of the patient and that the order for discharge, when made, will have no effect if, in the meantime, the responsible medical officer has reported to the managers that, in his opinion, the patient, if discharged, would be likely to act in a manner dangerous to other persons or to himself.

Subs. (1)
Order for the discharge: Power is given to the nearest relative to order the discharge of the patient from hospital by section 23(2)(*a*), above.
Liable to be detained in a hospital: This section does not effect the right of a nearest relative to order the discharge of a patient who is subject to guardianship; see section 23(2)(*b*), above.
Nearest relative: Or acting nearest relative appointed by the county court under section 29, below.
72 hours' notice: Which could cover weekend or holiday periods.
Beginning with: Including the date of the report (*Hare* v. *Gocher* [1962] 2 Q.B. 641).

Subs. (2)
Cause the nearest relative to be informed: So that the nearest relative could consider appealing to a Mental Health Review Tribunal (s.66(1)(*g*), (2)(*d*)). The nearest relative of a patient who has been detained for assessment does not have an equivalent right of appeal.

Functions of relatives of patients

Definition of "relative" and "nearest" relative

26.—(1) In this Part of this Act "relative" means any of the following persons:—
    (*a*) husband or wife;
    (*b*) son or daughter;
    (*c*) father or mother;
    (*d*) brother or sister;
    (*e*) grandparent;
    (*f*) grandchild;
    (*g*) uncle or aunt;
    (*h*) nephew or niece.
  (2) In deducing relationships for the purposes of this section, any relationship of the half-blood shall be treated as a relationship of the whole blood, and an illegitimate person shall be treated as the legitimate child of his mother.
  (3) In this Part of this Act, subject to the provisions of this section and to the following provisions of this Part of this Act, the "nearest relative" means the person first described in subsection (1) above who is for the time being surviving, relatives of the whole blood being preferred to relatives of the same description of the half-blood and the elder or eldest of two or more relatives described in any paragraph of that subsection being preferred to the other or others of those relatives, regardless of sex.
  (4) Subject to the provisions of this section and to the following provisions of this Part of this Act, where the patient ordinarily resides with or is cared for by one or more of his relatives (or, if he is for the time being an in-patient in a hospital, he last ordinarily resided with or was cared for by one or more of his relatives) his nearest relative shall be determined—
    (*a*) by giving preference to that relative or those relatives over the other or others; and
    (*b*) as between two or more such relatives, in accordance with subsection (3) above.

(5) Where the person who, under subsection (3) or (4) above, would be the nearest relative of a patient—

(*a*) in the case of a patient ordinarily resident in the United Kingdom, the Channel Islands or the Isle of Man, is not so resident; or

(*b*) is the husband or wife of the patient, but is permanently separated from the patient, either by agreement or under an order of a court, or has deserted or has been deserted by the patient for a period which has not come to an end; or

(*c*) is a person other than the husband, wife, father or mother of the patient, and is for the time being under 18 years of age; or

(*d*) is a person against whom an order divesting him of authority over the patient has been made under section 38 of the Sexual Offences Act 1956 (which relates to incest with a person under eighteen) and has not been rescinded,

the nearest relative of the patient shall be ascertained as if that person were dead.

(6) In this section "husband" and "wife" include a person who is living with the patient as the patient's husband or wife, as the case may be (or, if the patient is for the time being an in-patient in a hospital, was so living until the patient was admitted), and has been or had been so living for a period of not less than six months; but a person shall not be treated by virtue of this subsection as the nearest relative of a married patient unless the husband or wife of the patient is disregarded by virtue of paragraph (*b*) of subsection (5) above.

(7) A person, other than a relative, with whom the patient ordinarily resides (or, if the patient is for the time being an in-patient in a hospital, last ordinarily resided before he was admitted), and with whom he has or had been ordinarily residing for a period of not less than five years, shall be treated for the purposes of this Part of this Act as if he were a relative but—

(*a*) shall be treated for the purposes of subsection (3) above as if mentioned last in subsection (1) above; and

(*b*) shall not be treated by virtue of this subsection as the nearest relative of a married patient unless the husband or wife of the patient is disregarded by virtue of paragraph (*b*) of subsection (5) above.

DEFINITIONS
    "Hospital": ss.34(2), 145(1).
    "Patient": s.145(1).

TRANSITIONAL PROVISION
    Sched. 5, para. 11.

GENERAL NOTE
    This section, which defines "relative" and "nearest relative," is applied to patients who have been placed under hospital or guardianship orders by a court under s.37, below (Sched. 1, Pt. 1, para. 1).

Subs. (1)
    If a relative of a patient is not one of the relatives specified in this subsection, that person cannot be a relative for the purposes of this Act. However, such a person could be appointed by the county court to be the patient's acting nearest relative under s.29, below. For the occasions when relatives will be disregarded for the purposes of ascertaining the patient's "nearest relative," see subs. (5).
    Husband or wife: Even if the marital partner is under the age of 18 (subs. (5)(*c*)). Note that if the patient is unmarried or if the marital partner can be disregarded under subs. (5)(*b*), a person who had been living with the patient as the patient's husband or wife for at least six months will be treated as if they were the patient's husband or wife (subs. (6)).

Son or daughter: An adopted child is treated as if he were the child of his adoptive parents (Children Act 1975, Sched. 1) and an illegitimate child is treated as if he were the legitimate child of his mother (Subs. (2)). The child must be over the age of 18 (subs. (5)(c)).

Father or mother: Even if the parent is under the age of 18 (subs. (5)(c)). A father of an illegitimate child (subs. (2)) and a parent who has been divested of his authority over the child under the Sexual Offences Act 1956 (subs. (5)(d)) are to be disregarded. In cases where parental rights have been vested in a local authority or where a person has been given custody or guardianship over a child, that authority (s.27) or person (s.28) is deemed to be the child's nearest relative. If the child is a ward of court the functions of the nearest relative can only be exercised with the leave of the High Court (s.33(2)).

Subs. (3)

Nearest relative: If the patient has no nearest relative or if it is not reasonably practicable to ascertain whether he has such a relative, or who that relative is, an application may be made to the county court for the appointment of an acting nearest relative under s.29(3)(a), below.

Subs. (4)

This subsection provides that if the patient is either living with or being cared for by a relative, that relative becomes the patient's nearest relative.

Ordinarily resides: "Unless . . . it can be shown that the statutory framework or the legal context in which the words are used requires a different meaning. I unhesitatingly subscribe to the view that 'ordinarily resident' refers to a man's abode in a particular place or country which he has adopted voluntarily and for settled purposes as part of the regular order of his life for the time being, whether short or long duration": *Shah* v. *Barnet London Borough Council* [1983] 1 All E.R. 226, H.L., *per* Lord Scarman at p.235.

Cared for: The patient may be "cared for" on a daily basis by a relative even if they do not share a residence. This would include cases where a relative shopped, cooked and did housework for a handicapped or disturbed person who was not capable of looking after himself.

Subs. (5)

This subsection which disqualifies certain persons from acting as a patient's nearest relative, is applied to persons who have been deemed to be the patient's nearest relative by virtue of s.28, below (s.28(2)).

United Kingdom: This means Great Britain and Northern Ireland (Interpretation Act 1978, s.5, Sched. 1).

Deserted: Here means a desertion in fact rather than the desertion of two years required by s.1(2)(c) of the Matrimonial Causes Act 1973.

Under 18 years of age: Means before the commencement of his eighteenth birthday (Family Law Reform Act 1969, s.9(1)).

Subs. (6)

Living with the patient as the patient's husband or wife: Whether a couple are living together as husband and wife is a question of fact. For a discussion of "living together as husband and wife" in the context of social security law, see *The Law of Social Security*, Ogus and Barendt, 1982, pp.384–386.

Subs. (7)

This subsection provides that a person who has been living with the patient for five years or more shall be treated as if came last on the hierarchy of relatives set out in subs. (1). By virtue of subs. (4) that person would become the patient's nearest relative, unless a relative who came higher in the hierarchy was also living with the patient.

There may be difficulties in identifying the patient's nearest relative in cases where the patient has been residing with a number of people for five years or more. This situation could occur where, for example, the patient is a member of a religious community or if he lives in a residential institution. In this situation the provisions of subs. (3) would apply and the eldest person who had become a "relative" under this subsection would become the patient's nearest relative.

Ordinarily resides: Note that this provision does not require the patient and the person with whom he has resided for five years or more to regard each other as husband or wife, or to be lovers, or even to be friends. Also see the note on subs. (4).

Five years: Temporary separations resulting, for example, from separate holidays being taken should be disregarded in calculating this period.

Children and young persons in care of local authority

27. In any case where the rights and powers of a parent of a patient, being a child or young person, are vested in a local authority or other person by virtue of—

(a) section 3 of the Child Care Act 1980 (which relates to the assumption by a local authority of parental rights and duties in relation to a child in their care);

(b) section 10 of that Act (which relates to the powers and duties of local authorities with respect to persons committed to their care under the Children and Young Persons Act 1969); or

(c) section 17 of the Social Work (Scotland) Act 1968 (which makes corresponding provision for Scotland),

that authority or person shall be deemed to be the nearest relative of the patient in preference to any person except the patient's husband or wife (if any) and except, in a case where the said rights and powers are vested in a local authority by virtue of subsection (1) of the said section 3, any parent of the patient not being the person on whose account the resolution mentioned in that subsection was passed.

DEFINITIONS
   "Patient": s.145(1).
   "Nearest relative": ss.26(3), 145(1).

GENERAL NOTE
   This section provides that, except where a child is married, a local authority becomes the nearest relative of a child in any case where parental rights in respect of the child are vested in the authority. It is applied to children who have been placed under hospital or guardianship orders by a court under s.37, below (Sched. 1, Pt. I, para. 1).
   Any parent of the patient: If a local authority has assumed parental rights under s.3 of the Child Care Act 1980 in respect of one parent only, the other parent remains as the child's nearest relative if the child is unmarried. If the child is married, the marital partner becomes the child's nearest relative.

Nearest relative of minor under guardianship, etc.

28.—(1) Where a patient who has not attained the age of 18 years—

(a) is, by virtue of an order made by a court in the exercise of jurisdiction (whether under any enactment or otherwise) in respect of the guardianship of minors (including an order under section 38 of the Sexual Offences Act 1956), or by virtue of a deed or will executed by his father or mother, under the guardianship of a person who is not his nearest relative under the foregoing provisions of this Act, or is under the joint guardianship of two persons of whom one is such a person; or

(b) is, by virtue of an order made by a court in the exercise of such jurisdiction or in matrimonial proceedings, or by virtue of a separation agreement between his father and mother, in the custody of any such person,

the person or persons having the guardianship or custody of the patient shall, to the exclusion of any other person, be deemed to be his nearest relative.

(2) Subsection (5) of section 26 above shall apply in relation to a person who is, or who is one of the persons, deemed to be the nearest relative of a patient by virtue of this section as it applies in relation to a person who would be the nearest relative under subsection (3) of that section.

(3) A patient shall be treated for the purposes of this section as being in the custody of another person if he would be in that other person's custody apart from section 8 above.

(4) In this section "court" includes a court in Scotland or Northern Ireland, and "enactment" includes an enactment of the Parliament of Northern Ireland, a Measure of the Northern Ireland Assembly and an Order in Council under Schedule 1 of the Northern Ireland Act 1974.

DEFINITIONS
  "Patient": s.145(1).
  "Nearest relative": ss.26(3), 145(1).

GENERAL NOTE
  This section provides for a person who has guardianship or custody over a child to become the child's nearest relative. It is applied to children who have been placed under hospital or guardianship orders by a court under s.37, below. (Sched. 1, Pt. I, para. 1).

Subs. (1)
  Attained the age: At the commencement of his eighteenth birthday (Family Law Reform Act 1969, s.9(1)).
  Guardianship: This section does not apply to custodianship orders which a court will, at some time in the future, be able to make under s.33 of the Children Act 1975.
  Person or persons: Thus two persons, as co-guardians could have equal powers as the patients nearest relative. Compare this with s.26(3), above, where only a sole nearest relative is contemplated.

Appointment by court of acting nearest relative

29.—(1) The county court may, upon application made in accordance with the provisions of this section in respect of a patient, by order direct that the functions of the nearest relative of the patient under this Part of this Act and sections 66 and 69 below shall, during the continuance in force of the order, be exercisable by the applicant, or by any other person specified in the application, being a person who, in the opinion of the court, is a proper person to act as the patient's nearest relative and is willing to do so.

(2) An order under this section may be made on the application of—
  (*a*) any relative of the patient;
  (*b*) any other person with whom the patient is residing (or, if the patient is then an in-patient in a hospital, was last residing before he was admitted); or
  (*c*) an approved social worker;
but in relation to an application made by such a social worker, subsection (1) above shall have effect as if for the words "the applicant" there were substituted the words "the local social services authority."

(3) An application for an order under this section may be made upon any of the following grounds, that is to say—
  (*a*) that the patient has no nearest relative within the meaning of this Act, or that it is not reasonably practicable to ascertain whether he has such a relative, or who that relative is;
  (*b*) that the nearest relative of the patient is incapable of acting as such by reason of mental disorder or other illness;
  (*c*) that the nearest relative of the patient unreasonably objects to the making of an application for admission for treatment or a guardianship application in respect of the patient; or
  (*d*) that the nearest relative of the patient has exercised without due regard to the welfare of the patient or the interests of the public his power to discharge the patient from hospital or guardianship under this Part of this Act, or is likely to do so.

(4) If, immediately before the expiration of the period for which a patient is liable to be detained by virtue of an application for admission for assessment, an application under this section, which is an application made on the ground specified in subsection (3)(*c*) or (*d*) above, is pending in respect of the patient, that period shall be extended—

(*a*) in any case, until the application under this section has been finally disposed of; and

(*b*) if an order is made in pursuance of the application under this section, for a further period of seven days;

and for the purposes of this subsection an application under this section shall be deemed to have been finally disposed of at the expiration of the time allowed for appealing from the decision of the court or, if notice of appeal has been given within that time, when the appeal has been heard or withdrawn, and "pending" shall be construed accordingly.

(5) An order made on the ground specified in subsection (3)(*a*) or (*b*) above may specify a period for which it is to continue in force unless previously discharged under section 30 below.

(6) While an order made under this section is in force, the provisions of this Part of this Act (other than this section and section 30 below) and sections 66, 69, 132(4) and 133 below shall apply in relation to the patient as if for any reference to the nearest relative of the patient there were substituted a reference to the person having the functions of that relative and (without prejudice to section 30 below) shall so apply notwithstanding that the person who was the patient's nearest relative when the order was made is no longer his nearest relative; but this subsection shall not apply to section 66 below in the case mentioned in paragraph (*h*) of subsection (1) of that section.

DEFINITIONS
"Patient": s.145(1).
"Nearest relative": ss.26(3), 145(1).
"Hospital": ss.34(2), 145(1).
"Approved social worker": s.145(1).
"Local social services authority": s.145(1).
"Mental disorder": ss.1, 145(1).
"Application for admission for treatment": ss.3, 145(1).
"Application for admission for assessment": ss.2, 145(1).

GENERAL NOTE
The section gives the county court power to make an order directing that the functions of the nearest relative shall be exercised by another person, or by a local social services authority. A nearest relative who has been supplanted by an order under this section can apply to a Mental Health Review Tribunal (ss.66(1)(*h*), (2)(*g*)). An appeal lies from the county court to the Court of Appeal on a point of law.

Subs. (1)
County court: For the procedure on an application to the county court, see s.31, below.
Application: In *B.(A.)* v. *B.(L.)* (Mental Health Patient) [1980] 1 W.L.R. 116, the Court of Appeal held that under the provisions of the relevant county court rule (now see, the County Court Rules 1981, Ord. 49, r.12(4)) it was sufficient that the medical reports were handed to the applicant's legal adviser in circumstances where the adviser could give advice and take instructions.
Exercisable by the applicant: Except where the applicant is an approved social worker; see subs. (2).
Willing to do so: The consent of the relevant person or local services authority should be obtained prior to the application being made to the county court.

Subs. (2)
Relative: Is defined in s.26(1), above.

Subs. (3)

Para. (a): There is no obligation placed on an approved social worker to seek an order under this section if the patient has no nearest relative.

Para. (c):

Unreasonably objects: In *W.* v. *L.* [1974] Q.B. 711 the Court of Appeal held that the proper test for the county court to apply is an objective one: the court should ask what a reasonable person would do in all the circumstances, and not ask whether the actual nearest relative involved in the case was behaving reasonably from his own point of view. Also see, *S.* v. *G.*, Sheffield county court [1981] J.S.W.L. 174.

"The object of an application under [this para.] is to enable the provisions of [s.3] to be brought into operation, and until an application has been dealt with under [this section the approved social worker] is not in a position to make an application under [s.3]. It follows, so it seems to me, that if there were any defects for the purposes of [s.3] in the form of the reports tendered to the county court judge they were irrelevant for the purposes of . . . the application. The county court judge had to look at the reports for their medical content; he was not concerned with their statutory form"; *B.(A.)* v. *B.(L.)* (*Mental Health Patient*) *ibid.*, *per* Lawton L.J. at p.121.

Para. (d):

Power to discharge the patient: Under s.23, above.

Subs. (4)

This subsection provides that if the patient is detained for assessment and an application is made to the county court on ground (*c*) or (*d*), above, the period for which the patient may be detained is extended until the application is finally disposed of and, if an order is made, for a further period of seven days.

Subs. (6)

This subsection provides that an order made under this section remains in force notwithstanding that the person who was the patient's nearest relative when the order was made is no longer his nearest relative.

Discharge and variation of orders under s.29

30.—(1) An order made under section 29 above in respect of a patient may be discharged by the county court upon application made—

    (*a*) in any case, by the person having the functions of the nearest relative of the patient by virtue of the order;

    (*b*) where the order was made on the ground specified in paragraph (*a*) or paragraph (*b*) of section 29(3) above, or where the person who was the nearest relative of the patient when the order was made has ceased to be his nearest relative, on the application of the nearest relative of the patient.

(2) An order made under section 29 above in respect of a patient may be varied by the county court, on the application of the person having the functions of the nearest relative by virtue of the order or on the application of an approved social worker, by substituting for the first-mentioned person a local social services authority or any other person who in the opinion of the court is a proper person to exercise those functions, being an authority or person who is willing to do so.

(3) If the person having the functions of the nearest relative of a patient by virtue of an order under section 29 above dies—

    (*a*) subsections (1) and (2) above shall apply as if for any reference to that person there were substituted a reference to any relative of the patient, and

    (*b*) until the order is discharged or varied under those provisions the functions of the nearest relative under this Part of this Act and sections 66 and 69 below shall not be exercisable by any person.

(4) An order under section 29 above shall, unless previously discharged under subsection (1) above, cease to have effect at the expiration of the period, if any, specified under subsection (5) of that section or, where no such period is specified—

(a) If the patient was on the date of the order liable to be detained in pursuance of an application for admission for treatment or by virtue of an order or direction under Part III of this Act (otherwise than under section 35, 36 or 38) or was subject to guardianship under this Part of this Act or by virtue of such an order or direction, or becomes so liable or subject within the period of three months beginning with that date, when he ceases to be so liable or subject (otherwise than on being transferred in pursuance of regulations under section 19 above);

(b) if the patient was not on the date of the order, and has not within the said period become, so liable or subject, at the expiration of that period.

(5) The discharge or variation under this section of an order made under section 29 above shall not affect the validity of anything previously done in pursuance of the order.

DEFINITIONS
"Patient": s.145(1).
"Nearest relative": ss.26(3), 145(1).
"Approved social worker": s.145(1).
"Application for admission for treatment": ss.3, 145(1).

GENERAL NOTE
This section provides for the discharge or variation of an order made by a county court under s.29, above, for the appointment of an acting nearest relative. It also, in subs. (4), specifies when such an order will cease to have effect.

Supplemental

Procedure on applications to county court

31. County court rules which relate to applications authorised by this Part of this Act to be made to a county court may make provision—
(a) for the hearing and determination of such applications otherwise than in open court;
(b) for the admission on the hearing of such applications of evidence of such descriptions as may be specified in the rules notwithstanding anything to the contrary in any enactment or rule of law relating to the admissibility of evidence:
(c) for the visiting and interviewing of patients in private by or under the directions of the court.

DEFINITION
"Patient": s.145(1).

GENERAL NOTE
This section is applied to patients who have been placed under hospital or guardianship orders by a court under s.37, below. (Sched. 1, Pt. I, para. 1).
County court rules: See the County Court Rules 1981 (S.I. 1981 No. 1687), Ord. 49, r.12.
Otherwise than in open court: The publication of information relating to proceedings before a county court sitting in private is a contempt of court under s.12(1)(b) of the Administration of Justice Act 1960.

Regulations for purposes of Part II

32.—(1) The Secretary of State may make regulations for prescribing anything which, under this Part of this Act, is required or authorised to be prescribed, and otherwise for carrying this Part of this Act into full effect.

(2) Regulations under this section may in particular make provision—
(a) for prescribing the form of any application, recommendation,

report, order, notice or other document to be made or given under this Part of this Act;

(b) for prescribing the manner in which any such application, recommendation, report, order, notice or other document may be proved, and for regulating the service of any such application, report, order or notice;

(c) for requiring the managers of hospitals and local social services authorities to keep such registers or other records as may be prescribed by the regulations in respect of patients liable to be detained or subject to guardianship under this Part of this Act, and to furnish or make available to those patients, and their relatives, such written statements of their rights and powers under this Act as may be so prescribed;

(d) for the determination in accordance with the regulations of the age of any person whose exact age cannot be ascertained by reference to the registers kept under the Births and Deaths Registration Act 1953; and

(e) for enabling the functions under this Part of this Act of the nearest relative of a patient to be performed, in such circumstances and subject to such conditions (if any) as may be prescribed by the regulations, by any person authorised in that behalf by that relative;

and for the purposes of this Part of this Act any application, report or notice the service of which is regulated under paragraph (b) above shall be deemed to have been received by or furnished to the authority or person to whom it is authorised or required to be furnished, addressed or given if it is duly served in accordance with the regulations.

(3) Without prejudice to subsections (1) and (2) above, but subject to section 23(4) above, regulations under this section may determine the manner in which functions under this Part of this Act of the managers of hospitals, local social services authorities, Regional Health Authorities, District Health Authorities or special health authorities are to be exercised, and such regulations may in particular specify the circumstances in which, and the conditions subject to which, any such functions may be performed by officers of or other persons acting on behalf of those managers and authorities.

DEFINITIONS
"The managers": s.145(1).
"Hospital": ss.34(2), 145(1).
"Local social services authority": s.145(1).
"Patient": s.145(1).
"Nearest relative": ss.26(3), 145(1).

GENERAL NOTE
New regulations to replace the Mental Health (Hospital and Guardianship) Regulations 1960 will come into force on September 30, 1983.

Special provisions as to wards of court

33.—(1) An application for the admission to hospital of a minor who is a ward of court may be made under this Part of this Act with the leave of the court; and section 11(4) above shall not apply in relation to an application so made.

(2) Where a minor who is a ward of court is liable to be detained in a hospital by virtue of an application for admission under this Part of this Act, any power exercisable under this Part of this Act or under section 66 below in relation to the patient by his nearest relative shall be exercisable by or with the leave of the court.

(3) Nothing in this Part of this Act shall be construed as authorising the making of a guardianship application in respect of a minor who is a ward of court, or the transfer into guardianship of any such minor.

DEFINITIONS
  "Hospital": ss.34(2), 145(1).
  "Nearest relative": s.26(3), 145(1).

GENERAL NOTE
  This section provides that the leave of the High Court must be obtained before a ward of court can be compulsorily detained in hospital, and before the ward's nearest relative exercises his powers.

Interpretation of Part II

34.—(1) In this Part of this Act—
  "the nominated medical attendant", in relation to a patient who is subject to the guardianship of a person other than a local social services authority, means the person appointed in pursuance of regulations made under section 9(2) above to act as the medical attendant of the patient;
  "the responsible medical officer" means—
  (*a*) in relation to a patient liable to be detained by virtue of an application for admission for assessment or an application for admission for treatment, the registered medical practitioner in charge of the treatment of the patient;
  (*b*) in relation to a patient subject to guardianship, the medical officer authorised by the local social services authority to act (either generally or in any particular case or for any particular purpose) as the responsible medical officer.

(2) Except where otherwise expressly provided, this Part of this Act applies in relations to a mental nursing home, being a home in respect of which the particulars of registration are for the time being entered in the separate part of the register kept for the purposes of section 3(4)(*b*) of the Nursing Homes Act 1975, as it applies in relation to a hospital, and references in this Part of this Act to a hospital, and any reference in this Act to a hospital to which this Part of this Act applies, shall be construed accordingly.

(3) In relation to a patient who is subject to guardianship in pursuance of a guardianship application, any reference in this Part of this Act to the responsible local social services authority is a reference—
  (*a*) where the patient is subject to the guardianship of a local social services authority, to that authority;
  (*b*) where the patient is subject to the guardianship of a person other than a local social services authority, to the local social services authority for the area in which that person resides.

DEFINITIONS
  "Patient": s.145(1).
  "Local social services authority": s.145(1).
  "Application for admission for assessment": ss.2, 145(1).
  "Application for admission for treatment": ss.3, 145(1).
  "Mental nursing home": s.145(1).
  "Hospital": s.145(1).

GENERAL NOTE
  This section is applied, with modifications, to patients who have been placed under hospital, restriction or guardianship orders by a court under s.37 or 41 of this Act (Sched. 1, Pt. I, para. 1, Pt. II, para. 2).

Subs. (1)

Medical practitioner in charge of the treatment of the patient: This will usually be the consultant psychiatrist on the staff of the hospital under whose care the patient has been admitted. However, determining such a person is a question of fact and the medical practitioner need not necessarily have consultant status.

Subs. (2)

Register kept: By a District Health Authority by virtue of the National Health Service Functions (Direction to Authorities and Administration Arrangements) Regulations 1982 (S.I. 1982 No. 287).

Subs. (3)

Responsible local social services authority: Has the power to discharge a patient from guardianship by virtue of s.23(2)(*b*), below.

Resides: Temporary absences from the place where a person lives does not affect residence, as long as there is an intention to return (*R.* v. *St. Leonard's Shoreditch* (*Inhabitants*), (1865) L.R. 1 Q.B. 21).

Part III

Patients Concerned in Criminal Proceedings or Under Sentence

Remands to hospital

Remand to hospital for report on accused's mental condition

35.—(1) Subject to the provisions of this section, the Crown Court or a magistrates' court may remand an accused person to a hospital specified by the court for a report on his mental condition.

(2) For the purposes of this section an accused person is—

    (*a*) in relation to the Crown Court, any person who is awaiting trial before the court for an offence punishable with imprisonment or who has been arraigned before the court for such an offence and has not yet been sentenced or otherwise dealt with for the offence on which he has been arraigned;

    (*b*) in relation to a magistrates' court, any person who has been convicted by the court of an offence punishable on summary conviction with imprisonment and any person charged with such an offence if the court is satisfied that he did the act or made the omission charged or he has consented to the exercise by the court of the powers conferred by this section.

(3) Subject to subsection (4) below, the powers conferred by this section may be exercised if—

    (*a*) the court is satisfied, on the written or oral evidence of a registered medical practitioner, that there is reason to suspect that the accused person is suffering from mental illness, psychopathic disorder, severe mental impairment or mental impairment; and

    (*b*) the court is of the opinion that it would be impracticable for a report on his mental condition to be made if he were remanded on bail;

but those powers shall not be exercised by the Crown Court in respect of a person who has been convicted before the court if the sentence for the offence of which he has been convicted is fixed by law.

(4) The court shall not remand an accused person to a hospital under this section unless satisfied, on the written or oral evidence of the registered medical practitioner who would be responsible for making the report or of some other person representing the managers of the hospital, that arrangements have been made for his admission to that hospital and

for his admission to it within the period of seven days beginning with the
date of the remand; and if the court is so satisfied it may, pending his
admission, give directions for his conveyance to and detention in a place
of safety.

(5) Where a court has remanded an accused person under this section
it may further remand him if it appears to the court, on the written or
oral evidence of the registered medical practitioner responsible for making
the report, that a further remand is necessary for completing the assessment of the accused person's mental condition.

(6) The power of further remanding an accused person under this
section may be exercised by the court without his being brought before
the court if he is represented by counsel or a solicitor and his counsel or
solicitor is given an opportunity of being heard.

(7) An accused person shall not be remanded or further remanded
under this section for more than 28 days at a time or for more than 12
weeks in all; and the court may at any time terminate the remand if it
appears to the court that it is appropriate to do so.

(8) An accused person remanded to hospital under this section shall be
entitled to obtain at his own expense an independent report on his mental
condition from a registered medical practitioner chosen by him and to
apply to the court on the basis of it for his remand to be terminated under
subsection (7) above.

(9) Where an accused person is remanded under this section—
   (a) a constable or any other person directed to do so by the court
       shall convey the accused person to the hospital specified by the
       court within the period mentioned in subsection (4) above; and
   (b) the managers of the hospital shall admit him within that period
       and thereafter detain him in accordance with the provisions of
       this section.

(10) If an accused person absconds from a hospital to which he has
been remanded under this section, or while being conveyed to or from
that hospital, he may be arrested without warrant by any constable and
shall, after being arrested, be brought as soon as practicable before the
court that remanded him; and the court may thereupon terminate the
remand and deal with him in any way in which it could have dealt with
him if he had not been remanded under this section.

DEFINITIONS
   "Hospital": ss.55(5), 145(1).
   "Psychopathic disorder": ss.1, 145(1).
   "Severe mental impairment": ss.1, 145(1).
   "Mental impairment": ss.1, 145(1).
   "The managers": s.145(1).

GENERAL NOTE
   This section gives effect to the recommendation of the Butler Committee that courts
should have the option of remanding an accused person to hospital for the preparation of a
report on his mental condition (Butler Report, paras. 12.8 to 12.11). Magistrates' courts and
the Crown Court have this power if they are satisfied, on the evidence of an approved
doctor, that there is reason to suspect that the accused is suffering from one of the four
categories of mental disorder and that it would be impracticable for a report on his mental
condition to be made if he were remanded on bail. The remand, which can last for a
maximum of 12 weeks, cannot be made unless the court is also satisfied that arrangements
have been made for the accused's admission to hospital.
   The power to remand to hospital should be used as an alternative to a remand to prison,
and not as an alternative to a remand on bail. The Butler Committee emphasised that where
it is possible to do so, the first choice of the courts should "always to be to give bail" (Butler
Report, para. 12.10).
   A person remanded under this section is not subject to the consent to treatment provisions
contained in Part IV of this Act (s.56(1)(b)).

Commencement

This section will not come into operation on September 30, 1983 (s.149(3)).

Subs. (1)

Hospital: Or a mental nursing home registered under the Nursing Homes Act 1975 (s.55(5)).

Subs. (2)

Para. (*a*): *offence punishable with imprisonment.* This section applies to a person who has been accused, but not convicted, of murder (subs. (3)).

Para. (*b*): *offence punishable on summary conviction with imprisonment*: The offence could have been committed by a person under the age of 21 (s.55(2)).

Satisfied that he did the act: Without convicting him.

Subs. (3)

Para. (*a*): *evidence*: For general provisions as to medical evidence, see s.54, below.

Registered medical practitioner: Who must have been approved by the Secretary of State under s.12, above (s.54(1)).

Reason to suspect: A firm diagnosis is not required.

Para. (*b*): *impracticable*: This presumably refers to the impracticability of preparing a sufficiently thorough report if the accused were granted bail.

Fixed by law: The power to remand to hospital is not available in respect of a person who has been convicted of murder who must be sentenced to life imprisonment (Murder (Abolition of Death Penalty) Act 1965, s.1(1)). Note that s.34 of the Mental Health (Amendment) Act 1982 amends the Bail Act 1976 to oblige a court granting bail to a person accused of murder to impose conditions of bail requiring him to co-operate in the preparation of reports on his mental condition if satisfactory reports have not already been obtained.

Subs. (4)

Or of some other person: Who need not be a doctor.

Beginning with: Including the date of the remand (*Hare* v. *Gocher* [1962] 2 Q.B. 641).

Place of safety: Is defined in s.55(1), below.

Subs (5)

Further remand him: Up to a maximum of 12 weeks in all (subs. (7)).

Subs. (7)

At any time: "It will be open to the responsible medical officer in every case to inform the court if the object of the remand is achieved before the expiry of the stipulated time, so that the adjourned hearing may be brought forward accordingly or if necessary an alternative form of remand, either in custody or on bail, may be substituted" (Butler Report, para. 12.9).

Subs. (8)

This subs. was successfully moved during the passage of the 1982 Act against Government advice. The Government view was that this subsection would be unlikely to be of great benefit to the accused person, first because he already has the right to commission his own private medical report and, secondly, because the court is unlikely to end his remand on the basis of such a report.

Apply to the court on the basis of it. Once the accused has received his private medical report he has the right to apply to the court to seek an end to the remand even if the reports which the court has asked for are not available.

Subs. (9)

Convey: For general provisions relating to conveyance, see s.137, below.

Hospital specified by the court: "Remands to hospital may sometimes entail a requirement of secure custody. It will be for the court to decide whether the defendant should be sent on remand to a local psychiatric hospital or whether there is need for the greater security afforded by the regional secure units. Exceptionally the security of a special hospital might be required" (Butler Report, para. 12.12). Presumably the doctor referred to in subs. (3) would give evidence on this point.

Shall admit him: The hospital specified in the remand cannot refuse to admit the accused person.

Remand of accused person to hospital for treatment

36.—(1) Subject to the provisions of this section, the Crown Court may, instead of remanding an accused person in custody, remand him to a hospital specified by the court if satisfied, on the written or oral evidence of two registered medical practitioners, that he is suffering from mental illness or severe mental impairment of a nature or degree which makes it appropriate for him to be detained in a hospital for medical treatment.

(2) For the purposes of this section an accused person is any person who is in custody awaiting trial before the Crown Court for an offence punishable with imprisonment (other than an offence the sentence for which is fixed by law) or who at any time before sentence is in custody in the course of a trial before that court for such an offence.

(3) The court shall not remand an accused person under this section to a hospital unless it is satisfied, on the written or oral evidence of the registered medical practitioner who would be in charge of his treatment or of some other person representing the managers of the hospital, that arrangements have been made for his admission to that hospital and for his admission to it within the period of seven days beginning with the date of the remand; and if the court is so satisfied it may, pending his admission, give directions for his conveyance to and detention in a place of safety.

(4) Where a court has remanded an accused person under this section it may further remand him if it appears to the court, on the written or oral evidence of the responsible medical officer, that a further remand is warranted.

(5) The power of further remanding an accused person under this section may be exercised by the court without his being brought before the court if he is represented by counsel or a solicitor and his counsel or solicitor is given an opportunity of being heard.

(6) An accused person shall not be remanded or further remanded under this section for more than 28 days at a time or for more than 12 weeks in all; and the court may at any time terminate the remand if it appears to the court that it is appropriate to do so.

(7) An accused person remanded to hospital under this section shall be entitled to obtain at his own expense an independent report on his mental condition from a registered medical practitioner chosen by him and to apply to the court on the basis of it for his remand to be terminated under subsection (6) above.

(8) Subsections (9) and (10) of section 35 above shall have effect in relation to a remand under this section as they have effect in relation to a remand under that section.

DEFINITIONS
  "Hospital": ss.55(5), 145(1).
  "Severe mental impairment": ss.1, 145(1).
  "The managers": s.145(1).
  "Responsible medical officer": s.55(1).

GENERAL NOTE
  This section empowers the Crown Court to remand an accused person suffering from mental illness or severe mental impairment to hospital for treatment for a maximum of 12 weeks. A person remanded under this section is subject to the consent to treatment provisions contained in Part IV of this Act.

COMMENCEMENT
  This section will not come into operation on September 30, 1983 (s.149(3)).

Subs. (1)
  Hospital: Or a mental nursing home registered under the Nursing Homes Act 1975 (s.55(1)).

Evidence: For general provisions relating to medical evidence, see s.54, below.

Two registered medical practitioners: At least one of whom must have been approved by the Secretary of State under s.12, above (s.54(1)). There is no prohibition on both of the doctors being on the staff of the same hospital.

Mental illness or severe mental impairment: According to Dr. James Higgins the reason for limiting this section to those suffering from mental illness or severe mental impairment is "that these forms equate most closely to the medical model of illness and sufferers would be seriously disadvantaged by a long remand in custody whereas those felt to be suffering from psychopathic disorder and mental impairment would not" (*Tried and Treated*, Social Work Today, Vol. 14, No. 21, p.11).

Subs. (2)

Fixed by law: This section does not apply to a person who has been charged with murder.

Subs. (3)

Or of some other person: Who need not be a doctor.

Beginning with: Including the date of the remand (*Hare* v. *Gocher* [1962] 2 Q.B. 641).

Place of safety: Is defined in s.55(1), below.

Subs. (7)

See the notes on s.35(8), above.

Hospital and guardianship orders

Powers of courts to order hospital admission or guardianship

37.—(1) Where a person is convicted before the Crown Court of an offence punishable with imprisonment other than an offence the sentence for which is fixed by law, or is convicted by a magistrates' court of an offence punishable on summary conviction with imprisonment, and the conditions mentioned in subsection (2) below are satisfied, the court may by order authorise his admission to and detention in such hospital as may be specified in the order or, as the case may be, place him under the guardianship of a local social services authority or of such other person approved by a local social services authority as may be so specified.

(2) The conditions referred to in subsection (1) above are that—

    (*a*) the court is satisfied, on the written or oral evidence of two registered medical practitioners, that the offender is suffering from mental illness, psychopathic disorder, severe mental impairment or mental impairment and that either—

        (i) the mental disorder from which the offender is suffering is of a nature or degree which makes it appropriate for him to be detained in a hospital for medical treatment and, in the case of psychopathic disorder or mental impairment, that such treatment is likely to alleviate or prevent a deterioration of his condition; or

        (ii) in the case of an offender who has attained the age of 16 years, the mental disorder is of a nature or degree which warrants his reception into guardianship under this Act; and

    (*b*) the court is of the opinion, having regard to all the circumstances including the nature of the offence and the character and antecedents of the offender, and to the other available methods of dealing with him, that the most suitable method of disposing of the case is by means of an order under this section.

(3) Where a person is charged before a magistrates' court with any act or omission as an offence and the court would have power, on convicting him of that offence, to make an order under subsection (1) above in his case as being a person suffering from mental illness or severe mental impairment, then, if the court is satisfied that the accused did the act or

made the omission charged, the court may, if it thinks fit, make such an order without convicting him.

(4) An order for the admission of an offender to a hospital (in this Act referred to as "a hospital order") shall not be made under this section unless the court is satisfied on the written or oral evidence of the registered medical practitioner who would be in charge of his treatment or of some other person representing the managers of the hospital that arrangements have been made for his admission to that hospital in the event of such an order being made by the court, and for his admission to it within the period of 28 days beginning with the date of the making of such an order; and the court may, pending his admission within that period, give such directions as it thinks fit for his conveyance to and detention in a place of safety.

(5) If within the said period of 28 days it appears to the Secretary of State that by reason of an emergency or other special circumstances it is not practicable for the patient to be received into the hospital specified in the order, he may give directions for the admission of the patient to such other hospital as appears to be appropriate instead of the hospital so specified; and where such directions are given—

(*a*) the Secretary of State shall cause the person having the custody of the patient to be informed, and

(*b*) the hospital order shall have effect as if the hospital specified in the directions were substituted for the hospital specified in the order.

(6) An order placing an offender under the guardianship of a local social services authority or of any other person (in this Act referred to as "a guardianship order") shall not be made under this section unless the court is satisfied that that authority or person is willing to receive the offender into guardianship.

(7) A hospital order or guardianship order shall specify the form or forms of mental disorder referred to in subsection (2)(*a*) above from which, upon the evidence taken into account under that subsection, the offender is found by the court to be suffering; and no such order shall be made unless the offender is described by each of the practitioners whose evidence is taken into account under that subsection as suffering from the same one of those forms of mental disorder, whether or not he is also described by either of them as suffering from another of them.

(8) Where an order is made under this section, the court shall not pass sentence of imprisonment or impose a fine or make a probation order in respect of the offence or make any such order as is mentioned in paragraph (*b*) or (*c*) of section 7(7) of the Children and Young Persons Act 1969 in respect of the offender, but may make any other order which the court has power to make apart from this section; and for the purposes of this subsection "sentence of imprisonment" includes any sentence or order for detention.

DEFINITIONS
  "Hospital": ss.55(5), 145(1).
  "Local social services authority": s.145(1).
  "Psychopathic disorder": ss.1, 145(1).
  "Severe mental impairment": ss.1, 145(1).
  "Mental impairment": ss.1, 145(1).
  "Medical treatment": s.145(1).
  "Patient": s.145(1).
  "The managers": s.145(1).

GENERAL NOTE
  This section empowers a Crown Court or magistrates' court to make a hospital or guardianship order as an alternative to a penal disposal for offenders who are found to be

suffering from mental disorder such as to warrant their detention in hospital or reception into guardianship. The effect of hospital and guardianship orders are set out in s.40, below.

A juvenile court has power to make a hospital or guardianship order in respect of a juvenile who is found to be in need of care or control in proceedings under s.1 of the Children and Young Persons Act 1969, provided the provisions of this section are satisfied.

Both the patient who has been placed under a hospital or guardianship order and his nearest relative can apply to a Mental Health Review Tribunal (ss.40(4), 66(1), 69(1)).

Hospital orders: "In making a hospital order, the court is placing the patient in the hands of the doctors, foregoing any question of punishment, and relinquishing from then onwards its own control over him. When the doctor, or the Mental Health Review Tribunal, thinks it right, the patient will be discharged. If it appears quickly that the patient does not need in-patient treatment, or that he has no intention of co-operating, he may be discharged very soon" (Butler Report, para. 14.8, 9). Where the Crown Court makes a hospital order, it may also make an order under s.41, below, restricting the discharge of the offender from hospital, if it considers that it is necessary for the protection of the public from serious harm so to do.

The Court of Appeal has said that where a court is considering making a hospital order the defendant should, except in the rarest circumstances, be represented by counsel (*R.* v. *Blackwood* (1974) 59 Cr.App.R. 170).

District Health Authorities and local social services authorities have a duty to provide after-care services for hospital order patients who cease to be liable to be detained and leave hospital (s.117).

Guardianship orders: Little use has been made of guardianship orders by the courts even though, in the view of the Butler Committee, they "offer a useful form of control of some mentally disordered offenders who do not require hospital treatment [and are] particularly suited to the needs of subnormal offenders including those inadequate offenders who require help in managing their affairs" (Butler Report, para. 15.8). The Committee felt that in some circumstances a guardianship order is more effective than a probation order. A guardianship order differs from a probation order in that: (1) it can be used in cases where the offender does not consent; (2) there is no sanction available to the guardian if the patient breaches the order; and (3) the guardian has to be willing to receive the offender into guardianship.

Subs. (1)

Offence punishable with imprisonment: This is construed in accordance with s.47(5), below (s.55(6)).

Fixed by law: This section does not apply to persons who have been convicted of murder who must be sentenced to life imprisonment (Murder (Abolition of Death Penalty) Act 1965, s.1(1)).

Magistrates court: Including a juvenile court. By virtue of s.7(8) of the Children and Young Persons Act 1969 an adult magistrates' court cannot make a hospital or guardianship order in respect of a juvenile. If the adult court considers that such an order should be made it should remit the case to the juvenile court under s.56(1) of the Children and Young Persons Act 1933.

Offence punishable on summary conviction with imprisonment: See s.55(2), below.

The court may by order: A hospital order can be made despite the fact that there is no causal connection between the offender's mental disorder and the offence in respect of which the order is made (*R.* v. *McBride* [1972] Crim.L.R. 322). The offender's consent to the order is not required (*R.* v. *Gunnee* [1972] Crim.L.R. 261). A court is not obliged to make a hospital order if the conditions of this section are satisfied and a sentence of imprisonment could be imposed if, for example, there is a particular need to mark the gravity of the offence or if a secure hospital cannot be found for a dangerous offender; see *R.* v. *Morris* [1961] 2 Q.B. 237 and *R.* v. *Higginbotham* [1961] 1 W.L.R. 1277.

Hospital: Or a nursing home registered under the Nursing Homes Act 1975 (s.55(5)). A court may request information about the availability of hospital places under s.39, below, and the offender can be admitted to a hospital which is not situated in the locality where he is normally resident (*R.* v. *Marsden* (*Practice Note*) [1968] 1 W.L.R. 785).

Courts have occasionally been placed in the position of not being able to make orders under this section because of pressure from the nursing staff of the regional secure units who consider that certain offenders should not be sent to secure units without an accompanying increase in staffing levels. This situation was considered by Lawton L.J. in *R.* v. *Harding (Bernard), The Times*, June 15, 1983, C.A. His Lordship said that the time had come for those who in the past had been obstructive to the use of secure units to appreciate that once a court had made an order under this section, anyone who obstructed the execution of that order or counselled or procured others to obstruction, might be guilty of contempt of court.

Subs. (2)

Para. (*a*): *Evidence*: For general requirements as to medical evidence, see s.54, below.

Two registered medical practitioners: One of whom must be approved by the Secretary of State under s.12, above (s.54(1)). The Court of Appeal has advised that the trial judge should hear evidence from the doctor who will be treating the offender (*R.* v. *Blackwood, supra.*). The two doctors could be on the staff of the same hospital.

Suffering from: The offender's mental condition at the time when the offence was committed is not at issue.

The two medical practitioners must agree one of the forms of mental disorder from which the offender is suffering (subs. (7)). In *R.* v. *Nigel Gordon Smith*, July 30, 1974, (unreported), the court noted that it did not matter if one of the doctors made a general diagnosis as to the form of mental disorder, (*e.g.* mental illness) and the other doctor made a specific diagnosis coming within the same form (*e.g.* paranoid schizophrenia) (N.B. This case is referred to by Larry Gostin *A Human Condition*, Vol. 2 at p.31).

Appropriate for him to be detained in a hospital for medical treatment: Even though he might not benefit from treatment.

Likely to alleviate: See the note on s.3(2)(*b*), above.

Attained the age: At the commencement of his sixteenth birthday (Family Law Reform Act 1969, s.9(1)). Also see, s.55(7), below.

Para. (*b*):

Nature of the offence: "Although hospital orders are frequently made in cases involving grave offences of violence, the gravity of the offences is not an important consideration in making a hospital order (except in so far as it indicates a need for detention in secure conditions). Hospital orders have been upheld or imposed on appeal on offenders whose offences would not have justified a substantial term of imprisonment" (D. A. Thomas, *Principles of Sentencing*, 2nd ed., 1979, p.299).

Subs. (3)

The provisions of this subsection which empowers magistrates to make a hospital or guardianship order without proceeding to conviction where the defendant is suffering from mental illness or severe mental impairment, apply only where the court is satisfied that the defendant did the act or made the omission charged. "In trivial cases the magistrates may properly have recourse to the expedient of adjourning the proceedings *sine die* or of simply not proceeding" (Butler Report, para. 10.34).

In *R.* v. *Lincolnshire (Kesteven) Justices, ex p. O'Connor*, [1983] 1 All E.R. 901, D.C., Lord Lane said, at p.904, that "the circumstances in which it will be appropriate to exercise this unusual power are bound to be very rare and will usually require . . . the consent of those acting for the defendant if he is under a disability so that he cannot be tried."

Did the act or made the omission charged: There is no need for the court to be satisfied as to the *mens rea, i.e.* whether the accused had the state of mind required by the offence at the time when the act or omission occurred.

Make such an order: An order under this subsection can be made even though the court has not proceeded to trial. It can therefore be made in cases where the defendant is unable, by virtue of his mental disorder, to give his consent as to the mode of trial (*R.* v. *Lincolnshire (Kesteven) Justices, supra*).

Without convicting him: The person has the same right of appeal against the order as if it had been made on his conviction (s.45).

Subs. (4)

An order . . . shall not be made: A hospital order can only be made if a suitable hospital has agreed to make a bed available for the offender. See *R.* v. *Harding (Bernard)*, noted in subs. (1), above.

Registered medical practitioner: Who could be one of the doctors giving evidence under subs. (2)(*a*).

Some other person: Who need not be a doctor.

Managers: Note that the four special hospitals are managed by the Department of Health and Social Security (s.145(1)).

Beginning with: Including the date of the making of the order (*Hare* v. *Gocher* [1962] 2 Q.B. 641).

Conveyance . . . and detention: General provisions relating to conveyance and detention are set out in s.137, below.

Place of safety: Is defined in s.55(1), below. Home Office Circular No. 66/1980 draws attention to the problem which can arise when a hospital order has been made and the defendant is committed to a place of safety under this subsection pending admission to hospital, but the hospital subsequently withdraws its undertaking to admit him. If no alternative placement is arranged before the 28 days currency of the "place of safety" direction expires, the defendant must be released, and the hospital order is frustrated. A change of procedure was introduced in 1979 in the Crown Court, which attempts to deal with this problem. The Crown Court has power, under s.11(2) of the Crown Act 1971, to vary sentence on a defendant within 28 days, and the purpose of the new procedure is to ensure that the court is forewarned of the possible frustration of a hospital order and so has the opportunity to pass an alternative sentence before the authority to detain the person is extinguished. The Lord Chief Justice has directed that an additional direction be given by the court under this section, addressed to the governor of the prison which is to hold the person pending admission to hospital, which reads as follows: "but if at any time it appears to the person in whose custody the defendant is detained in a place of safety that the defendant might not be admitted to hospital in pursuance of this order within 28 days of this date, that person shall within 21 days of this date (or at once if it becomes apparent only after 21 days that the defendant might not be admitted to hospital) report the circumstances to the Chief Clerk of the Court and unless otherwise directed by the Chief Clerk shall bring the defendant before the Court forthwith so as to enable it within 28 days of this date to make such order as may be necessary". Magistrates' courts have re-sentencing powers, analogous to those of the Crown Court, under section 142 of the Magistrates' Courts Act 1980. It is the Home Secretary's opinion that this provision can properly be applied in these circumstances.

Subs. (8)

    Para. (b) or (c) of s.7(7).: Which refers to care orders and supervision orders.

    Any other order: For example, a compensation order or an order disqualifying the offender from driving.

Interim hospital orders

38.—(1) Where a person is convicted before the Crown Court of an offence punishable with imprisonment (other than an offence the sentence for which is fixed by law) or is convicted by a magistrates' court of an offence punishable on summary conviction with imprisonment and the court before or by which he is convicted is satisfied, on the written or oral evidence of two registered medical practitioners—

    (*a*) that the offender is suffering from mental illness, psychopathic disorder, severe mental impairment or mental impairment; and

    (*b*) that there is reason to suppose that the mental disorder from which the offender is suffering is such that it may be appropriate for a hospital order to be made in his case,

the court may, before making a hospital order or dealing with him in some other way, make an order (in this Act referred to as "an interim hospital order") authorising his admission to such hospital as may be specified in the order and his detention there in accordance with this section.

    (2) In the case of an offender who is subject to an interim hospital order the court may make a hospital order without his being brought before the court if he is represented by counsel or a solicitor and his counsel or solicitor is given an opportunity of being heard.

    (3) At least one of the registered medical practitioners whose evidence is taken into account under subsection (1) above shall be employed at the hospital which is to be specified in the order.

    (4) An interim hospital order shall not be made for admission of an offender to a hospital unless the court is satisfied, on the written or oral evidence of the registered medical practitioner who would be in charge of his treatment or of some other person representing the managers of the hospital, that arrangements have been made for his admission to that hospital and for his admission to it within the period of 28 days beginning with the date of the order; and if the court is so satisfied the court may,

pending his admission, give directions for his conveyance to and detention in a place of safety.

(5) An interim hospital order—

(*a*) shall be in force for such period, not exceeding 12 weeks; as the court may specify when making the order; but

(*b*) may be renewed for further periods of not more than 28 days at a time if it appears to the court, on the written or oral evidence of the responsible medical officer, that the continuation of the order is warranted;

but no such order shall continue in force for more than six months in all and the court shall terminate the order if it makes a hospital order in respect of the offender or decides after considering the written or oral evidence of the responsible medical officer to deal with the offender in some other way.

(6) The power of renewing an interim hospital order may be exercised without the offender being brought before the court if he is represented by counsel or a solicitor and his counsel or solicitor is given an opportunity of being heard.

(7) If an offender absconds from a hospital in which he is detained in pursuance of an interim hospital order, or while being conveyed to or from such a hospital, he may be arrested without warrant by a constable and shall, after being arrested, be brought as soon as practicable before the court that made the order; and the court may thereupon terminate the order and deal with him in any way in which it could have dealt with him if no such order had been made.

DEFINITIONS

"Psychopathic disorder": ss.1, 145(1).
"Mental impairment": ss.1, 145(1).
"Severe mental impairment": ss.1, 145(1).
"Hospital": ss.55(5), 145(1).
"Hospital order": ss.37, 145(1).
"The managers": s.145(1).

GENERAL NOTE

The Butler Committee "gained the impression that many doctors found it difficult to decide whether to recommend that a hospital order should be made where they have been able to examine the patient only briefly in a prison hospital under the pressure of impending court proceedings, since it was often impossible to know how he would react subsequently to the psychiatric hospital regime" (Butler Report, para. 12.5). This section responds to this concern by empowering a Crown Court or magistrates' court to send a convicted offender to hospital for up to six months to enable an assessment to be made on the appropriateness of making a hospital order in respect of him. An offender who is placed under an "interim hospital order" made under this section is subject to the consent to treatment provisions contained in Pt. IV of this Act.

COMMENCEMENT

This section will not come into operation on September 30, 1983 (s.149(3)).

Subs. (1)

Offence punishable with imprisonment: This is construed in accordance with s.47(5), below (s.55(6)).

Fixed by law: This section does not apply to persons who have been convicted of murder.

Magistrates' court: Including a juvenile court. By virtue of s.7(8) of the Children and Young Persons Act 1969 an adult magistrates' court cannot make an interim hospital order in respect of a juvenile. If the adult court considers that such an order should be made it should remit the case to the juvenile court under s.56(1) of the Children and Young Persons Act 1933.

Offence punishable on summary conviction with imprisonment: See s.55(2), below.

Evidence: For general requirements as to medical evidence, see s.54, below.

Two registered medical practitioners: One of whom must be approved by the Secretary of State under s.12, above (s.54(1)). Also see subs. (3).

Is suffering from: It is not sufficient that the doctors have a mere reason to suspect that the offender is suffering from one of the four forms of mental disorder (*cf.* s.35(3)(*a*)).

Interim hospital order: The effect of such an order is set out in s.40(3), below.

Hospital: Or a nursing home registered under the Nursing Homes Act 1975 (s.55(5)). A court may request information about the availability of hospital places under s.39, below.

Subs. (4)

Registered medical practitioners who would be in charge of his treatment: Who could be the doctor referred to in subs. (3).

Some other person: Who need not be a doctor.

Beginning with the date of the order: Including the date of the order (*Hare* v. *Gocher* [1962] 2 Q.B. 641).

Conveyance . . . and detention: For general provisions relating to conveyance and detention, see s.137, below.

Place of safety: See the note on s.37(4), above.

Subs. (5) provides that if doubts remain as to the appropriateness of a hospital order after three months the interim hospital order can be renewed at monthly intervals up to an overall total of six months.

The responsible medical officer: Is the medical practitioner in charge of the treatment of the patient (s.55(1)).

Information as to hospitals

39.—(1) Where a court is minded to make a hospital order or interim hospital order in respect of any person it may request—

    (*a*) the Regional Health Authority for the region in which that person resides or last resided; or

    (*b*) any other Regional Health Authority that appears to the court to be appropriate,

to furnish the court with such information as that Authority has or can reasonably obtain with respect to the hospital or hospitals (if any) in its region or elsewhere at which arrangements could be made for the admission of that person in pursuance of the order, and that Authority shall comply with any such request.

(2) In it application to Wales subsection (1) above shall have effect as if for any reference to any such Authority as is mentioned in paragraph (*a*) or (*b*) of that subsection there were substituted a reference to the Secretary of State, and as if for the words "in its region or elsewhere" there were substituted the words "in Wales".

DEFINITION

"Hospital order": ss.37, 145(1).
"Interim hospital order": ss.38, 145(1).
"Hospital": ss.55(5), 145(1).

GENERAL NOTE

This section provides that whenever a court is considering making a hospital order or interim hospital order it may ask the appropriate regional health authority (in Wales, the Secretary of State) to provide information as to the availability of suitable hospital places.

Subs. (1)

Resides: Temporary absences from the place where a person lives does not affect residence, as long as there is an intention to return (*R.* v. *St. Leonard's Shoreditch* (*Inhabitants*), (1865) L.R. 1 Q.B. 21).

Hospital: Or nursing home registered under the Nursing Homes Act 1975 (s.55(5)).

Effect of hospital orders, guardianship orders and interim hospital orders

40.—(1) A hospital order shall be sufficient authority—

    (*a*) for a constable, an approved social worker or any other person directed to do so by the court to convey the patient to the hospital specified in the order within a period of 28 days; and

(*b*) for the managers of the hospital to admit him at any time within that period and thereafter detain him in accordance with the provisions of this Act.

(2) A guardianship order shall confer on the authority or person named in the order as guardian the same powers as a guardianship application made and accepted under Part II of this Act.

(3) Where an interim hospital order is made in respect of an offender—

(*a*) a constable or any other person directed to do so by the court shall convey the offender to the hospital specified in the order within the period mentioned in section 38(4) above; and

(*b*) the managers of the hospital shall admit him within that period and thereafter detain him in accordance with the provisions of section 38 above.

(4) A patient who is admitted to a hospital in pursuance of a hospital order, or placed under guardianship by a guardianship order, shall, subject to the provisions of this subsection, be treated for the purposes of the provisions of this Act mentioned in Part I of Schedule 1 to this Act as if he had been so admitted or placed on the date of the order in pursuance of an application for admission for treatment or a guardianship application, as the case may be, duly made under Part II of this Act, but subject to any modifications of those provisions specified in that Part of that Schedule.

(5) Where a patient is admitted to a hospital in pursuance of a hospital order, or placed under guardianship by a guardianship order, any previous application, hospital order or guardianship order by virtue of which he was liable to be detained in a hospital or subject to guardianship shall cease to have effect; but if the first-mentioned order, or the conviction on which it was made, is quashed on appeal, this subsection shall not apply and section 22 above shall have effect as if during any period for which the patient was liable to be detained or subject to guardianship under the order, he had been detained in custody as mentioned in that section.

DEFINITIONS

"Hospital order": ss.37, 145(1).
"Approved social worker": s.145(1).
"The managers": s.145(1).
"Hospital": ss.55(5), 145(1).
"Guardianship order": ss.37, 145(1).
"Interim hospital order": ss.38, 145(1).
"Patient": s.145(1).
"Application for admission for treatment": ss.3, 145(1).

GENERAL NOTE

This section provides that, with very few exceptions, a patient who is admitted to hospital under a hospital order without restrictions or placed under guardianship by a guardianship order is treated the same as a patient who has been admitted to hospital or placed under guardianship under Part II of this Act. The necessary modifications to the provisions of Part II are made by Part I of Sched. I, below and are noted in subs. (4), below.

Any reference to hospital orders and guardianship orders in subs. (2), (4) or (5) of this section shall be construed as including a reference to any order or directions under this Part having the same effect as a hospital or guardianship order (s.55(4)).

COMMENCEMENT

Subs. (3) will not come into force on September 30, 1983 (s.149(3)).

Subs. (1)

Constable: Means the office of constable, and not the rank of constable (Police Act 1964, s.18, Sched. 2).

Convey the patient to hospital: For general provisions relating to conveyance, see s.137, below. Before proceeding to convey the patient to hospital the authorised person should confirm with the hospital that it is still willing to accept the patient, as this section does not give authority to convey the patient *from* hospital if admission is refused.

Within a period of 28 days: If the hospital specified in the order withdraws its agreement to accept the patient, the person having custody of him should bring him back to the Crown Court within the 28 day period so that the court can vary the sentence under s.11(2) of the Crown Court Act 1971; see the note on s.37(4), above.

Detain him: A patient placed under a hospital order is subject to the consent to treatment provisions contained in Pt. IV of this Act.

Subs. (2)
Some powers: As contained in s.8(1), above. A patient placed under a guardianship order is not subject to the consent to treatment provisions contained in Pt. IV of this Act.

Subs. (3)
Within the period mentioned in s.38(4): 28 days.
Shall admit him: The hospital specified in an interim hospital order cannot subsequently withdraw its agreement to accept the offender.
Detain him: A patient placed under an interim hospital order is subject to the consent to treatment provisions contained in Pt. IV of this Act.

Subs. (4)
Hospital order: The effect of this subs. is, with two exceptions, to place a patient who has been placed under a hospital order in the same legal position as a patient who has been admitted to hospital for treatment under s.3 of this Act. The two major exceptions are: (1) the nearest relative of a hospital order patient cannot order his discharge under s.23, above (Sched. 1, paras. 2, 8); and (2) unlike the s.3 patient, the hospital order patient cannot apply to a Mental Health Review Tribunal within the first six months of his detention (Sched. 1; paras. 2, 9). The first occasion on which either the hospital order patient or his nearest relative can apply to a Tribunal occurs in the period between six and 12 months of the order being made (ss.66(1)(*f*)(2)(*f*), 69(1)). Note that a hospital order patient could have his case automatically referred to a tribunal under s.68(2) below.

Guardianship order: The effect of a guardianship order made under s.37, above, is essentially the same as if the patient had been made the subject of a guardianship application under s.7, above. The major difference between the two is that with a guardianship order the power of the nearest relative to discharge the patient from guardianship does not apply (Sched. 1, paras. 2, 8).

Subs. (5)
Cease to have effect: Unless a restriction order made in respect of the patient under section 41, below, is in force at the material time (s.41(4)).

Restriction orders

Power of higher courts to restrict discharge from hospital

41.—(1) Where a hospital order is made in respect of an offender by the Crown Court, and it appears to the court, having regard to the nature of the offence, the antecedents of the offender and the risk of his committing further offences if set at large, that it is necessary for the protection of the public from serious harm so to do, the court may, subject to the provisions of this section, further order that the offender shall be subject to the special restrictions set out in this section, either without limit of time or during such period as may be specified in the order; and an order under this section shall be known as "a restriction order".

(2) A restriction order shall not be made in the case of any person unless at least one of the registered medical practitioners whose evidence is taken into account by the court under section 37(2)(*a*) above has given evidence orally before the court.

(3) The special restrictions applicable to a patient in respect of whom a restriction order is in force are as follows—

(*a*) none of the provisions of Part II of this Act relating to the duration, renewal and expiration of authority for the detention of patients shall apply, and the patient shall continue to be liable to be detained by virtue of the relevant hospital order until he is duly discharged under the said Part II or absolutely discharged under section 42, 73, 74 or 75 below;

(*b*) no application shall be made to a Mental Health Review Tribunal in respect of a patient under section 66 or 69(1) below;

(*c*) the following powers shall be exercisable only with the consent of the Secretary of State, namely—

(i) power to grant leave of absence to the patient under section 17 above;

(ii) power to transfer the patient in pursuance of regulations under section 19 above; and

(iii) power to order the discharge of the patient under section 23 above;

and if leave of absence is granted under the said section 17 power to recall the patient under that section shall vest in the Secretary of State as well as the responsible medical officer; and

(*d*) the power of the Secretary of State to recall the patient under the said section 17 and power to take the patient into custody and return him under section 18 above may be exercised at any time;

and in relation to any such patient section 40(4) above shall have effect as if it referred to Part II of Schedule 1 to this Act instead of Part I of that Schedule.

(4) A hospital order shall not cease to have effect under section 40(5) above if a restriction order in respect of the patient is in force at the material time.

(5) Where a restriction order in respect of a patient ceases to have effect while the relevant hospital order continues in force, the provisions of section 40 above and Part I of Schedule 1 to this Act shall apply to the patient as if he had been admitted to the hospital in pursuance of a hospital order (without a restriction order) made on the date on which the restriction order ceased to have effect.

(6) While a person is subject to a restriction order the responsible medical officer shall at such intervals (not exceeding one year) as the Secretary of State may direct examine and report to the Secretary of State on that person; and every report shall contain such particulars as the Secretary of State may require.

DEFINITIONS
 "Hospital order": ss.37, 145(1).
 "Patient": s.145(1).
 "Hospital": ss.55(5), 145(1).
 "Responsible medical officer": s.55(1).

GENERAL NOTE
 This section empowers the Crown Court, having made a hospital order under s.37, above, to make a further order (a "restriction order") restricting the discharge of the patient from hospital for a specified or unlimited period if it considers that it is necessary for the protection of the public from serious harm so to do. The aim of a restriction order is to protect the public from the inappropriate release of patients from hospital while there remains a real risk of further and serious crime being committed.
 In subs. (3) to (5) of this section any reference to a hospital order, a guardianship order or a restriction order are to be construed as including a reference to any order or direction under this Part having the same effect as such orders (s.55(4)).

A patient who is subject to a restriction order may apply to a Mental Health Review Tribunal (s.70) and the Home Secretary may, and in some circumstances must, refer such patients to a Tribunal (s.71). The powers of a Tribunal when considering the case of a restricted patient are set out in s.73, below.

If a court is considering making an order under this section the defendant should be represented by counsel (*R.* v. *Blackwood* (1974) 59 Cr.App.R. 170).

Subs. (1)

Hospital order is made: The offender must therefore have satisfied the conditions of s.37(2), above. Although this section implies that the offender will be kept in secure accommodation this might not be necessary in all cases. The Butler Committee gave the following example of a restricted patient who might not need to be accommodated in secure accommodation: "the persistent molester of small children may need the continuing supervision after discharge which a restriction order allows, and should not be permitted simply to walk out of hospital whenever he wishes, but is unlikely to need the secure containment of bolts and bars" (Butler Report, para. 14.21).

Before it makes an order under this section the court should ensure that the receiving hospital has the facilities for keeping the offender in the degree of custody that the court considers necessary; see *R.* v. *Morris* [1961] 2 Q.B. 237. There is no requirement that restricted patients must be sent to one of the special hospitals managed by the Department of Health and Social Security.

Crown Court: Although a magistrates' court cannot make a restriction order, it does have the power to commit the offender to the Crown Court with a view to such an order being made by that court (s.43).

Nature of the offence, the antecedents of the offender: "It is very advisable that [a restriction order] should be made in all cases where it is thought that the protection of the public is required. Thus in, for example, the case of crimes of violence, and of the more serious sexual offences, particularly if the prisoner has a record of such offences, or if there is a history of mental disorder involving violent behaviour, it is suggested that there must be compelling reasons to explain why a restriction order should not be made"; *R.* v. *Gardiner* [1967] 1 W.L.R. 464, *per* Lord Parker C.J. at 469.

Serious harm: The insertion of this phrase into the 1982 Act gave effect to recommendation 108 of the Butler Committee which proposed that the equivalent section in the 1959 Act should be revised to make it clear that the intention of a restriction order is to protect the public from serious harm. The court should not therefore impose restrictions on "the petty recidivist because of the virtual certainty that he will persist in similar offences in the future" (Butler Report, para. 14.24) or on the offender who has become a "social nuisance" by virtue of his criminal activities.

"Serious harm" refers to possible serious harm to the public in the future rather than to proven serious harm to the public in the past and an offender who has no history of violence but who, on the medical evidence, has a potentiality for serious violence could be made the subject of an order under this section. "Harm" is not restricted to physical harm and the arsonist or the offender who engages in serious destructive activities would be covered. It is doubtful whether a persistent burglar could be said to cause "serious harm" to the public and it is submitted that a restriction order cannot now be made in cases such as *R.* v. *Toland* (1973) 58 Cr.App.R. 453 where an order was made in respect of a young offender who had committed repeated burglaries during periods of absconding from hospital and who was described by the court as being a "pest" and a "social nuisance". There can be no doubt that the courts will no longer be able to make restriction orders in cases like *R.* v. *Eaton* [1976] Crim.L.R. 390, where an order was made in respect of a woman who had been convicted of damaging two window panes in a telephone kiosk and who had no potentiality for violence.

Further order: If the conditions of this section are satisfied the judge can make a restriction order notwithstanding the fact that the medical witnesses advised against such an order (*R.* v. *Royse* (1981) 3 Cr.App.R.(S.) 58).

During such period: Only a small number of restriction orders are made for a fixed period. In *R.* v. *Gardiner, supra,* Lord Parker C.J. said, at p.469: "Since in most cases the prognosis cannot be certain, the safer course is to make a restriction order unlimited in point of time. The only exception is where the doctors are able to assert confidently that recovery will take place within a fixed period when the restriction order can properly be limited to that period". This formulation has been criticised as seeming to be "faulty in attempting to equate complete recovery from mental disorder with duration of dangerousness. An offender may cease to be dangerous and yet continue to suffer from some degree of mental disorder; indeed many mentally disordered offenders will never be entirely free from mental disorder" (Cmnd. 7320, para. 5.27). The Butler Committee recommended that the power to make orders of limited duration should be removed from the statute book (Butler Report, para. 14.25) but this was rejected because in "certain cases where there is a good ground for expectation that an offender will soon recover from the disorder that has prompted his offence (for example, in cases of endogenous depression) it may be possible for the court, in the light of medical evidence, to make a reasonable prediction of when an offender will cease to be dangerous" (Cmnd. 7320, para. 5.28).

In *R.* v. *Haynes* (1981) 3 Cr.App.R.(S.) 330, the Court of Appeal held that it was wrong for the court to seek to equate the length of a restriction order with the length of the term of imprisonment which would have been appropriate to the offence.

Subs. (2)

One of the registered medical practitioners: Who need not necessarily be approved by the Secretary of State under s.12, above.

Subs. (3) specifies the restrictions that are placed upon patients who are subject to restriction orders. They are: (1) there is no periodic review of the authority to detain under s.20, above; (2) the patient cannot be discharged, transferred or granted leave of absence without the leave of the Home Secretary; and (3) the authority to detain lasts as long as the restriction order is in force and the patient cannot obtain his discharge under the provisions of s.17(5) or 18(4), above, or by reason of his mental disorder being reclassified under s.16, above. Note that the Home Secretary may, at any time, discharge a restricted patient from hospital either absolutely or subject to conditions (s.42).

Para. (*a*).

Provisions . . . relating to the duration, renewal and expiration of authority for the detention of patients: See sections 20 *et seq.*

Liable to be detained: The patient is subject to the consent to the treatment provisions contained in Pt. IV of this Act.

Para. (*b*)

Mental Health Review Tribunal: See the General Note to this Act.

Subs. (5)

This subsection provides that when a restriction order ceases to have effect either through lapse of time or by virtue of the direction of the Home Secretary (s.42(1)) the patient is to be treated as if he had been admitted to hospital under a hospital order without restrictions made on the date on which the restriction order ceased to have effect.

Cease to have effect: The patient can apply to a Mental Health Review Tribunal within six months of the restriction order ceasing to have effect (s.69(2)(*a*)).

Subs. (6)

This subsection which was enacted in response to recommendation 114 of the Butler Committee, is aimed at preventing restricted patients being detained for unjustifiably long periods.

Powers of Secretary of State in respect of patients subject to restriction orders

42.—(1) If the Secretary of State is satisfied that in the case of any patient a restriction order is no longer required for the protection of the public from serious harm, he may direct that the patient shall cease to be subject to the special restrictions set out in section 41(3) above; and where the Secretary of State so directs, the restriction order shall cease to have effect, and section 41(5) above shall apply accordingly.

(2) At any time while a restriction order is in force in respect of a patient, the Secretary of State may, if he thinks fit, by warrant discharge the patient from hospital, either absolutely or subject to conditions; and where a person is absolutely discharged under this subsection, he shall thereupon cease to be liable to be detained by virtue of the relevant hospital order, and the restriction order shall cease to have effect accordingly.

(3) The Secretary of State may at any time during the continuance in force of a restriction order in respect of a patient who has been conditionally discharged under subsection (2) above by warrant recall the patient to such hospital as may be specified in the warrant.

(4) Where a patient is recalled as mentioned in subsection (3) above—

   (a) if the hospital specified in the warrant is not the hospital from which the patient was conditionally discharged, the hospital order and the restriction order shall have effect as if the hospital specified in the warrant were substituted for the hospital specified in the hospital order;

   (b) in any case, the patient shall be treated for the purposes of section 18 above as if he had absented himself without leave from the hospital specified in the warrant, and, if the restriction order was made for a specified period, that period shall not in any event expire until the patient returns to the hospital or is returned to the hospital under that section.

(5) If a restriction order in respect of a patient ceases to have effect after the patient has been conditionally discharged under this section, the patient shall, unless previously recalled under subsection (3) above, be deemed to be absolutely discharged on the date when the order ceases to have effect, and shall cease to be liable to be detained by virtue of the relevant hospital order accordingly.

(6) The Secretary of State may, if satisfied that the attendance at any place in Great Britain of a patient who is subject to a restriction order is desirable in the interests of justice or for the purposes of any public inquiry, direct him to be taken to that place; and where a patient is directed under this subsection to be taken to any place he shall, unless the Secretary of State otherwise directs, be kept in custody while being so taken, while at that place and while being taken back to the hospital in which he is liable to be detained.

DEFINITIONS
   "Patient": s.145.
   "Restriction order": ss.41, 145(1).
   "Hospital": ss.55(5), 145(1).
   "Hospital order": ss.37, 145(1).
   "Absent without leave": ss.18(6), 145(1).

GENERAL NOTE
   This section empowers the Home Secretary to take the following action in respect of patients who have been placed on restriction orders: (1) to direct that the order shall cease to have effect; (2) to discharge the patient from hospital absolutely; and (3) to discharge the patient from hospital subject to conditions.
   Any reference in this section to a hospital order, a guardianship order or a restriction order shall be construed as including a reference to any other order or direction under this Part having the same effect as such orders (s.55(4)).

Subs. (1)
   Is satisfied: The Home Secretary will receive advice from the responsible medical officer (*cf.* s.41(6)), and the Department of Health and Social Security, as managers of the special hospitals, will be consulted on proposals for the discharge of patients detained in special hospitals.
   In June 1972 a committee was set up under the chairmanship of Sir Carl Aarvold to advise whether any changes, within the existing law, were required in the procedures for the discharge and supervision of patients who had been placed on restriction orders. The committee, which reported in January 1973 (Cmnd. 5191), recommended that special precautions needed to be taken in the discharge of a patient who had been identified by his responsible medical officers as requiring "special care in assessment" because of an unfavourable or unpredictable psychiatric prognosis and an indication of risk of the patient harming other persons. This recommendation was accepted by the Government and the following procedure has been adopted. If the Home Secretary is considering the discharge of a patient identified as needing "special care in assessment", or his transfer from secure to open conditions, he will refer the case to an Advisory Board called the "Aarvold Board" for its opinion. This Board comprises a legal chairman, a forensic psychiatrist and a social

worker and, as it is a purely advisory body, it is not bound by the rules of natural justice, nor are its decisions amenable to judicial review (*R.* v. *Secretary of State for Home Department, ex p. Powell*, December 21, 1978, (unreported): a transcript of this case is reproduced as Appendix C to L. Gostin and E. Rassaby, *Representing the Mentally Ill and Handicapped*, 1980).

The Butler Committee identified two main elements that need to be satisfied before a "restricted patient" is discharged: "from a medical point of view he must have sufficiently recovered his health; and from the point of view of society there must be, so far as can be assessed, little risk of further serious offending" (Butler Report, para. 7.24).

The restriction order shall cease to have effect: And the patient will continue to be detained as if he had been admitted to hospital under a hospital order made without restrictions (s.41(5)).

Subs. (2)

Absolutely: An absolute discharge from hospital has the effect of extinguishing both the hospital order and the restriction order.

Subject to conditions: The main purpose of a conditional discharge is to provide compulsory supervision of the patient in the community. The supervisor, who will either be a probation officer or a local authority social worker will "assist the patient to settle down in the community and to this end to help him cope with his problems by providing him with professional guidance, support and control while he does do". He is, "sometimes in a position to recognise that the discharged patient may be moving into a similar situation to that which originally precipitated an offence of violence; or to perceive other signs indicating the likelihood of a repetition of dangerous behaviour. Where this is so he can take steps to warn the patient and if necessary arrange for him to be recalled to hospital" (Butler Report, para. 4.31).

The supervising officer would also be in a position to advise the Home Secretary when the behaviour and circumstances of the discharged patient had been satisfactory for a sufficient time to justify consideration being given to converting the conditional discharge into an absolute one. The Butler Committee were informed that "in practice the formal supervision of a conditionally discharged patient is normally maintained for five years if he has a history of serious violence or sexual offences and for two years where he has no such history" (*ibid.*, para. 4.32).

A conditionally discharged patient has a right to appeal to a Mental Health Review Tribunal under the section 75(2), below.

Subs. (3)

Recall the patient: As a result of criticisms made by the European Commission of Human Rights the Government have introduced the following two stage procedure for informing restricted patients of the reasons for their recall:

"Stage 1—the person taking the patient 'into custody' should inform him in simple terms that he is being recalled to hospital by the Home Secretary under the Mental Health Act and that a further explanation will be given later.

Stage 2—will take place as soon as possible after admission to hospital and in any event within 72 hours. The responsible medical officer or his deputy should explain to the patient the reasons for his recall. He should ensure that, so far as the patient's mental condition allows, he understands those reasons. The responsible medical officer will also be responsible for informing the patient's supervising officer in the community and a responsible member of the patient's family (or his legal adviser) of the reasons for his recall" (D.H.S.S. Circular LASSL (80) 7, paras. 3, 4).

A conditionally discharged patient who has been recalled to hospital must have his case referred to a Mental Health Review Tribunal by the Home Secretary within a month of his return to hospital (s.75(1)).

Hospital: Or a nursing home registered under the Nursing Homes Act 1975 (s.55(5)). There is no statutory requirement for the Home Secretary to obtain the agreement of the hospital doctors to re-admit a recalled patient.

Subs. (4)

Para. (*b*) This subsection provides: (1) that a recalled patient can be taken into custody and conveyed to the specified hospital by any approved social worker, officer on the staff of the hospital or any other person authorised by the hospital managers; and, (2) that a patient whose restriction order was made for a specified period shall not cease to be liable to be detained if that period expires after the recall has been issued and before the patient can be returned to hospital.

Subs. (5)

This subsection provides that if a restriction order ceases to have effect while the patient is on conditional discharge from hospital he will cease to be liable to be detained.

Subs. (6)

Great Britain: England, Wales and Scotland (Union with Scotland Act 1706, preamble, art. 1).

Taken to that place: For general provisions relating to custody, conveyance and detention, see s.137, below.

Power of magistrates' courts to commit for restriction order

43.—(1) If in the case of a person of or over the age of 14 years who is convicted by a magistrates' court of an offence punishable on summary conviction with imprisonment—

(*a*) the conditions which under section 37(1) above are required to be satisfied for the making of a hospital order are satisfied in respect of the offender; but

(*b*) it appears to the court, having regard to the nature of the offence, the antecedents of the offender and the risk of his committing further offences if set at large, that if a hospital order is made a restriction order should also be made,

the court may, instead of making a hospital order or dealing with him in any other manner, commit him in custody to the Crown Court to be dealt with in respect of the offence.

(2) Where an offender is committed to the Crown Court under this section, the Crown Court shall inquire into the circumstances of the case and may—

(*a*) if that court would have power so to do under the foregoing provisions of this Part of this Act upon the conviction of the offender before that court of such an offence as is described in section 37(1) above, make a hospital order in his case, with or without a restriction order;

(*b*) if the court does not make such an order, deal with the offender in any other manner in which the magistrates' court might have dealt with him.

(3) The Crown Court shall have the same power to make orders under sections 35, 36 and 38 above in the case of a person committed to the court under this section as the Crown Court has under those sections in the case of an accused person within the meaning of section 35 or 36 above or of a person convicted before that court as mentioned in section 38 above.

(4) The power of a magistrates' court under section 38 of the Magistrates' Courts Act 1980 (which enables such a court to commit an offender to the Crown Court where the court is of the opinion that greater punishment should be inflicted for the offence than the court has power to inflict) shall also be exercisable by a magistrates' court where it is of the opinion that greater punishment should be inflicted as aforesaid on the offender unless a hospital order is made in his case with a restriction order.

(5) The power of the Crown Court to make a hospital order, with or without a restriction order, in the case of a person convicted before that court of an offence may, in the same circumstances and subject to the same conditions, be exercised by such a court in the case of a person committed to the court under section 5 of the Vagrancy Act 1824 (which provides for the committal to the Crown Court of persons who are incorrigible rogues within the meaning of that section).

DEFINITIONS
    "Hospital order": ss.37, 145(1).
    "Restriction order": ss.41, 145(1).

GENERAL NOTE
    This section empowers a magistrates' court to commit a convicted person who is over the age of 14 years to the Crown Court with a view to a restriction order being made.

Subs. (1)
    Age: See s.55(7), below. A person attains the age of 14 at the commencement of his fourteenth birthday (Family Law Reform Act 1969, s.9(1)).
    Magistrates' court: Including a juvenile court.
    Offence punishable on summary conviction with imprisonment: See s.55(2), below.
    Risk of his committing further offences: Note that the magistrates' court does not need to be satisfied as to the "serious harm" test set out in s.41(1), above.
    Commit him in custody: Or order him to be admitted to a hospital if the conditions of s.44, below, are satisfied. Note that the Home Secretary has power to transfer a mentally ill or severely mentally impaired offender from custody to hospital under section 48(2)(*b*), below.

Subs. (2)
    Committed to the Crown Court under this section: Or under s.38 of the Magistrates' Courts Act 1980; see subs. (4).

Committal to hospital under s.43

44.—(1) Where an offender is committed under section 43(1) above and the magistrates' court by which he is committed is satisfied on written or oral evidence that arrangements have been made for the admission of the offender to a hospital in the event of an order being made under this section, the court may, instead of committing him in custody, by order direct him to be admitted to that hospital, specifying it, and to be detained there until the case is disposed of by the Crown Court, and may give such directions as it thinks fit for his production from the hospital to attend the Crown Court by which his case is to be dealt with.

(2) The evidence required by subsection (1) above shall be given by the registered medical practitioner who would be in charge of the offender's treatment or by some other person representing the managers of the hospital in question.

(3) The power to give directions under section 37(4) above, section 37(5) above and section 40(1) above shall apply in relation to an order under this section as they apply in relation to a hospital order, but as if references to the period of 28 days mentioned in section 40(1) above were omitted; and subject as aforesaid an order under this section shall, until the offender's case is disposed of by the Crown Court, have the same effect as a hospital order together with a restriction order, made without limitation of time.

DEFINITIONS
    "Hospital": ss.55(5), 145(1).
    "Hospital order": ss.37, 145(1).
    "Restriction order": ss.41, 145(1).
    "Guardianship order": ss.37, 145(1).
    "The managers": s.145(1).

GENERAL NOTE
    If a magistrates' court on committing an offender to the Crown Court under s.43, above, is satisfied that arrangements have been made for the admission of the offender to a hospital, it may direct him to be admitted to that hospital until the case is disposed of by the Crown Court.

Subs. (1)

Admitted to that hospital: Once the offender has been admitted to the hospital, subs. (5) and (6) of s.51, below, shall apply to him as if he were a person subject to a transfer direction made under s.47, below (s.51(3)).

Subs. (2)

Some other person: Who need not be a medical practitioner.

Subs. (3)

This subsection provides that the magistrates' court can direct that the offender be detained in a place of safety for up to 28 days pending his admission to hospital. It also authorises a constable, approved social worker or any other person directed to do so by the court to convey the offender to hospital at any time within the 28 day period provided for by s.40(1), above. Subject to this exception, an order under this section has the same effect as a restriction order made without limit of time.

Appeals from magistrates' courts

45.—(1) Where on the trial of an information charging a person with an offence a magistrates' court makes a hospital order or guardianship order in respect of him without convicting him, he shall have the same right of appeal against the order as if it had been made on his conviction; and on any such appeal the Crown Court shall have the same powers as if the appeal had been against both conviction and sentence.

(2) An appeal by a child or young person with respect to whom any such order has been made, whether the appeal is against the order or against the finding upon which the order was made, may be brought by him or by his parent or guardian on his behalf.

DEFINITIONS

"Hospital order": ss.37, 145(1).
"Guardianship order": ss.37, 145(1).
"Child": s.55(1).
"Young person": s.55(1).
"Guardian": s.55(1).

GENERAL NOTE

This section provides a right of appeal for a person who has been made the subject of a hospital order or a guardianship order made by a magistrates' court under s.37(3), above.

Detention during Her Majesty's pleasure

Persons ordered to be kept in custody during Her Majesty's pleasure

46.—(1) The Secretary of State may by warrant direct that any person who, by virtue of any enactment to which this subsection applies, is required to be kept in custody during Her Majesty's pleasure or until the directions of Her Majesty are known shall be detained in such hospital (not being a mental nursing home) as may be specified in the warrant and, where that person is not already detained in the hospital, give directions for his removal there.

(2) The enactments to which subsection (1) above applies are section 16 of the Courts-Martial (Appeals) Act 1968, section 116 of the Army Act 1955, section 116 of the Air Force Act 1955 and section 63 of the Naval Discipline Act 1957.

(3) A direction under this section in respect of any person shall have the same effect as a hospital order together with a restriction order, made without limitation of time; and where such a direction is given in respect of a person while he is in the hospital, he shall be deemed to be admitted in pursuance of, and on the date of, the direction.

DEFINITIONS
  "Hospital": ss.55(5), 145(1).
  "Mental nursing home": s.145(1).
  "Hospital order": ss.37, 145(1).
  "Restriction order": ss.41, 145(1).

TRANSITIONAL PROVISION
  Sched. 5, para. 21.

GENERAL NOTE
  This section provides that a serviceman who has been ordered to be detained "during Her Majesty's pleasure" (*i.e.* indefinitely) may be directed by the Home Secretary to be detained in a hospital. Such a direction has the same effect as a restriction order made with limit of time under section 41, above.

Subs. (3)
  Direction: The patient may make an application to a Mental Health Review Tribunal within six months of the date of the direction (s.69(2)(*b*)).

Transfer to hospital of prisoners, etc.

Removal to hospital of persons serving sentences of imprisonment, etc.

47.—(1) If in the case of a person serving a sentence of imprisonment the Secretary of State is satisfied, by reports from at least two registered medical practitioners—

(*a*) that the said person is suffering from mental illness, psychopathic disorder, severe mental impairment or mental impairment; and

(*b*) that the mental disorder from which that person is suffering is of a nature or degree which makes it appropriate for him to be detained in a hospital for medical treatment and, in the case of psychopathic disorder or mental impairment, that such treatment is likely to alleviate or prevent a deterioration of his condition;

the Secretary of State may, if he is of the opinion having regard to the public interest and all the circumstances that it is expedient so to do, by warrant direct that that person be removed to and detained in such hospital (not being a mental nursing home) as may be specified in the direction; and a direction under this section shall be known as "a transfer direction".

(2) A transfer direction shall cease to have effect at the expiration of the period of 14 days beginning with the date on which it is given unless within that period the person with respect to whom it was given has been received into the hospital specified in the direction.

(3) A transfer direction with respect to any person shall have the same effect as a hospital order made in his case.

(4) A transfer direction shall specify the form or forms of mental disorder referred to in paragraph (*a*) of subsection (1) above from which, upon the reports taken into account under that subsection, the patient is found by the Secretary of State to be suffering; and no such direction shall be given unless the patient is described in each of those reports as suffering from the same form of disorder, whether or not he is also described in either of them as suffering from another form.

(5) References in this Part of this Act to a person serving a sentence of imprisonment include references—

(*a*) to a person detained in pursuance of any sentence or order for detention made by a court in criminal proceedings (other than an order under any enactment to which section 46 above applies);

(*b*) to a person committed to custody under section 115(3) of the Magistrates' Courts Act 1980 (which relates to persons who fail to comply with an order to enter into recognisances to keep the peace or be of good behaviour); and

    (c) to a person committed by a court to a prison or other institution to which the Prison Act 1952 applies in default of payment of any sum adjudged to be paid on his conviction.

DEFINITIONS
    "Psychopathic disorder": ss.1, 145(1).
    "Severe mental impairment": ss.1, 145(1).
    "Mental impairment": ss.1, 145(1).
    "Hospital": ss.55(5), 145(1).
    "Medical treatment": s.145(1).
    "Mental nursing home": s.145(1).
    "Hospital order": ss.37, 145(1).
    "Patient": s.145(1).

GENERAL NOTE
    This section enables the Home Secretary to direct that a person serving a sentence of imprisonment or other detention be removed to and detained in a hospital. A direction made under this section (a "transfer direction") has the same effect as a hospital order made without restrictions under s.37, above. When giving a transfer direction under this section the Home Secretary may, and in most cases will, also impose the restrictions provided for under s.49, below (so that the patient cannot be transferred to another hospital, sent on leave or discharged without his consent). The Home Secretary must make a further direction under s.49 in respect of certain prisoners (s.49(1)).

    District Health Authorities and local social services authorities have a duty to provide after-care services for patients who cease to be liable to be detained and leave hospital after having been transferred by the Home Secretary under this section (s.117).

Subs. (1)
    Sentence of imprisonment: See s.55(6), below, and subs. (5).
    Two registered medical practitioners: One of whom must be approved by the Secretary of State under s.12, above (s.54(1)).

Subs. (2)
    Beginning with: Including the day on which the transfer direction is given (*Hare* v. *Gocher* [1962] 2 Q.B. 641).
    Received into the hospital: The Butler Committee was informed that although there is no requirement under this section for the consent of the receiving hospital to be obtained, the Home Secretary observes the practice of seeking such consent before directing transfers from prison (Butler Report, para. 2.29).

Subs. (3)
    Transfer direction: The patient may make an application to a Mental Health Review Tribunal within six months of the date of the direction (s.69(2)(b)).
    Same effect as a hospital order: See section 40, above.

Subs. (4)
    Suffering from: See the note on s.37(2), above.

Removal to hospital of other prisoners

    48.—(1) If in the case of a person to whom this section applies the Secretary of State is satisfied by the same reports as are required for the purposes of section 47 above that that person is suffering from mental illness or severe mental impairment of a nature or degree which makes it appropriate for him to be detained in a hospital for medical treatment and that he is in urgent need of such treatment, the Secretary of State shall the same power of giving a transfer direction in respect of him under that section as if he were serving a sentence of imprisonment.

    (2) This section applies to the following persons, that is to say—

        (a) persons detained in a prison or remand centre, not being

persons serving a sentence of imprisonment or persons falling
within the following paragraphs of this subsection;
(*b*) persons remanded in custody by a magistrates' court;
(*c*) civil prisoners, that is to say, persons committed by a court to
prison for a limited term (including persons committed to
prison in pursuance of a writ of attachment), who are not
persons falling to be dealt with under section 47 above;
(*d*) persons detained under the Immigration Act 1971.
(3) Subsections (2) to (4) of section 47 above shall apply for the
purposes of this section and of any transfer direction given by virtue of
this section as they apply for the purposes of that section and of any
transfer direction under that section.

DEFINITIONS
"Severe mental impairment": ss.1, 145(1).
"Hospital": ss.55(5), 145(1).
"Medical treatment": s.145(1).
"Transfer direction": ss.47, 145(1).
"Civil prisoner": s.55(1).

GENERAL NOTE
This section, which only applies to persons suffering from mental illness or severe mental
impairment, empowers the Home Secretary to direct the removal from prison to hospital of
certain categories of *unsentenced* prisoners. A person removed to hospital under this section
is placed in the same position as a person who has been made the subject of a transfer
direction under s.47, above.
District Health Authorities and local social services authorities have a duty to provide
after-care services for patients who have ceased to be liable to be detained and leave hospital
after having been transferred under this section (s.117).
Urgent need of treatment: The Home Office informed the Butler Committee that the
procedure under this section is adopted only where a prisoner's condition is such that
immediate removal to a hospital is necessary and that normally when he is well enough he
is either produced at court from hospital or returned to prison to await trial (Butler Report,
para. 3.38).
Transfer direction: Which will cease to have effect unless the prisoner is admitted to
hospital within 14 days of it being given (s.47(2)).

Subs. (2)
A transfer direction made in respect of persons coming within categories (*a*) or (*b*) *must*
be made subject to the restrictions provided for under s.49, below (s.49(1)).
para. (*a*): persons coming within this category are subject to the further provisions
provided for under s.51, below.
para. (*b*): persons coming within this category are subject to the further provisions
provided for under s.52, below.
paras. (*c*) and (*d*): persons coming within these categories are subject to the further
provisions provided for under s.53, below.

Subs. (3)
Transfer direction given by virtue of this section: The patient may make an application to
a Mental Health Review Tribunal within six months of the date of the direction (s.69(2)(*b*)).
Also note s.74(4), below.

Restriction on discharge of prisoners removed to hospital

49.—(1) Where a transfer direction is given in respect of any person,
the Secretary of State, if he thinks fit, may by warrant further direct that
that person shall be subject to the special restrictions set out in section 41
above; and where the Secretary of State gives a transfer direction in
respect of any such person as is described in paragraph (*a*) or (*b*) of
section 48(2) above, he shall also give a direction under this section
applying those restrictions to him.

(2) A direction under this section shall have the same effect as a restriction order made under section 41 above and shall be known as "a restriction direction".

(3) While a person is subject to a restriction direction the responsible medical officer shall at such intervals (not exceeding one year) as the Secretary of State may direct examine and report to the Secretary of State on that person; and every report shall contain such particulars as the Secretary of State may require.

DEFINITIONS
  "Transfer direction": ss.47, 145(1).
  "Responsible medical officer": s.55(1).

GENERAL NOTE
  This section provides that the Home Secretary may, and in respect of certain prisoners must, add an order restricting the patient's discharge from hospital (a "restriction direction") to a transfer direction made under s.47 above. A restriction direction has the same effect as a restriction order made by the court under s.41, above.
  A patient who is subject to a restriction direction may apply to a Mental Health Review Tribunal (ss.70, 79).

Subs. (1)
  May: In the majority of cases, when a sentenced prisoner is transferred to hospital a restriction direction is added by the Home Secretary (Cmnd. 7320, para. 5.40).

Subs. (2)
  Restriction direction: For further provisions, see s.50, below.

Further provisions as to prisoners under sentence

50.—(1) Where a transfer direction and a restriction direction have been given in respect of a person serving a sentence of imprisonment and before the expiration of that person's sentence the Secretary of State is notified by the responsible medical officer, any other registered medical practitioner or a Mental Health Review Tribunal that that person no longer requires treatment in hospital for mental disorder or that no effective treatment for his disorder can be given in the hospital to which he has been removed, the Secretary of State may—

(a) by warrant direct that he be remitted to any prison or other institution in which he might have been detained if he had not been removed to hospital, there to be dealt with as if he had not been so removed; or

(b) exercise any power of releasing him on licence or discharging him under supervision which would have been exercisable if he had been remitted to such a prison or institution as aforesaid.

and on his arrival in the prison or other institution or, as the case may be, his release or discharge as aforesaid, the transfer direction and the restriction direction shall cease to have effect.

(2) A restriction direction in the case of a person serving a sentence of imprisonment shall cease to have effect on the expiration of the sentence.

(3) Subject to subsection (4) below, references in this section to the expiration of a person's sentence are references to the expiration of the period during which he would have been liable to be detained in a prison or other institution if the transfer direction had not been given and that period shall be treated as expiring on the date on which he could have been discharged if he had not forfeited remission of any part of the sentence after his removal pursuant to the direction.

(4) For the purposes of section 49(2) of the Prison Act 1952 (which provides for discounting from the sentences of certain prisoners periods while they are unlawfully at large) a patient who, having been transferred

in pursuance of a transfer direction from any such institution as is referred to in that section, is at large in circumstances in which he is liable to be taken into custody under any provision of this Act, shall be treated as unlawfully at large and absent from that institution.

DEFINITIONS
   "Transfer direction": ss.47, 145(1).
   "Restriction direction": ss.49, 145(1).
   "Hospital": ss.55(5), 145(1).
   "Mental disorder": ss.1, 145(1).
   "Patient": s.145(1).
   "Responsible medical officer": s.55(1).

GENERAL NOTE
   This section provides that if the Home Secretary is informed that a patient who has been placed on a restriction direction no longer requires treatment he may either direct that the patient be returned to prison to serve the remainder of his sentence or release him from hospital on the same terms on which he could be released from prison. It also provides for a restriction direction to cease to have effect on what would have been the patient's earliest date of release if he had remained in prison.

Subs. (1)
   Serving a sentence of imprisonment: See section 55(6), below.
   Expiration of that persons sentence: See subs. (3), below.

Subs. (2)
   Cease to have effect: The patient will remain in hospital as a detained patient subject to a hospital order made without restrictions under s.37, above.

Further provisions as to detained persons

   51.—(1) This section has effect where a transfer direction has been given in respect of any such person as is described in paragraph (*a*) of section 48(2) above and that person is in this section referred to as "the detainee".
   (2) The transfer direction shall cease to have effect when the detainee's case is disposed of by the court having jurisdiction to try or otherwise deal with him, but without prejudice to any power of that court to make a hospital order or other order under this Part of this Act in his case.
   (3) If the Secretary of State is notified by the responsible medical officer, any other registered medical practitioner or a Mental Health Review Tribunal at any time before the detainee's case is disposed of by that court—
   (*a*) that the detainee no longer requires treatment in hospital for mental disorder; or
   (*b*) that no effective treatment for his disorder can be given at the hospital to which he has been removed,
the Secretary of State may by warrant direct that he be remitted to any place where he might have been detained if he had not been removed to hospital, there to be dealt with as if he had not been so removed, and on his arrival at the place to which he is so remitted the transfer direction shall cease to have effect.
   (4) If (no direction having been given under subsection (3) above) the court having jurisdiction to try or otherwise deal with the detainee is satisfied on the written or oral evidence of the responsible medical officer—
   (*a*) that the detainee no longer requires treatment in hospital for mental disorder; or
   (*b*) that no effective treatment for his disorder can be given at the hospital to which he has been removed,

the court may order him to be remitted to any such place as is mentioned in subsection (3) above or released on bail and on his arrival at that place or, as the case may be, his release on bail the transfer direction shall cease to have effect.

(5) If (no direction or order having been given or made under subsection (3) or (4) above) it appears to the court having jurisdiction to try or otherwise deal with the detainee—

(*a*) that it is impracticable or inappropriate to bring the detainee before the court; and

(*b*) that the conditions set out in subsection (6) below are satisfied,

the court may make a hospital order (with or without a restriction order) in his case in his absence and, in the case of a person awaiting trial, without convicting him.

(6) A hospital order may be made in respect of a person under subsection (5) above if the court—

(*a*) is satisfied, on the written or oral evidence of at least two registered medical practitioners, that the detainee is suffering from mental illness or severe mental impairment of a nature or degree which makes it appropriate for the patient to be detained in a hospital for medical treatment; and

(*b*) is of the opinion, after considering any depositions or other documents required to be sent to the proper officer of the court, that it is proper to make such an order.

(7) Where a person committed to the Crown Court to be dealt with under section 43 above is admitted to a hospital in pursuance of an order under section 44 above, subsections (5) and (6) above shall apply as if he were a person subject to a transfer direction.

DEFINITIONS
  "Transfer direction": ss.47, 145(1).
  "Hospital order": ss.37, 145(1).
  "Responsible medical officer".
  "Hospital": ss.55(5), 145(1).
  "Mental disorder": ss.1, 145(1).
  "Restriction order": ss.41, 145(1).
  "Severe mental impairment": ss.1, 145(1).
  "Medical treatment": s.145(1).

GENERAL NOTE
  This section provides that a transfer direction made in respect of a person detained in a prison or remand centre shall cease to have effect when the case has been finally dealt with by the appropriate court (subs. (2)). In the meanwhile the Home Secretary has power to direct the patient's return to prison (subs. (3)). If the Home Secretary does not exercise this power the court can, on receiving the requisite evidence, either order the patient to be returned to prison or released on bail (subs. (4)). The transfer direction will cease to have effect if the Home Secretary or court exercise their powers under subs. (3) and (4). If the patient has not been sent back to prison or released on bail the court can make a hospital order in respect of a mentally ill or severely mentally impaired patient in his absence and without convicting him (subs. (5)(6)).

Subs. (4)
  Written or oral evidence: For general requirements as to medical evidence, see s.54, below.

Subs. (6)
  Two registered medical practitioners: One of whom must be approved by the Secretary of State under s.12, above.

Further provisions as to persons remanded by magistrates' courts

52.—(1) This section has effect where a transfer direction has been given in respect of any such person as is described in paragraph (*b*) of section 48(2) above; and that person is in this section referred to as "the accused".

(2) Subject to subsection (5) below, the transfer direction shall cease to have effect on the expiration of the period of remand unless the accused is committed in custody to the Crown Court for trial or to be otherwise dealt with.

(3) Subject to subsection (4) below, the power of further remanding the accused under section 128 of the Magistrates' Courts Act 1980 may be exercised by the court without his being brought before the court; and if the court further remands the accused in custody (whether or not he is brought before the court) the period of remand shall, for the purposes of this section, be deemed not to have expired.

(4) The court shall not under subsection (3) above further remand the accused in his absence unless he has appeared before the court within the previous six months.

(5) If the magistrates' court is satisfied, on the written or oral evidence of the responsible medical officer—

(a) that the accused no longer requires treatment in hospital for mental disorder; or

(b) that no effective treatment for his disorder can be given in the hospital to which he has been removed,

the court may direct that the transfer direction shall cease to have effect notwithstanding that the period of remand has not expired or that the accused is committed to the Crown Court as mentioned in subsection (2) above.

(6) If the accused is committed to the Crown Court as mentioned in subsection (2) above and the transfer direction has not ceased to have effect under subsection (5) above, section 51 above shall apply as if the transfer direction given in his case were a direction given in respect of a person falling within that section.

(7) The magistrates' court may, in the absence of the accused, inquire as examining justices into an offence alleged to have been committed by him and commit him for trial in accordance with section 6 of the Magistrates' Courts Act 1980 if—

(a) the court is satisfied, on the written or oral evidence of the responsible medical officer, that the accused is unfit to take part in the proceedings; and

(b) where the court proceeds under subsection (1) of that section, the accused is represented by counsel or a solicitor.

DEFINITIONS
"Transfer direction": ss.47, 145(1).
"Responsible medical officer": s.55(1).
"Hospital": s.55(5), 145(1).
"Mental disorder": ss.1, 145(1).

GENERAL NOTE
This section provides that a transfer direction made in respect of a person who has been remanded in custody by a magistrates' court ceases to have effect at the expiration of the period of remand unless the accused is then committed in custody to the Crown Court (subs. (2)). However, if the magistrates' court further remands the accused under subs. (3) the direction will not expire. Alternatively, if the court is satisfied, on receiving the requisite evidence, that the accused no longer requires treatment in hospital it may direct that the transfer direction shall cease to have effect (subs. (5)). The court also has power to conduct committal proceedings in the absence of the accused if it is satisfied that he is unfit to take part in the proceedings (subs. (7)).

Subs. (4)
Months: Means calendar months (Interpretation Act, s.5, Sched. 1).

Subs. (5)
   Written or oral evidence: See s.54, below.

Further provisions as to civil prisoners and persons detained under the Immigration Act 1971

53.—(1) Subject to subsection (2) below, a transfer direction given in respect of any such person as is described in paragraph (c) or (d) of section 48(2) above shall cease to have effect on the expiration of the period during which he would, but for his removal to hospital, be liable to be detained in the place from which he was removed.

(2) Where a transfer direction and a restriction direction have been given in respect of any such person as is mentioned in subsection (1) above, then, if the Secretary of State is notified by the responsible medical officer, any other registered medical practitioner or a Mental Health Review Tribunal at any time before the expiration of the period there mentioned—

   (a) that that person no longer requires treatment in hospital for mental disorder; or

   (b) that no effective treatment for his disorder can be given in the hospital to which he has been removed,

the Secretary of State may by warrant direct that he be remitted to any place where he might have been detained if he had not been removed to hospital, and on his arrival at the place to which he is so remitted the transfer direction and the restriction direction shall cease to have effect.

DEFINITIONS
   "Transfer direction": ss.47, 145(1).
   "Hospital": ss.55(5), 145(1).
   "Restriction direction": ss.49, 145(1).
   "Responsible medical officer": s.55(1).
   "Mental disorder": ss.1, 145(1).

GENERAL NOTE
   This section provides that a transfer direction made in respect of a civil prisoner or a person detained under the Immigration Act 1971 ceases to have effect on the expiration of the period of detention that would have occurred had the removal to hospital not taken place (subs. (1)). Where a transfer direction *and* a restriction direction have been made the Home Secretary has power to direct that the patient be returned to prison, and on his arrival there both the transfer direction and the restriction direction shall cease to have effect (subs. (2)).

Supplemental

Requirements as to medical evidence

54.—(1) The registered medical practitioner whose evidence is taken into account under section 35(3)(a) above and at least one of the registered medical practitioners whose evidence is taken into account under sections 36(1), 37(2)(a), 38(1) and 51(6)(a) above and whose reports are taken into account under sections 47(1) and 48(1) above shall be a practitioner approved for the purposes of section 12 above by the Secretary of State as having special experience in the diagnosis or treatment of mental disorder.

(2) For the purposes of any provision of this Part of this Act under which a court may act on the written evidence of—

   (a) a registered medical practitioner or a registered medical practitioner of any description; or

   (b) a person representing the managers of a hospital,

a report in writing purporting to be signed by a registered medical practitioner or a registered medical practitioner of such a description or by a person representing the managers of a hospital may, subject to the provisions of this section, be received in evidence without proof of the signature of the practitioner or that person and without proof that he has the requisite qualifications or authority or is of the requisite description; but the court may require the signatory of any such report to be called to give oral evidence.

(3) Where, in pursuance of a direction of the court, any such report is tendered in evidence otherwise than by or on behalf of the person who is the subject of the report, then—

(*a*) if that person is represented by counsel or a solicitor, a copy of the report shall be given to his counsel or solicitor;

(*b*) if that person is not so represented, the substance of the report shall be disclosed to him or, where he is a child or young person, to his parent or guardian if present in court; and

(*c*) except where the report relates only to arrangements for his admission to a hospital, that person may require the signatory of the report to be called to give oral evidence, and evidence to rebut the evidence contained in the report may be called by or on behalf of that person.

DEFINITIONS

"Mental disorder": ss.1, 145(1).
"The managers": s.145(1).
"Hospital": ss.55(5), 145(1).
"Child": s.55(1).
"Young person": s.55(1).
"Guardian": s.55(1).

GENERAL NOTE

This section specifies when medical evidence must be given by a doctor who has been approved by the Secretary of State under s.12, above, and provides for the circumstances when written evidence by a doctor or a person representing the managers of a hospital may be accepted by a court.

Subs. (1)

Note that the general requirement relating to civil admissions under Pt. II of this Act that the two doctors making medical recommendations cannot be on the staff of the same hospital (s.12(3)) does not apply to medical recommendations made under this Part.

Interpretation of Part III

55.—(1) In this Part of this Act—

"child" and "young person" have the same meaning as in the Children and Young Persons Act 1933;

"civil prisoner" has the meaning given to it by section 48(2)(*c*) above;

"guardian", in relation to a child or young person, has the same meaning as in the Children and Young Persons Act 1933;

"place of safety", in relation to a person who is not a child or young person, means any police station, prison or remand centre, or any hospital the managers of which are willing temporarily to receive him, and in relation to a child or young person has the same meaning as in the Children and Young Persons Act 1933;

"responsible medical officer", in relation to a person liable to be detained in a hospital within the meaning of Part II of this Act, means the registered medical practitioner in charge of the treatment of the patient.

(2) Any reference in this Part of this Act to an offence punishable on summary conviction with imprisonment shall be construed without regard

to any prohibition or restriction imposed by or under any enactment relating to the imprisonment of young offenders.

(3) Where a patient who is liable to be detained in a hospital in pursuance of an order or direction under this Part of this Act is treated by virtue of any provision of this Part of this Act as if he had been admitted to the hospital in pursuance of a subsequent order or direction under this Part of this Act or a subsequent application for admission for treatment under Part II of this Act, he shall be treated as if the subsequent order, direction or application had described him as suffering from the form or forms of mental disorder specified in the earlier order by direction or, where he is treated as if he had been so admitted by virtue of a direction under section 42(1) above, such form of mental disorder as may be specified in the direction under that section.

(4) Any reference to a hospital order, a guardianship order or a restriction order in section 40(2), (4) or (5), section 41(3) to (5), or section 42 above or section 69(1) below shall be construed as including a reference to any order or direction under this Part of this Act having the same effect as the first-mentioned order; and the exceptions and modifications set out in Schedule 1 to this Act in respect of the provisions of this Act described in that Schedule accordingly include those which are consequential on the provisions of this subsection.

(5) Section 34(2) above shall apply for the purposes of this Part of this Act as it applies for the purposes of Part II of this Act.

(6) References in this Part of this Act to persons serving a sentence of imprisonment shall be construed in accordance with section 47(5) above.

(7) Section 99 of the Children and Young Persons Act 1933 (which relates to the presumption and determination of age) shall apply for the purposes of this Part of this Act as it applies for the purposes of that Act.

DEFINITIONS
"Hospital": s.145(1).
"The managers": s.145(1).
"Patient": s.145(1).
"Application for admission for treatment": ss.3, 145(1).
"Mental disorder": ss.1, 145(1).
"Hospital order": ss.37, 145(1).
"Guardianship order": ss.73, 145(1).
"Restriction order": ss.41, 145(1).

Subs. (1)
Under s.107(1) of the Children and Young Persons Act 1933, "child" means a person under the age of 14 years, "young person" means a person who has attained the age of fourteen years and is under the age of seventeen years, "guardian", in relation to a child or young person, includes any person who, in the opinion of the relevant court, has for the time being the charge of or control over the child or young person, and "place of safety" means a community home provided by a local authority or a controlled community home, any police station, or any hospital, surgery, or any other suitable place, the occupier of which is willing temporarily to receive a child or young person.

Medical practitioner in charge of the treatment of the patient: In most cases this will be the consultant psychiatrist on the staff of the hospital under whose care the patient has been admitted. However, determining the "medical practitioner in charge" is a question of fact, and he need not necessarily have consultant status.

PART IV

CONSENT TO TREATMENT

GENERAL NOTE
The extent to which the 1959 Act gave authority to the responsible medical officer to treat a patient without his consent was unclear. The opinion of the Department of Health and

Social Security was that where the purpose of detention was treatment, the Act gave implied authority for treatment to be imposed. In recent years this opinion had been brought into doubt and, in particular, the Confederation of Health Service Employees in their publication *The Management of Violent or Potentially Violent Patients* (1977) quoted the view of their legal adviser that the 1959 Act could not be taken to confer on staff any right to impose treatment. The purpose of this Part, which derives from Pt. VI of the 1982 Act, is to clarify the extent to which treatment for mental disorder can be imposed on detained patients in hospitals and mental nursing homes. It provides for two categories of treatment which have different legal consequences. They are: (*a*) the most serious treatments which require the patient's consent *and* a second opinion (s.57); and (2) other serious treatments which require the patient's consent *or* a second opinion (s.58). Treatments that do not come within either of these categories can be imposed on a detained patient who understands the nature and purpose of the treatment, but expressly withholds consent (s.63). The safeguards provided for by ss.57 and 58 can be overriden if the treatment is required urgently (s.62).

This Part only applies to treatment relating to the patient's mental disorder. As far as treatment for other conditions is concerned the patient is in the same position as a non-psychiatric patient who can only be treated without his consent in certain emergency situations. There will be some patients, particularly the severely mentally impaired, who will not be capable of giving valid consent even to routine medical treatment. "In these cases it would clearly not be right for the hospital to withhold such treatment until an emergency arises . . . In these circumstances some reliance must be placed on professional judgment in providing routine medication for minor illnesses. Where more serious medical intervention is required and need is not in doubt, the best course would seem to be for the nearest relative to be consulted" (Cmnd. 7320, para. 6.24). See further, P. D. G. Skegg, "A Justification for Medical Procedures Performed Without Consent" (1974) 90 L.Q.R. 512 and Brenda Hoggett *Mental Health*, 1976, pp.126 to 129.

The Code of Practice, published by the Secretary of State under s.118, below, will provide guidance on the medical treatment of mental disorder.

Patients to whom Part IV applies

56.—(1) This Part of this Act applies to any patient liable to be detained under this Act except—

(*a*) a patient who is liable to be detained by virtue of an emergency application and in respect of whom the second medical recommendation referred to in section 4(4)(*a*) above has not been given and received;

(*b*) a patient who is liable to be detained by virtue of section 5(2) or (4) or 35 above or section 135 or 136 below or by virtue of a direction under section 37(4) above; and

(*c*) a patient who has been conditionally discharged under section 42(2) above or section 73 or 74 below and has not been recalled to hospital.

(2) Section 57 and, so far as relevant to that section, sections 59, 60 and 62 below, apply also to any patient who is not liable to be detained under this Act.

DEFINITIONS
"Patient": s.145(1).
"Hospital": ss.64(1), 145(1).

GENERAL NOTE
The section establishes that the provisions of this Part shall apply to all detained patients, except those mentioned in paras. (*a*) to (*c*) of subs. (1) and provides for the safeguards for the most serious treatments to apply to informal patients.

Subs. (1)
Liable to be detained: Patients who are subject to guardianship and informal patients are not "liable to be detained". Patients who have been granted leave of absence under s.17, above, continue to be "liable to be detained" under this Act.
Hospital: Or a mental nursing home (s.64(1)).

Subs. (2)

This subsection extends the protection provided by s.57 to voluntary patients. It was enacted as a result of an opposition amendment to the 1982 Act which found favour with the Minister for Health who accepted the argument that "if a course of treatment is so drastic that a detained patient's consent alone should not justify it and that there should be further safeguards, it is difficult to see why the same provisions should not apply to an informal patient" (H.C. Vol. 29, col. 81).

Treatment requiring consent and a second opinion

57.—(1) This section applies to the following forms of medical treatment for mental disorder—

  (a) any surgical operation for destroying brain tissue or for destroying the functioning of brain tissue; and

  (b) such other forms of treatment as may be specified for the purposes of this section by regulations made by the Secretary of State.

(2) Subject to section 62 below, a patient shall not be given any form of treatment to which this section applies unless he has consented to it and—

  (a) a registered medical practitioner appointed for the purposes of this Part of this Act by the Secretary of State (not being the responsible medical officer) and two other persons appointed for the purposes of this paragraph by the Secretary of State (not being registered medical practitioners) have certified in writing that the patient is capable of understanding the nature, purpose and likely effects of the treatment in question and has consented to it; and

  (b) the registered medical practitioner referred to in paragraph (a) above has certified in writing that, having regard to the likelihood of the treatment alleviating or preventing a deterioration of the patient's condition, the treatment should be given.

(3) Before giving a certificate under subsection (2)(b) above the registered medical practitioner concerned shall consult two other persons who have been professionally concerned with the patient's medical treatment, and of those persons one shall be a nurse and the other shall be neither a nurse nor a registered medical practitioner.

(4) Before making any regulations for the purpose of this section the Secretary of State shall consult such bodies as appear to him to be concerned.

DEFINITIONS

  "Medical treatment": s.145(1).
  "Mental disorder": ss.1, 145(1).
  "Patient": s.145(1).
  "Responsible medical officer": s.64(1).

GENERAL NOTE

This section provides that certain of the most serious forms of medical treatment can only be given if the patient has consented to it and three independent people, one being a medical practitioner, have certified that the patient understands the treatment and has consented to it. The medical practitioner who is involved in the certification process is placed under an obligation to consult with two other persons who have been professionally concerned with the patients' treatment.

This section applies to voluntary patients (s.56(2)) as well as to patients who are liable to be detained. It does not apply to patients who are detained under the powers set out in paras. (a) to (c) of s.56(1) and only the consent of such patients is required before the treatments covered by this section can be given. In view of the argument accepted by the Minister for Health relating to voluntary patients (see the note on s.56(2)) this exclusion would appear to have been an oversight and, although it is highly unlikely that the very serious forms of treatment provided for in this section would ever be given to patients who are being detained under one of the short term powers, it is submitted that the spirit of this section requires that its protection be afforded to all categories of mentally disordered patients.

If a patient is given treatment under this section his responsible medical officer must provide the Mental Health Act Commission with reports on the treatment and the patient's condition (ss.61, 121(2)(*b*)).

Subs. (1), para (*a*): at the Special Standing Committee the Under-Secretary of State announced that from 1979 to 1982 in England and Wales there had been 207 psycho-surgical operations on informal patients and 4 on detained patients (Sitting of June 29, 1982). See further, Larry Gostin, "Psycho-surgery: A Hazardous and Unestablished Treatment? A Case for the Importation of American Legal Safeguards to Great Britain", [1982] J.S.W.L. 83.

para. (*b*)

Other forms of treatment: "[This section] will also apply to the most serious treatments that are irreversible or drastic, such as certain hormone treatments", *per* the Minister for Health, H.C., Vol. 29, col. 80.

Regulations: See subs. (4). The Code of Practice will also specify treatments to which this section will apply (s.118(2)).

Subs. (2)

Consented to it: "Valid consent implies the ability, given an explanation in simple terms to understand the nature, purpose and effect of the proposed treatment" (Cmnd. 7320, para. 6.23). The consent should be given in an atmosphere which is uncontaminated by fear or intimidation. A patient can withdraw his consent to treatment under s.60, below.

para. (*a*)

Secretary of State: The Mental Health Act Commission will appoint the medical practitioner and the two other persons referred to in this paragraph (s.121(2)(*a*)). They must be allowed to interview the patient and inspect his records, and the medical practitioner must be allowed to examine the patient; see ss.119 and 129, below.

Consented: Both the patient's consent and the medical practitioner's certificate may apply to a plan of treatment (s.59).

para. (*b*)

Certified: In the prescribed form (s.64(2)). During the passage of the 1982 Act the Minister for Health said that there "is nothing in the [Act] to stop an independent psychiatrist putting a time limit on a certificate. If he thinks that it is an unusual or difficult decision he can specify whatever time limit he deems appropriate" (H.C., Vol. 29, col. 58).

Subs. (3)

Shall consult: It is submitted that the process of consultation should include the exchange of information and the seeking and giving of advice.

Who have been professionally concerned: And who would therefore have some knowledge of the patient's history and needs.

With the patient's medical treatment: It is submitted that it would not be sufficient for the two people consulted merely to have had general responsibilities on the ward where the patient is being treated.

The other: Who could be a psychologist, occupational therapist, psychotherapist or a social worker. It will not be possible for the medical practitioner to give a certificate if no other professionals, apart from nurses, have been involved in the patient's treatment.

Treatment requiring consent or a second opinion

58.—(1) This section applies to the following forms of medical treatment for mental disorder—

(*a*) such forms of treatment as may be specified for the purposes of this section by regulations made by the Secretary of State;

(*b*) the administration of medicine to a patient by any means (not being a form of treatment specified under paragraph (*a*) above or section 57 above) at any time during a period for which he is liable to be detained as a patient to whom this Part of this Act applies if three months or more have elapsed since the first occasion in that period when medicine was administered to him by any means for this mental disorder.

(2) The Secretary of State may by order vary the length of the period mentioned in subsection (1)(*b*) above.

(3) Subject to section 62 below, a patient shall not be given any form of treatment to which this section applies unless—

(*a*) he has consented to that treatment and either the responsible medical officer or a registered medical practitioner appointed for the purposes of this Part of this Act by the Secretary of State has certified in writing that the patient is capable of understanding its nature, purpose and likely effect and has consented to it; or

(*b*) a registered medical practitioner appointed as aforesaid (not being the responsible medical officer) has certified in writing that the patient is not capable of understanding the nature, purpose and likely effects of that treatment or has not consented to it but that, having regard to the likelihood of its alleviating or preventing a deterioration of his condition, the treatment should be given.

(4) Before giving a certificate under subsection (3)(*b*) above the registered medical practitioner concerned shall consult two other persons who have been professionally concerned with the patient's medical treatment, and of those persons one shall be a nurse and the other shall be neither a nurse nor a registered medical practitioner.

(5) Before making any regulations for the purposes of this section the Secretary of State shall consult such bodies as appear to him to be concerned.

DEFINITIONS
"Medical treatment": s.145(1).
"Mental disorder": ss.1, 145(1).
"Patient": s.145(1).
"Responsible medical officer": s.64(1).

TRANSITIONAL PROVISION
Sched. 5, para. 18:

GENERAL NOTE
This section provides that certain forms of treatment shall not be given to a patient unless the patient consents *or* an independent medical practitioner has certified that either the patient is incapable of giving his consent or that the patient should receive the treatment even though he has not consented to it. If the patient consents to the treatment either the patient's responsible medical officer or an independent medical practitioner must certify that the consent has been properly given.

If a patient is given treatment under this section his responsible medical officer must provide the Mental Health Act Commission with reports on the treatment and the patient's condition (ss.61, 121(2)(*b*)).

Subs. (1)
Such forms of treatment: The Government has announced that E.C.T. treatment will be specified in regulations as a form of treatment to which this section applies. E.C.T. was not mentioned in this section because it was felt that as practice developed a future Secretary of State might wish to "promote it or relegate it from one division to another", *per* the Minister for Health, H.C., Vol. 29, col. 86.

Regulations: See subs. (5). There is no power for treatments to be specified for the purposes of this section by the Code of Practice. Para. (*b*) enables a course of medication to be imposed on a patient for up to three months without the patient's consent and without the need to consult or to obtain an independent medical opinion. The protection provided by this section does not come into play until three months have elapsed since the commencement of the treatment.

Patient: See section 56(1), above.

Three months or more: "The three months gives time for the psychiatrist to consider a treatment programme which suits the patient. Three months seems to fit in best with both clinical experience and clinical practice. It is long enough to allow a proper valuation and assessment of what, if any, long term treatment may be needed. It is also short enough to ensure that patients' consent, or a second opinion, is obtained before a long term course of drug treatment gets too far ahead", *per* the Under-Secretary of State, Special Standing Committee, June 29, 1982.

Subs. (3)
  para. (*a*)
  Consented to that treatment: see the note on s.57(2), above. Both the patient's consent and the medical practitioner's certificate may relate to a plan of treatment (s.59). A patient can withdraw his consent to treatment under s.60, below.
  Appointed . . . by the Secretary of State: The Mental Health Act Commission will make the appointment (s.112(2)(*a*)). Provisions relating to the payment and powers of the appointed medical practitioner are contained in section 119, below.
  para. (*b*): The Minister of Health has said that it would probably be very unusual for the psychiatrist who gives a certificate under this paragraph to give an open-ended opinion which would allow the treatment to go on for years. Most psychiatrists would be likely to suggest that a course of treatment should be tried for a finite period. (Special Standing Committee, June 29, 1982.)
  Certified: In the prescribed form (s.64(2)).
  Not consented to it: The 1978 White Paper suggested that the following principle be adopted in cases where the patient's consent is not forthcoming: "where it is not possible to agree with the patient the form the treatment is to take and the consultant feels the imposition of treatment is essential he should, wherever there is a choice, select the method of treatment the patient finds least objectionable or which would represent the minimum interference with the patient" (Cmnd. 7320, para. 6.18).

Plans of treatment

59. Any consent or certificate under section 57 or 58 above may relate to a plan of treatment under which the patient is to be given (whether within a specified period or otherwise) one or more of the forms of treatment to which that section applies.

DEFINITION
  "Patient": s.145(1).

GENERAL NOTE
  This section enables any consent or certificate obtained for the purposes of s.57 or 58 to relate to a plan of treatment which would involve one or more of the treatments specified under the same section. Such a plan would allow for variations in treatment within the context of the treatment objectives and enable the responsible medical officer to respond rapidly to the patient's reaction to a particular drug or dosage. The plan could include a time scale for the administration of treatments. A patient may withdraw his consent to a plan of treatment under s.60(2), below.

Withdrawal of consent

60.—(1) Where the consent of a patient to any treatment has been given for the purposes of section 57 or 58 above, the patient may, subject to section 62 below, at any time before the completion of the treatment withdraw his consent, and those sections shall then apply as if the remainder of the treatment were a separate form of treatment.

(2) Without prejudice to the application of subsection (1) above to any treatment given under the plan of treatment to which a patient has consented, a patient who has consented to such a plan may, subject to section 62 below, at any time withdraw his consent to further treatment, or to further treatment of any description, under the plan.

DEFINITION
  "Patient": s.145(1).

GENERAL NOTE
  This section provides for a patient to withdraw his consent to treatment under s.57 or 58 or to a plan of treatment. Treatment can be continued if the criteria for urgent treatment set out in s.62, below, apply.

Subs. (1)

Separate form of treatment: If the patient withdraws his consent to a s.57 treatment, it must cease immediately. If a s.58 treatment is involved the responsible medical officer must cease treatment until the requirements of that section relating to non-consenting patients can be complied with. If the patient withdraws his consent to the administration of medication under s.58(1)(*b*) it would seem that the three-month rule specified in that para. would begin to run from the date of the withdrawal of the consent.

Review of treatment

61.—(1) Where a patient is given treatment in accordance with section 57(2) or 58(3)(*b*) above a report on the treatment and the patient's condition shall be given by the responsible medical officer to the Secretary of State—
  (*a*) on the next occasion on which the responsible medical officer furnishes a report in respect of the patient under section 20(3) above; and
  (*b*) at any other time if so required by the Secretary of State.
  (2) In relation to a patient who is subject to a restriction order or restriction direction subsection (1) above shall have effect as if paragraph (*a*) required the report to be made—
  (*a*) in the case of treatment in the period of six months beginning with the date of the order or direction, at the end of that period;
  (*b*) in the case of treatment at any subsequent time, on the next occasion on which the responsible medical officer makes a report in respect of the patient under section 41(6) or 49(3) above.
  (3) The Secretary of State may at any time give notice to the responsible medical officer directing that, subject to section 62 below, a certificate given in respect of a patient under section 57(2) or 58(3)(*b*) above shall not apply to treatment given to him after a date specified in the notice and sections 57 and 58 above shall then apply to any such treatment as if that certificate had not been given.

DEFINITIONS

This section provides for the periodic review by the Mental Health Act Commission of treatment which is being given under s.57 or 58.

Subs. (1)

Report on the treatment and the patient's condition: The responsible medical officer should report on the treatment and the patient's response to it.

Secretary of State: The functions of the Secretary of State under this section will be performed by the Mental Health Act Commission (s.121(2)(*b*)).

On the next occasion: And on each subsequent occasion when the authority to detain the patient is renewed.

Any other time: It is likely that the Mental Health Act Commission will require a more frequent review than is provided for in para. (*a*) if the treatment is particularly controversial or if the independent psychiatrist is of the opinion that there are special factors involved in the treatment which should be looked at after a short period.

Subs. (2)

This subsection specifies the timing of the treatment review in respect of patients who are subject to a restriction order or restriction direction.

Subs. (3)

This subsection provides that the Mental Health Act Commission may at any time give notice to the responsible medical officer that a certificate given under s.57(2) or 58(3)(*b*) shall cease to apply after the date it specifies. If the responsible medical officer wished to continue with the treatment specified in the notice he would need to start afresh with the procedures laid down in s.57 or 58, unless the criteria for urgent treatment set out in s.62 were satisfied.

Urgent treatment

62.—(1) Sections 57 and 58 above shall not apply to any treatment—
(a) which is immediately necessary to save the patient's life; or
(b) which (not being irreversible) is immediately necessary to prevent a serious deterioration of his condition; or
(c) which (not being irreversible or hazardous) is immediately necessary to alleviate serious suffering by the patient; or
(d) which (not being irreversible or hazardous) is immediately necessary and represents the minimum interference necessary to prevent the patient from behaving violently or being a danger to himself or to others.

(2) Sections 60 and 61(3) above shall not preclude the continuation of any treatment or of treatment under any plan pending compliance with section 57 or 58 above if the responsible medical officer considers that the discontinuance of the treatment or of treatment under the plan would cause serious suffering to the patient.

(3) For the purposes of this section treatment is irreversible if it has unfavourable irreversible physical or psychological consequences and hazardous if it entails significant physical hazard.

DEFINITIONS
"Patient": s.145(1).
"Responsible medical officer": s.64(1).

GENERAL NOTE
This section provides that ss.57 and 58 shall not apply to certain categories of urgent treatment. Because of the immediacy of the situations covered by this section it is submitted that any doctor who is concerned with the patient's treatment could impose treatment if he considered that it satisfied one of the criteria set out in paras. (a) to (d) of subs. (1).

Subs. (1)
Shall not apply: The treatment can be given to the patient without his consent.
Treatment: Treatment of physical disorder is not covered by this Act. Treatment must cease as soon as the crisis has been successfully resolved.

Subs. (2)
This subsection provides that a course of treatment or a plan of treatment can continue notwithstanding that the patient has withdrawn his consent if the responsible medical officer considers that discontinuing the treatment or plan of treatment would cause the patient *serious* suffering.
S.57: Cannot be complied with unless the patient consents to the treatment.
S.58: A certificate under s.58(2)(b) should be obtained as soon as possible after the patient has withdrawn his consent.
Serious suffering: Treatment must cease as soon as its cessation would no longer cause the patient serious suffering.

Subs. (3)
Unfavourable: At the Special Standing Committee the Under-Secretary of State cited the removal of a brain tumour and the removal of a diseased thyroid as examples of treatments which are irreversible and which can be reasonably expected to have favourable consequences. (Sitting of June 29, 1982.)

Treatment not requiring consent

63. The consent of a patient shall not be required for any medical treatment given to him for the mental disorder from which he is suffering, not being treatment falling within section 57 or 58 above, if the treatment is given by or under the direction of the responsible medical officer.

DEFINITIONS
"Patient": s.145(1).
"Medical treatment": s.145(1).
"Mental disorder": ss.1, 145(1).
"Responsible medical officer": s.64(1).

GENERAL NOTE
This section provides that the consent of a detained patient is not required for treatment which does not fall within s.57 or 58. The Minister for Health's response to the argument that detained patients should not be forced to receive treatment is contained in the following passage from his speech to the Special Standing Committee: "[That argument would] lead us to conclude that those who were forcibly detained and had lost their liberty against their will . . . should be kept in custody in places in which they received no treatment despite the fact that those who looked after them would have to gaze on them knowing perfectly well that some treatment could be given to alleviate their suffering and distress and enable them eventually to recover their liberty. Hospitals are places of treatment and we cannot have hospitals in which people are locked up and left to wander about without receiving treatment" (sitting of June 29, 1982).

Medical treatment: Is given a wide meaning in this Act, and although treatment which does not come within s.57 or 58 may be given to a detained patient without his consent, "in practice it is impossible to undertake many of the therapies concerned without a patient's co-operation" (Cmnd. 8405, para. 37).

Supplementary provisions for Part IV

64.—(1) In this Part of this Act "the responsible medical officer" means the registered medical practitioner in charge of the treatment of the patient in question and "hospital" includes a mental nursing home.

(2) Any certificate for the purposes of this Part of this Act shall be in such form as may be prescribed by regulations made by the Secretary of State.

DEFINITIONS
"Patient": s.145(1).
"Hospital": s.145(1).
"Mental nursing home": s.145(1).

Subs. (1)
Medical practitioner in charge: See the note on s.55(1), above.

PART V

MENTAL HEALTH REVIEW TRIBUNALS

Constitution etc.

Mental Health Review Tribunals

65.—(1) There shall continue to be a tribunal known as a Mental Health Review Tribunal for every region for which a Regional Health Authority is established in pursuance of the National Health Service Act 1977 and for Wales, for the purpose of dealing with applications and references by and in respect of patients under the provisions of this Act.

(2) The provisions of Schedule 2 to this Act shall have effect with respect to the constitution of Mental Health Review Tribunals.

(3) Subject to the provisions of Schedule 2 to this Act, and to rules made by the Lord Chancellor under this Act, the jurisdiction of a Mental Health Review Tribunal may be exercised by any three or more of its members, and references in this Act to a Mental Health Review Tribunal shall be construed accordingly.

(4) The Secretary of State may pay to the members of Mental Health Review Tribunals such remuneration and allowances as he may with the consent of the Treasury determine, and defray the expenses of such tribunals to such amount as he may with the consent of the Treasury determine, and may provide for each such tribunal such officers and servants, and such accommodation, as the tribunal may require.

DEFINITION
"Patient": s.145(1).

GENERAL NOTE
The Royal Commission recommended that psychiatric patients should be provided with a safeguard against unjustified detention or control under guardianship by means of a review of their cases from both medical and non-medical points of view. They proposed that the review should be undertaken by a local tribunal which would consist of medical and non-medical members selected from a panel of suitable people (Cmnd. 169, para. 442). This proposal was carried into effect by the 1959 Act which provided for the setting up of Mental Health Review Tribunals. The procedure to be followed in the Tribunals were laid down by the Mental Health Review Tribunal Rules 1960 (S.I. 1960 No. 1139). These rules are being revised and it is expected that new Tribunal Rules will come into force on September 30, 1983. Tribunals are obliged to follow the procedure laid down in the Rules and where the Rules are silent on a point of procedure the Tribunal is probably bound to follow the rules of natural justice, *i.e.* it should act in an unbiased way and provide an opportunity for each party to adequately state his case; see further L. Gostin and E. Rassaby *Representing the Mentally Ill and Handicapped*, 1980, chapter 8.

If a patient considers that his initial admission was unlawful he can attempt to secure his release by making an application to the High Court for a writ of *habeas corpus*. Although the court will examine the papers relating to the admission of the patient to ensure that the requirements of the relevant section have been met, Gostin and Rassaby consider that "the court is unlikely to go beyond what appears on the face of the papers or the court order to question the substantive justification of the detention. If, on the face of it, the applicable legal procedures have been strictly observed, the court will not examine whether the detention is justified, either psychiatrically or socially" (*supra* p.36); see further L. Gostin, "Human Rights, Judicial Review and the Mentally Disordered Offender", [1982] Crim.L.R. 779.

Legal assistance is available under the "Green Form Scheme" to help patients and other applicants prepare their case for the Tribunal hearing. Applicants can also apply for free legal representation at the hearing under the Assistance by Way of Representation Scheme; see the Legal Advice and Assistance (Amendment) Regulations 1982 (S.I. 1982 No. 1582).

The Law Society is establishing a panel of solicitors with experience of tribunal work to assist applicants in finding a suitable legal representative (Law Society's Gazette, January 19, 1983); see further, "Extending 'Assistance by Way of Representation' to the Mental Health Review Tribunal: Note for Guidance", *Guardian Gazette*, November 24, 1982.

The publication of information relating to proceedings before a Mental Health Review Tribunal sitting in private is a contempt of court (Administration of Justice Act 1960, s.12(1)(*b*)).

Provisions relating to the constitution of Mental Health Review Tribunals are contained in Sched. 2 to this Act.

Applications and references concerning Part II patients

Applications to tribunals

66.—(1) Where—
    (*a*) a patient is admitted to a hospital in pursuance of an application for admission for assessment; or
    (*b*) a patient is admitted to a hospital in pursuance of an application for admission for treatment; or
    (*c*) a patient is received into guardianship in pursuance of a guardianship application; or
    (*d*) a report is furnished under section 16 above in respect of a patient; or

(e) a patient is transferred from guardianship to a hospital in pursuance of regulations made under section 19 above; or

(f) a report is furnished under section 20 above in respect of a patient and the patient is not discharged; or

(g) a report is furnished under section 25 above in respect of a patient who is detained in pursuance of an application for admission for treatment; or

(h) an order is made under section 29 above in respect of a patient who is or subsequently becomes liable to be detained or subject to guardianship under Part II of this Act,

an application may be made to a Mental Health Review Tribunal within the relevant period—

    (i) by the patient (except in the cases mentioned in paragraphs (g) and (h) above) or, in the case mentioned in paragraph (d) above, by his nearest relative, and

    (ii) in the cases mentioned in paragraphs (g) and (h) above, by his nearest relative.

(2) In subsection (1) above "the relevant period" means—

    (a) in the case mentioned in paragraph (a) of that subsection, 14 days beginning with the day on which the patient is admitted as so mentioned;

    (b) in the case mentioned in paragraph (b) of that subsection, six months beginning with the day on which the patient is admitted as so mentioned;

    (c) in the case mentioned in paragraph (c) of that subsection, six months beginning with the day on which the application is accepted;

    (d) in the cases mentioned in paragraphs (d) and (g) of that subsection, 28 days beginning with the day on which the applicant is informed that the report has been furnished;

    (e) in the case mentioned in paragraph (e) of that subsection, six months beginning with the day on which the patient is transferred;

    (f) in the case mentioned in paragraph (f) of that subsection, the period for which authority for the patient's detention or guardianship is renewed by virtue of the report;

    (g) in the case mentioned in paragraph (h) of that subsection, 12 months beginning with the date of the order, and in any subsequent period of 12 months during which the order continues in force.

(3) Section 32 above shall apply for the purposes of this section as it applies for the purposes of Part II of this Act.

DEFINITIONS
"Patient": s.145(1).
"Hospital": ss.79(6), 145(1).
"Application for admission for assessment": ss.2, 145(1).
"Application for admission for treatment": ss.3, 145(1).
"Nearest relative": ss.26(3), 145(1).

TRANSITIONAL PROVISION
Sched. 5, para. 12.

GENERAL NOTE
This section identifies the occasions on which a patient or his nearest relative may make an application to a Tribunal. It is applied, with modifications, to patients who have been placed under hospital or guardianship orders by a court under s.37, above (Sched. 1, Pt. 1, para. 2).

Subs. (1)

Para. (*a*): *Application for admission for assessment:* Made under s.2, above.

Para. (*b*): *Application for admission for treatment:* Made under s.3, above. If the patient does not make an application within six months of his admission (subs. (2)(*b*)) the hospital managers will automatically refer the case to the Tribunal (s.68(1)).

Para. (*c*): *Received into guardianship:* Under s.7, above.

Para. (*d*): *Report under s.16:* Reclassifying the patient's mental disorder.

Para. (*e*): A patient who does not exercise his right to apply to a Tribunal within six months of his transfer (subs. (2)(*e*)) will have his case automatically referred to a Tribunal by the hospital managers (s.68(1)).

Para. (*f*): *Report . . . under s.20:* Renewing the authority to detain a patient who has been admitted to hospital treatment or renewing the authority for a patient's guardianship. In certain situations a patient who has been admitted to hospital for treatment will have his case automatically referred to a Tribunal by the hospital managers; see s.68(2), below.

Para. (*g*): *Report . . . under s.25:* By the responsible medical officer nullifying the nearest relative's power to discharge the patient.

Para. (*h*): *Order . . . under 29:* By the county court directing that the functions of the patient's nearest relative be exercised by an acting nearest relative.

An application: Only one application can be made during the period specified in subs. (2). Withdrawn applications do not count for this purpose (s.77(2)).

Nearest relative: Or, except in relation to para. (*h*), an acting nearest relative (s.29(6)). If the patient is a ward of court the nearest relative cannot make an application to a Tribunal without the leave of the High Court (s.33(2)).

Subs. (2)

Beginning with: Means "including" (*Hare* v. *Gocher* [1962] 2 Q.B. 641).

References to tribunals by Secretary of State concerning Part II patients

67.—(1) The Secretary of State may, if he thinks fit, at any time refer to a Mental Health Review Tribunal the case of any patient who is liable to be detained or subject to guardianship under Part II of this Act.

(2) For the purpose of furnishing information for the purposes of a reference under subsection (1) above any registered medical practitioner authorised by or on behalf of the patient may, at any reasonable time, visit the patient and examine him in private and require the production of and inspect any records relating to the detention or treatment of the patient in any hospital.

(3) Section 32 above shall apply for the purposes of this section as it applies for the purposes of Part II of this Act.

DEFINITIONS

"Patient": s.145(1).

"Hospital": ss.79(6), 145(1).

GENERAL NOTE

This section, which is rarely invoked, enables the Home Secretary to refer a patient to a Tribunal at any time. It is applied to patients who have been placed under hospital or guardianship orders by a court under section 37, above (Sched. 1, Pt. 1, para. 1).

Subs. (1)

If he thinks fit: A reference could be made if the Home Secretary considered that there were good reasons for a Tribunal hearing to take place before the date when the patient would be next eligible to make an application under s.66, above.

Subs. (2)

This subsection provides for a patient whose case has been referred to a Tribunal under this section to call for an independent medical opinion. A failure to allow the doctor to examine the patient could amount to an offence under s.129, below.

Duty of managers of hospitals to refer cases to tribunal

68.—(1) Where a patient who is admitted to a hospital in pursuance of an application for admission for treatment or a patient who is transferred from guardianship to hospital does not exercise his right to apply to a Mental Health Review Tribunal under section 66(1) above by virtue of his case falling within paragraph (*b*) or, as the case may be, paragraph (*e*) of that section, the managers of the hospital shall at the expiration of the period for making such an application refer the patient's case to such a tribunal unless an application or reference in respect of the patient has then been made under section 66(1) above by virtue of his case falling within paragraph (*d*), (*g*) or (*h*) of that section or under section 67(1) above.

(2) If the authority for the detention of a patient in a hospital is renewed under section 20 above and a period of three years (or, if the patient has not attained the age of sixteen years, one year) has elapsed since his case was last considered by a Mental Health Review Tribunal, whether on his own application or otherwise, the managers of the hospital shall refer his case to such a tribunal.

(3) For the purpose of furnishing information for the purpose of any reference under this section, any registered medical practitioner authorised by or on behalf of the patient may at any reasonable time visit and examine the patient in private and require the production of and inspect any records relating to the detention or treatment of the patient in any hospital.

(4) The Secretary of State may by order vary the length of the periods mentioned in subsection (2) above.

(5) For the purposes of subsection (1) above a person who applies to a tribunal but subsequently withdraws his application shall be treated as not having exercised his right to apply, and where a person withdraws his application on a date after the expiration of the period mentioned in that subsection, the managers shall refer the patient's case as soon as possible after that date.

DEFINITIONS
  "Patients": s.145(1).
  "Hospital": ss.79(6), 145(1).
  "Application for admission for treatment": ss.3, 145(1).
  "The managers": s.145(1).

TRANSITIONAL PROVISION
  Sched. 5, para. 13.

GENERAL NOTE
  This section requires the hospital managers to refer a patient who has been admitted for treatment, or a patient who has been transferred from guardianship to hospital, to a Tribunal where no application has been made during the first six months of his detention or within six months of his transfer (subs. (1)). It also requires the managers to refer to a Tribunal a patient whose authority to detain is being renewed and who has not had a Tribunal hearing during the preceding three years (or one year in case of a child under 16) (subs. (2)). The purpose of these provisions is to "ensure that patients who lack the ability or initiative to make an application to a Tribunal . . . have the safeguard of an independent review of their case" (Cmnd. 8405, para. 24).
  The Law Society is establishing a panel of solicitors with relevant experience to assist patients who are automatically referred to a Tribunal under this section to find legal representatives; see the General Note to s.65.

Subs. (2)
  Patient in a hospital: Including a patient who is subject to a hospital order made under s.37 above (s.40(4)).
  Attained the age: At the commencement of his sixteenth birthday (Family Law Reform Act 1969, s.9(1)).

Subs. (3)

Medical practitioner: A failure to allow the medical practitioners to perform his functions under this section could amount to an offence under s.129, below.

Subs. (4)

By order: See s.143(1), below.

Applications and references concerning Part III patients

Applications to tribunals concerning patients subject to hospital and guardianship orders

69.—(1) Without prejudice to any provision of section 66(1) above as applied by section 40(4) above, an application to a Mental Health Review Tribunal may also be made—

(*a*) in respect of a patient admitted to a hospital in pursuance of a hospital order, by the nearest relative of the patient in the period between the expiration of six months and the expiration of 12 months beginning with the date of the order and in any subsequent period of 12 months; and

(*b*) in respect of a patient placed under guardianship by a guardianship order—

(i) by the patient, within the period of six months beginning with the date of the order;

(ii) by the nearest relative of the patient, within the period of 12 months beginning with the date of the order and in any subsequent period of 12 months.

(2) Where a person detained in a hospital—

(*a*) is treated as subject to a hospital order or transfer direction by virtue of section 41(5) above, 82(2) or 85(2) below, section 73(2) of the Mental Health (Scotland) Act 1960 or section 5(1) of the Criminal Procedure (Insanity) Act 1964; or

(*b*) is subject to a direction having the same effect as a hospital order by virtue of section 46(3), 47(3) or 48(3) above,

then, without prejudice to any provision of Part II of this Act as applied by section 40 above, that person may make an application to a Mental Health Review Tribunal in the period of six months beginning with the date of the order or direction mentioned in paragraph (*a*) above or, as the case may be, the date of the direction mentioned in paragraph (*b*) above.

DEFINITIONS

"Patient": s.145(1).
"Hospital": ss.79(6), 145(1).
"Hospital order": ss.37, 145(1).
"Transfer direction": ss.47, 145(1).
"Nearest relative": ss.26(3), 145(1).

TRANSITIONAL PROVISION

Sched. 5, para. 6.

GENERAL NOTE

This section and s.66(1)(*f*), (2)(*f*), above, specify when a Tribunal application can be made by or on behalf of a patient who has been placed under a hospital or guardianship order made by a court under s.37 above. It also provides an opportunity for certain other patients who have been admitted to hospital after having committed offences to have their cases reviewed by a Tribunal.

Subs. (1)

This subsection provides that the nearest relative of a patient detained in hospital under a hospital order can apply to a Tribunal during the *second* six months of the patient's detention, and thereafter at yearly intervals. Under the 1959 Act an application could be made to a Tribunal within the first six months of the admission and a Tribunal only had advisory powers in relation to restricted patients. This latter provision was declared by the European Court of Human Rights to be a contravention of art. 5(4) of the European Convention of Human Rights which is concerned with the rights of individuals to have the lawfulness of their detention reviewed by a court; see *X.* v. *United Kingdom* (1982) 7 E.L. Review 435. The Government's response to this decision is contained in s.70 of this Act which provides for a restricted patient to make his initial Tribunal application during the second six months of his detention. The Government were advised that a continuance of the right of unrestricted patients to apply to a Tribunal within the first six months of their detention would contravene art. 14 of the European Convention which states that the "enjoyment of rights and freedoms set forth in [the] Convention shall be secured without discrimination on any ground". It was also pointed out during the Parliamentary debate on this provision that the patient's case would have been examined at the outset by the sentencing court which must have considered the medical evidence. These considerations led to this provision being enacted, together with Sched. 1, Pt. 1, paras. 2, 9, below, which has the effect of postponing the first opportunity for an unrestricted patient to apply to a Tribunal from the first six months to the second six months of his detention.

Hospital order: See s.55(4), above.

Nearest relative: Or acting nearest relative appointed by the county court under s.29, above. The patient has a right to apply to a Tribunal during the second six months of his detention and at yearly intervals thereafter by virtue of s.66(1)(*f*), (2)(*f*), above.

Beginning with: Including the date of the order (*Hare* v. *Gocher* [1962] 2 Q.B. 641).

Guardianship order: See s.55(4), above.

Within the period of six months: A patient who has been placed under a guardianship order can make subsequent applications to the Tribunal by virtue of s.66(1)(*f*), (2)(*f*), above.

Subs. (2)

This subsection affects "certain categories of patient whose cases have not recently been looked at by a court but who are, simply by reason of the way the [this Act is] put together, deemed to be detained as though subject to a fresh hospital order. I am referring chiefly to restricted patients whose restrictions expire or are removed; patients transferred from prison to hospital subject to restrictions, and whose restrictions subsequently expire; and patients transferred to the English hospital system from Scotland, Northern Ireland, the Isle of Man or the Channel Islands. As a result of [Sched. 1, Pt. 1, paras. 2, 9], such patients, who may already have been in hospital for a substantial period, would have a six months' gap during which they were not entitled to apply to a Tribunal and had not just had their cases looked at by a court . . . [This subsection removes] that gap. In addition, [it] seeks to meet the concern which has been expressed . . . about the position of patients immediately after they have been transferred from prison. Again, the grounds for their detention in hospital will not previously have been considered by a court. The Government now accept that such people should have an immediate right to a Tribunal hearing", *per* Lord Belstead, H.L. Vol. 427, col. 868.

S.5(1) of the Criminal Procedure (Insanity) Act: If such a patient does not exercise his right to apply to a Tribunal within six months of the order being made the Secretary of State will refer the patient to a Tribunal (s.71(5)).

Applications to tribunals concerning restricted patients

70. A patient who is a restricted patient within the meaning of section 79 below and is detained in a hospital may apply to a Mental Health Review Tribunal—

    (*a*) in the period between the expiration of six months and the expiration of 12 months beginning with the date of the relevant hospital order or transfer direction; and

    (*b*) in any subsequent period of 12 months.

DEFINITIONS

  "Patient": s.145(1).

  "Restricted patient": s.79(1).

  "Hospital": s.79(6), 145(1).

This section provides for a Tribunal application to be made by a restricted patient during the second six months of the duration of the hospital order or transfer direction, and at yearly intervals thereafter. Tribunals hearing applications by restricted patients will be chaired by a lawyer who has had substantial experience in the criminal courts; see the note on s.78(4), below.

Beginning with: Including the date of the hospital order or transfer direction (*Hare* v. *Gocher* [1962] 2 Q.B. 641).

References by Secretary of State concerning restricted patients

71.—(1) The Secretary of State may at any time refer the case of a restricted patient to a Mental Health Review Tribunal.

(2) The Secretary of State shall refer to a Mental Health Review Tribunal the case of any restricted patient detained in a hospital whose case has not been considered by such a tribunal, whether on his own application or otherwise, within the last three years.

(3) The Secretary of State may by order vary the length of the period mentioned in subsection (2) above.

(4) Any reference under subsection (1) above in respect of a patient who has been conditionally discharged and not recalled to hospital shall be made to the tribunal for the area in which the patient resides.

(5) Where a person who is treated as subject to a hospital order and a restriction order by virtue of an order under section 5(1) of the Criminal Procedure (Insanity) Act 1964 does not exercise his right to apply to a Mental Health Review Tribunal in the period of six months beginning with the date of that order, the Secretary of State shall at the expiration of that period refer his case to a tribunal.

(6) For the purposes of subsection (5) above a person who applies to a tribunal but subsequently withdraws his application shall be treated as not having exercised his right to apply, and where a patient withdraws his application on a date after the expiration of the period there mentioned the Secretary of State shall refer his case as soon as possible after that date.

DEFINITIONS
 "Restricted patient": s.79(1).
 "Hospital": ss.79(6), 145(1).
 "Hospital order": ss.37, 145(1).
 "Restriction order": ss.41, 145(1).
 "Patient": s.145(1).

This section provides that the Home Secretary may, and in certain circumstances must, refer the case of a restricted patient to a Tribunal.

Subs. (5)
S.5(1) of the Criminal Procedure (Insanity) Act 1964 provides that a court must make a hospital order with restrictions without limit of time in respect of an offender who has been found to be not guilty by reason of insanity.

Discharge of patients

Powers of tribunals

72.—(1) Where application is made to a Mental Health Review Tribunal by or in respect of a patient who is liable to be detained under this Act, the tribunal may in any case direct that the patient be discharged, and—

　(*a*) the tribunal shall direct the discharge of a patient liable to be detained under section 2 above if they are satisfied—

    (i) that he is not then suffering from mental disorder or from mental disorder of a nature or degree which warrants his detention in a hospital for assessment (or for assessment followed by a medical treatment) for at least a limited period; or

    (ii) that his detention as aforesaid is not justified in the interests of his own health or safety or with a view to the protection of other persons;

  (*b*) the tribunal shall direct the discharge of a patient liable to be detained otherwise than under section 2 above if they are satisfied—

    (i) that he is not then suffering from mental illness, psychopathic disorder, severe mental impairment or mental impairment or from any of those forms of disorder of a nature or degree which makes it appropriate for him to be liable to be detained in a hospital for medical treatment; of

    (ii) that it is not necessary for the health or safety of the patient or for the protection of other persons that he should receive such treatment; or

    (iii) in the case of an application by virtue of paragraph (*g*) of section 66(1) above, that the patient, if released, would not be likely to act in a manner dangerous to other persons or to himself.

(2) In determining whether to direct the discharge of a patient detained otherwise than under section 2 above in a case not falling within paragraph (*b*) of subsection (1) above, the tribunal shall have regard—

  (*a*) to the likelihood of medical treatment alleviating or preventing a deterioration of the patient's condition; and

  (*b*) in the case of a patient suffering from mental illness or severe mental impairment, to the likelihood of the patient, if discharged, being able to care for himself, to obtain the care he needs or to guard himself against serious exploitation.

(3) A tribunal may under subsection (1) above direct the discharge of a patient on a future date specified in the direction; and where a tribunal do not direct the discharge of a patient under that subsection the tribunal may—

  (*a*) with a view to facilitating his discharge on a future date, recommend that he be granted leave of absence or transferred to another hospital or into guardianship; and

  (*b*) further consider his case in the event of any such recommendation not being complied with.

(4) Where application is made to a Mental Health Review Tribunal by or in respect of a patient who is subject to guardianshp under this Act, the tribunal may in any case direct that the patient be discharged, and shall so direct if they are satisfied—

  (*a*) that he is not then suffering from mental illness, psychopathic disorder, severe mental impairment or mental impairment; or

  (*b*) that it is not necessary in the interests of the welfare of the patient, or for the protection of other persons, that the patient should remain under such guardianship.

(5) Where application is made to a Mental Health Review Tribunal under any provision of this Act by or in respect of a patient and the tribunal do not direct that the patient be discharged, the tribunal may, if satisfied that the patient is suffering from a form of mental disorder other than the form specified in the application, order or direction relating to him, direct that that application, order or direction be amended by substituting for the form of mental disorder specified in it such other form of mental disorder as appears to the tribunal to be appropriate.

(6) Subsections (1) to (5) above apply in relation to references to a Mental Health Review Tribunal as they apply in relation to applications made to such a tribunal by or in respect of a patient.

(7) Subsection (1) above shall not apply in the case of a restricted patient except as provided in sections 73 and 74 below.

DEFINITIONS
"Patient": s.145(1).
"Mental disorder": ss.1, 145(1).
"Hospital": ss.79(6), 145(1).
"Medical treatment": s.145(1).
"Psychopathic disorder": ss.1, 145(1).
"Severe mental impairment": ss.1, 145(1).
"Mental impairment": ss.1, 145(1).

GENERAL NOTE
This section empowers Mental Health Review Tribunals to discharge patients from hospital or guardianship and directs Tribunals to discharge such patients if specified criteria are satisfied. It also enables Tribunals to reclassify the mental disorder of a patient who is not discharged.

Subs. (1)
Application: Or a reference made by the Home Secretary (subs. (6)). Note that this subsection only applies to restricted patients to the extent provided for in s.73 and 74, below (subs. (7)).
May in any case direct that the patient be discharged: The Tribunal has power to discharge the patient even though the legal grounds for compulsory detention still subsist. The discharge could take place some time after the Tribunal's decision (subs. (3)).

Para. (*a*).
Shall direct: If either sub-paragraph (i) or (ii) is satisfied the patient must be discharged.
Detained under s.2: For assessment.

Para. (*b*).
Shall direct: If either paragraph (i), (ii) or (iii) is satisfied the patient must be discharged.
Para. (*g*) *of s.66(1):* Which provides for an application to a Tribunal to be made by a nearest relative on the issue by the responsible medical officer of a report under s.25, above, nullifying the nearest relative's discharge powers.

Subs. (2)
This subsection provides that if an application is made by a patient who is detained for treatment and the Tribunal does not have to discharge the patient under subs. (1)(*b*), the Tribunal must have regard to the provisions of this subsection when exercising its discretion to discharge.

Subs. (3)
On a future date: Which would enable preparations to be made to receive a patient back into the community. This power of delayed discharge could also be used if the Tribunal came to the conclusion that the patient would be fit for discharge at the expiration of a further short period of treatment.
Recommend: "The distinction between ordering and recommending is an important one and takes account of the need for agreement of others, *e.g.* the receiving hospital or social services department" (Cmnd. 7320, para. 6.5).

Power to discharge restricted patients

73.—(1) Where an application to a Mental Health Review Tribunal is made by a restricted patient who is subject to a restriction order, or where the case of such a patient is referred to such a tribunal, the tribunal shall direct the absolute discharge of the patient if satisfied—

(*a*) as to the matters mentioned in paragraph (*b*)(i) or (ii) of section 72(1) above; and

(b) that it is not appropriate for the patient to remain liable to be recalled to hospital for further treatment.

(2) Where in the case of any such patient as is mentioned in subsection (1) above the tribunal are satisfied as to the matters referred to in paragraph (a) of that subsection but not as to the matter referred to in paragraph (b) of that subsection the tribunal shall direct the conditional discharge of the patient.

(3) Where a patient is absolutely discharged under this section he shall thereupon cease to be liable to be detained by virtue of the relevant hospital order, and the restriction order shall cease to have effect accordingly.

(4) Where a patient is conditionally discharged under this section—

> (a) he may be recalled by the Secretary of State under subsection (3) of section 42 above as if he had been conditionally discharged under subsection (2) of that section; and
>
> (b) the patient shall comply with such conditions (if any) as may be imposed at the time of discharge by the tribunal or at any subsequent time by the Secretary of State.

(5) The Secretary of State may from time to time vary any condition imposed (whether by the tribunal or by him) under subsection (4) above.

(6) Where a restriction order in respect of a patient ceases to have effect after he has been conditionally discharged under this section the patient shall, unless previously recalled, be deemed to be absolutely discharged on the date when the order ceases to have effect and shall cease to be liable to be detained by virtue of the relevant hospital order.

(7) A tribunal may defer a direction for the conditional discharge of a patient until such arrangements as appear to the tribunal to be necessary for that purpose have been made to their satisfaction; and where by virtue of any such deferment no direction has been given on an application or reference before the time when the patient's case comes before the tribunal on a subsequent application or reference, the previous application or reference shall be treated as one on which no direction under this section can be given.

(8) This section is without prejudice to section 42 above.

DEFINITIONS
"Restricted patient": s.79(1).
"Restriction order": ss.41, 145(1).
"Hospital": ss.79(6), 145(1).
"Relevant hospital order": s.79(2).

GENERAL NOTE
This section specifies when a Mental Health Review Tribunal must direct either the absolute or conditional discharge of restricted patients.

Subs. (1)
Subject to a restriction order: Made under s.41, above.
Shall direct: The Tribunal must direct the absolute discharge of a patient if paras. (a) *and* (b) are satisfied.
Subs. (2) provides that a Tribunal must order the conditional discharge of a restricted patient if it is satisfied as to the matters referred to in para. (b)(i) or (ii) of s.72(1), above.
Direct the conditional discharge: The direction may be deferred under subs. (7).

Subs. (8)
Section 42: Which, *inter alia*, empowers the Home Secretary to discharge the patient from hospital either absolutely or subject to conditions.

Restricted patients subject to restriction directions

74.—(1) Where an application to a Mental Health Review Tribunal is made by a restricted patient who is subject to a restriction direction, or

where the case of such a patient is referred to such a tribunal, the tribunal—
- (*a*) shall notify the Secretary of State whether, in their opinion, the patient would, if subject to a restriction order, be entitled to be absolutely or conditionally discharged under section 73 above; and
- (*b*) if they notify him that the patient would be entitled to be conditionally discharged, may recommend that in the event of his not being discharged under this section he should continue to be detained in hospital.

(2) If in the case of a patient not falling within subsection (4) below—
- (*a*) the tribunal notify the Secretary of State that the patient would be entitled to be absolutely or conditionally discharged; and
- (*b*) within the period of 90 days beginning with the date of that notification the Secretary of State gives notice to the tribunal that the patient may be so discharged,

the tribunal shall direct the absolute or, as the case may be, the conditional discharge of the patient.

(3) Where a patient continues to be liable to be detained in a hospital at the end of the period referred to in subsection (2)(*b*) above because the Secretary of State has not given the notice there mentioned, the managers of the hospital shall, unless the tribunal have made a recommendation under subsection (1)(*b*) above, transfer the patient to a prison or other institution in which he might have been detained if he had not been removed to hospital, there to be dealt with as if he had not been so removed.

(4) If, in the case of a patient who is subject to a transfer direction under section 48 above, the tribunal notify the Secretary of State that the patient would be entitled to be absolutely or conditionally discharged, the Secretary of State shall, unless the tribunal have made a recommendation under subsection (1)(*b*) above, by warrant direct that the patient be remitted to a prison or other institution in which he might have been detained if he had not been removed to hospital, there to be dealt with as if he had not been so removed.

(5) Where a patient is transferred or remitted under subsection (3) or (4) above the relevant transfer direction and the restriction direction shall cease to have effect on his arrival in the prison or other institution.

(6) Subsections (3) to (8) of section 73 above shall have effect in relation to this section as they have effect in relation to that section, taking references to the relevant hospital order and the restriction order as references to the transfer direction and the restriction direction.

(7) This section is without prejudice to sections 50 to 53 above in their application to patients who are not discharged under this section.

DEFINITIONS
  "Restricted patient": s.79(1).
  "Restriction direction": ss.49, 145(1).
  "Restriction order": ss.41, 145(1).
  "Hospital": ss.79(6), 145(1).
  "The managers": s.145(1).
  "Transfer direction": ss.47, 145(1).

GENERAL NOTE
  This section provides for the procedure to be adopted on an application to a Mental Health Review Tribunal by a patient who has been transferred from prison to hospital subject to the special restrictions set out in s.41, above. It also applies to references to Tribunals made in respect of such patients by the Home Secretary.

Subs. (2)
  Beginning with: Including the date of the notification (*Hare* v. *Gocher* [1962] 2 Q.B. 641).

Subs. (5)
Relevant transfer direction: See s.79(2), below.

Subs. (6)
Relevant hospital order: See s.79(2), below.

Applications and references concerning conditionally discharged restricted patients

75.—(1) Where a restricted patient has been conditionally discharged under section 42(2), 73 or 74 above and is subsequently recalled to hospital—

(a) the Secretary of State shall, within one month of the day on which the patient returns or is returned to hospital, refer his case to a Mental Health Review Tribunal; and

(b) section 70 above shall apply to the patient as if the relevant hospital order or transfer direction had been made on that day.

(2) Where a restricted patient has been conditionally discharged as aforesaid but has not been recalled to hospital he may apply to a Mental Health Review Tribunal—

(a) in the period between the expiration of 12 months and the expiration of two years beginning with the date on which he was conditionally discharged; and

(b) in any subsequent period of two years.

(3) Sections 73 and 74 above shall not apply to an application under subsection (2) above but on any such application the tribunal may—

(a) vary any condition to which the patient is subject in connection with his discharge or impose any condition which might have been imposed in connection therewith; or

(b) direct that the restriction order or restriction direction to which he is subject shall cease to have effect;

and if the tribunal give a direction under paragraph (b) above the patient shall cease to be liable to be detained by virtue of the relevant hospital order or transfer direction.

DEFINITIONS
"Restricted patient": s.79(1).
"Hospital": ss.79(6), 145(1).
"Relevant hospital order": s.79(2).
"Relevant transfer direction": s.79(2).
"Restriction order": ss.41, 145(1).
"Restriction direction": ss.49, 145(1).

GENERAL NOTE
This section directs the Home Secretary to refer the case of a conditionally discharged restricted patient who has been recalled to hospital to a Mental Health Review Tribunal. It also provides for a Tribunal application to be made by a conditionally discharged restricted patient who has not been recalled to hospital. On such an application the Tribunal can either vary the conditions of the discharge, impose new conditions, or direct that the restriction order or direction shall cease to have effect.

Subs. (1)
Restricted patient: Is a patient who is subject to a restriction order or direction (s.79(1)).
Within one month: Disregarding the day of the patient's return to hospital (*Stewart* v. *Chapman* [1951] 2 K.B. 792).

Subs. (2)
Beginning with: Including the date of his conditional discharge (*Hare* v. *Gocher* [1962] 2 Q.B. 641).

General

Visiting and examination of patients

76.—(1) For the purpose of advising whether an application to a Mental Health Review Tribunal should be made by or in respect of a patient who is liable to be detained or subject to guardianship under Part II of this Act or of furnishing information as to the condition of a patient for the purposes of such an application, any registered medical practitioner authorised by or on behalf of the patient or other person who is entitled to make or has made the application—

(*a*) may at any reasonable time visit the patient and examine him in private, and

(*b*) may require the production of and inspect any records relating to the detention or treatment of the patient in any hospital.

(2) Section 32 above shall apply for the purposes of this section as it applies for the purposes of Part II of this Act.

DEFINITIONS
 "Patient": s.145(1).
 "Hospital": ss.79(6), 145(1).

GENERAL NOTE
 This section is applied to patients who have been placed under hospital, restriction or guardianship orders by a court under s.37 or 41 of this Act (Sched. 1, Pt. 1, para. 1; Pt. 2, para. 1). A failure to allow medical practitioners or authorised persons to carry out their functions under this section could amount to an obstruction under s.129, below.

General provisions concerning tribunal applications

77.—(1) No application shall be made to a Mental Health Review Tribunal by or in respect of a patient except in such cases and at such times as are expressly provided by this Act.

(2) Where under this Act any person is authorised to make an application to a Mental Health Review Tribunal within a specified period, not more than one such application shall be made by that person within that period but for that purpose there shall be disregarded any application which is withdrawn in accordance with rules made under section 78 below.

(3) Subject to subsection (4) below an application to a Mental Health Review Tribunal authorised to be made by or in respect of a patient under this Act shall be made by notice in writing addressed to the tribunal for the area in which the hospital in which the patient is detained is situated or in which the patient is residing under guardianship as the case may be.

(4) Any application under section 75(2) above shall be made to the tribunal for the area in which the patient resides.

DEFINITIONS
 "Patient": s.145(1).
 "Hospital": ss.79(6), 145(1).

GENERAL NOTE
 On December 9, 1981, the European Commission on Human Rights declared admissible an application where the complainant alleged that a delay of nearly 18 weeks that had occurred between his application to a Mental Health Review Tribunal and his hearing date contravened art. 5(4) of the European Convention of Human Rights. Art. 5(4) provides for questions relating to a person's loss of liberty to be decided "speedily". (*Barclay-Maguire* v. *United Kingdom,* referred to by Gostin at [1982] Crim.L.R. 792.)

Subs. (3)
 Residing: Temporary absences from the place where a person resides does not affect residence, as long as there is an intention to return (*R.* v. *St. Leonard's Shoreditch* (*Inhabitants*) (1865) L.R. 1 Q.B. 21).

   Application under s.75(2): By a restricted patient who has been conditionally discharged from hospital.

Procedure of tribunals

   78.—(1) The Lord Chancellor may make rules with respect to the making of applications to Mental Health Review Tribunals and with respect to the proceedings of such tribunals and matters incidental to or consequential on such proceedings.
   (2) Rules made under this section may in particular make provision—
   (*a*) for enabling a tribunal, or the chairman of a tribunal, to postpone the consideration of any application by or in respect of a patient, or of any such application of any specified class, until the expiration of such period (not exceeding 12 months) as may be specified in the rules from the date on which an application by or in respect of the same patient was last considered and determined by that or any other tribunal under this Act;
   (*b*) for the transfer of proceedings from one tribunal to another in any case where, after the making of the application, the patient is removed out of the area of the tribunal to which it was made;
   (*c*) for restricting the persons qualified to serve as members of a tribunal for the consideration of any application, or of an application of any specified class;
   (*d*) for enabling a tribunal to dispose of an application without a formal hearing where such a hearing is not requested by the applicant or it appears to the tribunal that such a hearing would be detrimental to the health of the patient;
   (*e*) for enabling a tribunal to exclude members of the public, or any specified class of members of the public, from any proceedings of the tribunal, or to prohibit the publication of reports of any such proceedings or the names of any persons concerned in such proceedings;
   (*f*) for regulating the circumstances in which, and the persons by whom, applicants and patients in respect of whom applications are made to a tribunal may, if not desiring to conduct their own case, be represented for the purposes of those applications;
   (*g*) for regulating the methods by which information relevant to an application may be obtained by or furnished to the tribunal, and in particular for authorising the members of a tribunal, or any one or more of them, to visit and interview in private any patient by or in respect of whom an application has been made;
   (*h*) for making available to any applicant, and to any patient in respect of whom an application is made to a tribunal, copies of any documents obtained by or furnished to the tribunal in connection with the application, and a statement of the substance of any oral information so obtained or furnished except where the tribunal considers it undesirable in the interests of the patient or for other special reasons;
   (*i*) for requiring a tribunal, if so requested in accordance with the rules, to furnish such statements of the reasons for any decision given by the tribunal as may be prescribed by the rules, subject to any provision made by the rules for withholding such a statement from a patient or any other person in cases where the tribunal considers that furnishing it would be undesirable in the interests of the patient or for other special reasons;
   (*j*) for conferring on the tribunals such ancillary powers as the

Lord Chancellor thinks necessary for the purposes of the exercise of their functions under this Act;

(k) for enabling any functions of a tribunal which relate to matters preliminary or incidental to an application to be performed by the chairman of the tribunal.

(3) Subsections (1) and (2) above apply in relation to references to Mental Health Review Tribunals as they apply in relation to applications to such tribunals by or in respect of patients.

(4) Rules under this section may make provision as to the procedure to be adopted in cases concerning restricted patients and, in particular—

(a) for restricting the persons qualified to serve as president of a tribunal for the consideration of an application or reference relating to a restricted patient;

(b) for the transfer of proceedings from one tribunal to another in any case where, after the making of a reference or application in accordance with section 71(4) or 77(4) above, the patient ceases to reside in the area of the tribunal to which the reference or application was made.

(5) Rules under this section may be so framed as to apply to all applications or references or to applications or references of any specified class and may make different provision in relation to different cases.

(6) Any functions conferred on the chairman of a Mental Health Review Tribunal by rules under this section may, if for any reason he is unable to act, be exercised by another member of that tribunal appointed by him for the purpose.

(7) A Mental Health Review Tribunal may pay allowances in respect of travelling expenses, subsistence and loss of earnings to any person attending the tribunal as an applicant or witness, to the patient who is the subject of the proceedings if he attends otherwise than as the applicant or a witness and to any person (other than counsel or a solicitor) who attends as the representative of an applicant.

(8) A Mental Health Review Tribunal may, and if so required by the High Court shall, state in the form of a special case for determination by the High Court any question of law which may arise before them.

(9) The Arbitration Act 1950 shall not apply to any proceedings before a Mental Health Review Tribunal except so far as any provisions of that Act may be applied, with or without modifications, by rules made under this section.

DEFINITION
"Patient": s.145(1).

GENERAL NOTE
The Mental Health Review Tribunal Rules 1960, S.I. 1960 No. 1139, are being revised and it is expected that new procedural rules will come into operation on September 30, 1983.

Subs. (2)
para. (a): *chairman of a tribunal:* see Sched. 2, para. 2, below.
para. (b): *area of the tribunal:* see s.65(1), above.
para. (f): *represented:* assistance by way of representation under the Legal Aid and Advice Act 1974 is available for tribunal hearings; see the General Note to s.65, above.

Subs. (4)
Qualified to serve as president of a tribunal: "The Government recognise that the power to release restricted patients who may have been convicted of very serious offences carries with it a formidable responsibility. We regard it as essential that the exercise of this responsibility . . . should command the confidence not only of the public but also of members of the judiciary who, in the Crown Court, must decide in an individual case

whether a restriction order ought to be made. Those considerations led us to conclude that when the tribunal exercises this . . . jurisdiction it should have in the chair as its president a lawyer with substantial judicial experience in the criminal courts. . . . The Lord Chancellor will therefore be appointing to the legal panels of the tribunals a number of circuit judges" (*per* Lord Belstead, H.L. Vol. 426, col. 761).

Subs. (8)
State in the form of a special case: For the procedure to be adopted, see the Rules of the Supreme Court, Ord. 56.

Interpretation of Part V

79.—(1) In this Part of this Act "restricted patient" means a patient who is subject to a restriction order or restriction direction and this Part of this Act shall, subject to the provisions of this section, have effect in relation to any person who—
   (*a*) is subject to a direction which by virtue of section 46(3) above has the same effect as a hospital order and a restriction order; or
   (*b*) is treated as subject to a hospital order and a restriction order by virtue of an order under section 5(1) of the Criminal Procedure (Insanity) Act 1964 or section 6 or 14(1) of the Criminal Appeal Act 1968; or
   (*c*) is treated as subject to a hospital order and a restriction order or to a transfer direction and a restriction direction by virtue of section 82(2) or 85(2) below or section 73(2) of the Mental Health (Scotland) Act 1960,
as it has effect in relation to a restricted patient.
   (2) Subject to the following provisions of this section, in this Part of this Act "the relevant hospital order" and "the relevant transfer direction", in relation to a restricted patient, mean the hospital order or transfer direction by virtue of which he is liable to be detained in a hospital.
   (3) In the case of a person within paragraph (*a*) of subsection (1) above, references in this Part of this Act to the relevant hospital order or restriction order shall be construed as references to the direction referred to in that paragraph.
   (4) In the case of a person within paragraph (*b*) of subsection (1) above, references in this Part of this Act to the relevant hospital order or restriction order shall be construed as references to the order under the provisions mentioned in that paragraph.
   (5) In the case of a person within paragraph (*c*) of subsection (1) above, references in this Part of this Act to the relevant hospital order, the relevant transfer direction, the restriction order or the restriction direction or to a transfer direction under section 48 above shall be construed as references to the hospital order, transfer direction, restriction order, restriction direction or transfer direction under that section to which that person is treated as subject by virtue of the provisions mentioned in that paragraph.
   (6) In this Part of this Act, unless the context otherwise requires, "hospital" means a hospital within the meaning of Part II of this Act.

DEFINITIONS
   "Patient": s.145(1).
   "Restriction order": ss.41, 145(1).
   "Restriction direction": ss.49, 145(1).
   "Hospital order": ss.37, 145(1).
   "Transfer direction": ss.47, 145(1).

Subs. (6)
Hospital: See s.34(2), above.

PART VI

REMOVAL AND RETURN OF PATIENTS WITHIN UNITED KINGDOM, ETC.

Removal to Scotland

Removal of patients to Scotland

80.—(1) If it appears to the Secretary of State, in the case of a patient who is for the time being liable to be detained or subject to guardianship under this Act (otherwise than by virtue of section 35, 36 or 38 above), that it is in the interests of the patient to remove him to Scotland, and that arrangements have been made for admitting him to a hospital or, as the case may be, for receiving him into guardianship there, the Secretary of State may authorise his removal to Scotland and may give any necessary directions for his conveyance to his destination.

(2) Subject to the provisions of subsection (4) below, where a patient liable to be detained under this Act by virtue of an application, order or direction under any enactment in force in England and Wales is removed under this section and admitted to a hospital in Scotland, he shall be treated as if on the date of his admission he had been so admitted in pursuance of an application forwarded to the Health Board responsible for the administration of the hospital, or an order or direction made or given, on that date under the corresponding enactment in Scotland, and, where he is subject to a restriction order or restriction direction under any enactment in this Act, as if he were subject to an order or direction under the corresponding enactment in force in Scotland.

(3) Where a patient subject to guardianship under this Act by virtue of an application, order or direction under any enactment in force in England and Wales is removed under this section and received into guardianship in Scotland, he shall be treated as if on the date on which he arrives at the place where he is to reside he had been so received in pursuance of an application, order or direction under the corresponding enactment in force in Scotland, and as if the application had been forwarded or, as the case may be, the order or direction had been made or given on that date.

(4) Where a person removed under this section was immediately before his removal liable to be detained by virtue of an application for admission for assessment under this Act, he shall, on his admission to a hospital in Scotland, be treated as if he had been admitted to the hospital in pursuance of an emergency recommendation under the Mental Health (Scotland) Act 1960 made on the date of his admission.

(5) Where a patient removed under this section was immediately before his removal liable to be detained under this Act by virtue of a transfer direction given while he was serving a sentence of imprisonment (within the meaning of section 47(5) above) imposed by a court in England and Wales, he shall be treated as if the sentence had been imposed by a court in Scotland.

(6) Where a person removed under this section was immediately before his removal subject to a restriction order or restriction direction of limited duration, the order or direction restricting his discharge to which he is subject by virtue of subsection (2) above shall expire on the date on which the restriction order or restriction direction would have expired if he had not been so removed.

(7) In this section "hospital" has the same meaning as in the Mental Health (Scotland) Act 1960.

DEFINITIONS
   "Patient": s.145(1).
   "Hospital": subs. (7).

"Restriction order": ss.41, 145(1).
"Restriction direction": ss.49, 145(1).
"Application for admission for assessment": ss.2, 145(1).
"Transfer direction": ss.47, 145(1).

GENERAL NOTE

This section enables the Secretary of State to transfer a patient who is detained or subject to guardianship in England or Wales to Scotland without a break in the powers of detention or guardianship. The Secretary of State must be satisfied that such a move is in the interests of the patient and that suitable arrangements have been made for admitting him to hospital or receiving him into guardianship in Scotland. On his arrival in Scotland the patient will become subject to the equivalent Scottish legislation.

Subs. (1)

Remove him to Scotland: The position of the nearest relative on the patient's transfer to Scotland is covered by s.76 of the Mental Health (Scotland) Act 1960.
Hospital: See subs. (7).
Conveyance to his destination: General provisions relating to the custody, conveyance and detention of patients are contained in s.137, below.

Subs. (4)

Emergency recommendation: Made under s.31 of the Mental Health (Scotland) Act 1960 and lasting for seven days. There is no equivalent in the Scottish legislation to an admission for assessment made under s.2 of this Act.

Subs. (7)

Hospital: Is defined in s.111(1) of the 1960 Act as: "(a) any hospital vested in the Secretary of State under the National Health Service (Scotland) Act 1978; (b) any private hospital registered under Part III of [the 1960] Act; and (c) any State hospital".

Removal to and from Northern Ireland

Removal of patients to Northern Ireland

81.—(1) If it appears to the Secretary of State, in the case of a patient who is for the time being liable to be detained or subject to guardianship under this Act (otherwise than by virtue of section 35, 36 or 38 above), that it is in the interests of the patient to remove him to Northern Ireland, and that arrangements have been made for admitting him to a hospital or, as the case may be, for receiving him into guardianship there, the Secretary of State may authorise his removal to Northern Ireland and may give any necessary directions for his conveyance to his destination.

(2) Subject to the provisions of subsections (4) and (5) below, where a patient liable to be detained under this Act by virtue of an application, order or direction under any enactment in force in England and Wales is removed under this section and admitted to a hospital in Northern Ireland, he shall be treated as if on the date of his admission he had been so admitted in pursuance of an application made, or an order or direction made or given, on that date under the corresponding enactment in force in Northern Ireland, and, where he is subject to a restriction order or restriction direction under any enactment in this Act, as if he were subject to an order or direction under the corresponding enactment in force in Northern Ireland.

(3) Where a patient subject to guardianship under this Act by virtue of an application, order or direction under any enactment in force in England and Wales is removed under this section and received into guardianship in Northern Ireland, he shall be treated as if on the date on which he arrives at the place where he is to reside he had been so received in pursuance of an application, order or direction under the corresponding enactment in force in Northern Ireland, and as if the application had been

accepted or, as the case may be, the order or direction had been made or given on that date.

(4) Where a person removed under this section was immediately before his removal liable to be detained by virtue of an application for admission for assessment under this Act, he shall, on his admission to a hospital in Northern Ireland, be treated as if he had been admitted to the hospital in pursuance of an application for admission under section 12 of the Mental Health Act (Northern Ireland) 1961 made on the date of his admission.

(5) Where a person removed under this section was immediately before his removal liable to be detained by virtue of an application for admission for treatment under this Act, he shall, on his admission to a hospital in Northern Ireland, be treated as if—

(*a*) he had been admitted to the hospital in pursuance of an application for admission under section 12 of the Mental Health Act (Northern Ireland) 1961 made on the date of his admission; and

(*b*) a medical report under section 19 of that Act had been made in respect of him on that date.

(6) Where a patient removed under this section was immediately before his removal liable to be detained under this Act by virtue of a transfer direction given while he was serving a sentence of imprisonment (within the meaning of section 47(5) above) imposed by a court in England and Wales, he shall be treated as if the sentence had been imposed by a court in Northern Ireland.

(7) Where a person removed under this section was immediately before his removal subject to a restriction order or restriction direction of limited duration, the order or direction restricting his discharge to which he is subject by virtue of subsection (2) above shall expire on the date on which the restriction order or restriction direction would have expired if he had not been so removed.

(8) In this section "hospital" has the same meaning as in the Mental Health Act (Northern Ireland) 1961.

Definitions
"Patient": s.145(1).
"Hospital": subs. (8).
"Restriction order": ss.41, 145(1).
"Restriction direction": ss.49, 145(1).
"Application for admission for assessment": ss.2, 145(1).
"Application for admission for treatment": ss.3, 145(1).
"Transfer direction": ss.47, 145(1).

General Note
This section enables the Secretary of State to transfer a patient who is detained or subject to guardianship in England or Wales to Northern Ireland without a break in the powers of detention or guardianship. The Secretary of State must be satisfied that such a move is in the interests of the patient and that suitable arrangements have been made for admitting him to hospital or receiving him into guardianship in Northern Ireland. On his arrival in Northern Ireland the patient will become subject to the equivalent Northern Irish legislation.

Subs. (1)
Hospital: See subs. (8).

Subs. (4)
S.12 of the Mental Health Act (Northern Ireland) 1961: Which provides for compulsory admission to hospital for up to 28 days.

Subs. (5)
S.19: Once a medical report under s.19 has been made the patient can be detained for up to six months from the date of his admission.

Subs. (8)
 Hospital: Is defined in s.113(1) of the 1961 Act.

Removal to England and Wales of patients from Northern Ireland

82.—(1) If it appears to the responsible authority, in the case of a patient who is for the time being liable to be detained or subject to guardianship under the Mental Health Act (Northern Ireland) 1961, that it is in the interests of the patient to remove him to England and Wales, and that arrangements have been made for admitting him to a hospital or, as the case may be, for receiving him into guardianship there, the responsible authority may authorise his removal to England and Wales and may give any necessary directions for his conveyance to his destination.

(2) Subject to the provisions of subsection (4) below, where a patient who is liable to be detained under the said Act of 1961 by virtue of an application, order or direction under any enactment in force in Northern Ireland is removed under this section and admitted to a hospital in England and Wales, he shall be treated as if on the date of his admission he had been so admitted in pursuance of an application made, or an order or direction made or given, on that date under the corresponding enactment in force in England and Wales and, where he is subject to an order or direction under any enactment in the said Act of 1961 restricting his discharge, as if he were subject to a restriction order or restriction direction.

(3) Where a patient subject to guardianship under the said Act of 1961 by virtue of an application, order or direction under any enactment in force in Northern Ireland is removed under this section and received into guardianship in England and Wales, he shall be treated as if on the date on which he arrives at the place where he is to reside he had been so received in pursuance of an application, order or direction under the corresponding enactment in force in England and Wales and as if the application had been accepted or, as the case may be, the order or direction had been made or given on that date.

(4) Where a person removed under this section was immediately before his removal liable to be detained by virtue of an application for admission under section 12 of the said Act of 1961 he shall—

  (*a*) if a report under section 19 of that Act has not been made in respect of him, be treated, on his admission to a hospital in England and Wales, as if he had been admitted to the hospital in pursuance of an application for admission for assessment made on the date of his admission;

  (*b*) if a report under the said section 19 has been made in respect of him, be treated, on his admission to a hospital in England and Wales, as if he had been admitted to the hospital in pursuance of an application for admission for treatment made on the date of his admission.

(5) Where a patient removed under this section was immediately before his removal liable to be detained under the said Act of 1961 by virtue of a transfer direction given while he was serving a sentence of imprisonment (within the meaning of section 58(6) of that Act) imposed by a court in Northern Ireland, he shall be treated as if the sentence had been imposed by a court in England and Wales.

(6) Where a person removed under this section was immediately before his removal subject to an order or direction restricting his discharge, being an order or direction of limited duration, the restriction order or restriction direction to which he is subject by virtue of subsection (2) above shall expire on the date on which the first-mentioned order or direction would have expired if he had not been so removed.

(7) In this section "the responsible authority" means the Department of Health and Social Services for Northern Ireland or, in relation to a patient who is subject to an order or direction restricting his discharge, the Secretary of State.

DEFINITIONS
    "Patient": s.145(1).
    "Hospital": ss.92(1), 145(1).
    "Application for admission for assessment": ss.2, 145(1).
    "Application for admission for treatment": ss.3, 145(1).
    "Transfer direction": ss.47, 145(1).
    "Restriction order": ss.41, 145(1).
    "Restriction direction": ss.49, 145(1).

GENERAL NOTE
    This section provides that a patient who is detained or subject to guardianship in Northern Ireland may be transferred to England or Wales without a break in the powers of detention or guardianship. On his arrival in England or Wales the patient will become subject to detention or guardianship under this Act. A patient who has been transferred under this section has a right to apply to a Mental Health Review Tribunal within six months of his transfer (ss.66(1), 69(2)(*a*)).

Subs. (1)
    Responsible authority: See subs. (7).

Removal to and from Channel Islands and Isle of Man

Removal of patients to Channel Islands or Isle of Man

83. If it appears to the Secretary of State, in the case of a patient who is for the time being liable to be detained or subject to guardianship under this Act (otherwise than by virtue of section 35, 36 or 38 above), that it is in the interests of the patient to remove him to any of the Channel Islands or to the Isle of Man, and that arrangements have been made for admitting him to a hospital or, as the case may be, for receiving him into guardianship there, the Secretary of State may authorise his removal to the island in question and may give any necessary directions for his conveyance to his destination.

DEFINITIONS
    "Patient": s.145(1).
    "Hospital": s.92(1), 145(1).

GENERAL NOTE
    This section provides for patients who are detained or subject to guardianship in England or Wales to be transferred to the Channel Islands or the Isle of Man without a break in the powers of detention or guardianship.
    Conveyance: General provisions relating to the custody, conveyance and detention of patients are contained in s.137, below.

Removal to England and Wales of offenders found insane in Channel Islands and Isle of Man

84.—(1) The Secretary of State may by warrant direct that any offender found by a court in any of the Channel Islands or in the Isle of Man to be insane or to have been insane at the time of the alleged offence, and ordered to be detained during Her Majesty's pleasure, be removed to a hospital in England and Wales.
    (2) A patient removed under subsection (1) above shall, on his reception into the hospital in England and Wales, be treated as if he had been

removed to that hospital in pursuance of a direction under section 46 above.

(3) The Secretary of State may by warrant direct that any patient removed under this section from any of the Channel Islands or from the Isle of Man be returned to the island from which he was so removed, there to be dealt with according to law in all respects as if he had not been removed under this section.

DEFINITIONS
"Hospital": ss.92(1), 145(1).
"Patient": s.145(1).

GENERAL NOTE
This section enables the Home Secretary to transfer to a hospital in England or Wales an offender who has been found to be insane by a court in the Channel Islands or Isle of Man.

Patients removed from Channel Islands or Isle of Man

85.—(1) This section applies to any patient who is removed to England and Wales from any of the Channel Islands or the Isle of Man under a provision corresponding to section 83 above and who immediately before his removal was liable to be detained or subject to guardianship in the island in question under a provision corresponding to an enactment contained in this Act (other than section 35, 36 or 38 above).

(2) Where the patient is admitted to a hospital in England and Wales he shall be treated as if on the date of his admission he had been so admitted in pursuance of an application made, or an order or direction made or given, on that date under the corresponding enactment contained in this Act and, where he is subject to an order or direction restricting his discharge, as if he were subject to a restriction order or restriction direction.

(3) Where a patient is received into guardianship in England and Wales, he shall be treated as if on the date on which he arrives at the place where he is to reside he had been so received in pursuance of an application, order or direction under the corresponding enactment contained in this Act and as if the application had been accepted or, as the case may be, the order or direction had been made or given on that date.

(4) Where the patient was immediately before his removal liable to be detained by virtue of a transfer direction given while he was serving a sentence of imprisonment imposed by a court in the island in question, he shall be treated as if the sentence had been imposed by a court in England and Wales.

(5) Where the patient was immediately before his removal subject to an order or direction restricting his discharge, being an order or direction of limited duration, the restriction order or restriction direction to which he is subject by virtue of subsection (2) above shall expire on the date on which the first-mentioned order or direction would have expired if he had not been removed.

(6) While being conveyed to the hospital referred to in subsection (2) or, as the case may be, the place referred to in subsection (3) above, the patient shall be deemed to be in legal custody, and section 138 below shall apply to him as if he were in legal custody by virtue of section 137 below.

(7) In the case of a patient removed from the Isle of Man the reference in subsection (4) above to a person serving a sentence of imprisonment includes a reference to a person detained as mentioned in section 60(6)(*a*) of the Mental Health Act 1974 (an Act of Tynwald).

DEFINITIONS
DEFINITIONS
"Patient": s.145(1).
"Hospital": ss.92(1), 145(1).
"Restriction order": ss.41, 145(1).
"Restriction direction": ss.49, 145(1).
"Transfer direction": ss.47, 145(1).

GENERAL NOTE
This section provides for a patient who is detained or subject to guardianship in the Channel Islands or the Isle of Man to be transferred to England or Wales without a break in the powers of detention or guardianship. On his arrival in this country the patient will be subject to the corresponding legislative provision in this Act. A patient who has been transferred under this section has a right to appeal to a Mental Health Review Tribunal within six months of his transfer (ss.66(1), 69(2)(*a*)).

Removal of aliens

Removal of alien patients

86.—(1) This section applies to any patient who is neither a British citizen nor a Commonwealth citizen having the right of abode in the United Kingdom by virtue of section 2(1)(*b*) of the Immigration Act 1971, being a patient who is receiving treatment for mental illness as an in-patient in a hospital in England and Wales or a hospital within the meaning of the Mental Health Act (Northern Ireland) 1961 and is detained pursuant to—

(*a*) an application for admission for treatment or an application under section 12 of the said Act of 1961;

(*b*) a hospital order under section 37 above or section 48 of the said Act of 1961; or

(*c*) an order or direction under this Act (other than under section 35, 36 or 38 above) or the said Act of 1961 having the same effect as such a hospital order.

(2) If it appears to the Secretary of State that proper arrangements have been made for the removal of a patient to whom this section applies to a country or territory outside the United Kingdom, the Isle of Man and the Channel Islands and for his care or treatment there and that it is in the interests of the patient to remove him, the Secretary of State may, subject to subsection (3) below—

(*a*) by warrant authorise the removal of the patient from the place where he is receiving treatment as mentioned in subsection (1) above, and

(*b*) give such directions as the Secretary of State thinks fit for the conveyance of the patient to his destination in that country or territory and for his detention in any place or on board any ship or aircraft until his arrival at any specified port or place in any such country or territory.

(3) The Secretary of State shall not exercise his powers under subsection (2) above in the case of any patient except with the approval of a Mental Health Review Tribunal or, as the case may be, of the Mental Health Review Tribunal for Northern Ireland.

DEFINITIONS
"Patient": s.145(1).
"Hospital": ss.92(2), 145(1).
"Application for admission for treatment": ss.3, 145(1).
"Hospital order": ss.37, 145(1).

GENERAL NOTE
This section empowers the Home Secretary to authorise the removal to any country abroad of certain detained patients who do not have a right of abode in this country and

who are receiving in-patient treatment for mental illness. Before he exercises his powers under this section the Home Secretary must have obtained the approval of a Mental Health Review Tribunal. The main purpose of this section is to "enable patients who are either irrationally opposed to their removal, or are unable to express a view, to be compulsorily removed to another country when this is judged to be in their best interests. It is also used to enable patients to be kept under escort on their journey home if this is necessary" (Cmnd. 7320, para. 8.26). There is nothing to prevent a patient who has been removed under this section from applying for re-admission to the United Kingdom. If the patient was subject to a restriction order when he was removed, note s.91(2), below.

Subs. (1)
    United Kingdom: Means Great Britain and Northern Ireland (Interpretation Act 1978, s.5, Sched. 1).
    Mental illness: This section only applies to patients who are currently receiving treatment for mental illness. It could apply to a patient who was originally detained after being diagnosed as suffering from one of the other categories of mental disorder but had subsequently been reclassified as being mentally ill under s.16, above.
    Detained: This section does not apply to informal patients.

Subs. (2)
    Conveyance . . . and for his detention: General provisions relating to the custody, conveyance and detention of patients are contained in s.137, below.

Return of patients absent without leave
Patients absent from hospitals in Northern Ireland

87.—(1) Any person who—
    (*a*) under section 30 or section 108 of the Mental Health Act (Northern Ireland) 1961 (which provide, respectively, for the retaking of patients absent without leave and for the retaking of patients escaping from custody); or
    (*b*) under the said section 30 as applied by section 34 of the said Act of 1961 (which makes special provision as to persons sentenced to imprisonment),
may be taken into custody in Northern Ireland, may be taken into custody in, and returned to Northern Ireland from, England and Wales by an approved social worker, by any constable or by any person authorised by or by virtue of the said Act of 1961 to take him into custody.

(2) This section does not apply to any person who is subject to guardianship.

DEFINITIONS
    "Patient": s.145(1).
    "Absent without leave": ss.18(6), 145(1).
    "Approved social worker": s.145(1).

GENERAL NOTE
    This section permits a patient from Northern Ireland who has either escaped from custody or who in absent without leave from a hospital, to be taken into custody in England or Wales and returned to Northern Ireland. An equivalent provision in respect of patients from Scotland is made by s.83 of the Mental Health (Scotland) Act 1960.

Subs. (1)
    Returned: For the powers of a constable or approved social worker on taking the patient into custody and returning him to Northern Ireland, see s.137, below.

Patients absent from hospitals in England and Wales

88.—(1) Subject to the provisions of this section, any person who, under section 18 above or section 138 below or under the said section 18 as applied by section 22 above, may be taken into custody in England and Wales may be taken into custody in, and returned to England and Wales from, any other part of the United Kingdom or the Channel Islands or the Isle of Man.

(2) For the purposes of the enactments referred to in subsection (1) above, in their application by virtue of this section to Scotland, Northern Ireland, the Channel Islands or the Isle of Man, the expression "constable" includes a Scottish constable, an officer or constable of the Royal Ulster Constabulary, a member of the police in Jersey, an officer of police within the meaning of section 43 of the Larceny (Guernsey) Law 1958 or any corresponding law for the time being in force, or a constable in the Isle of Man, as the case may be.

(3) For the purposes of the said enactments in their application by virtue of this section to Scotland or Northern Ireland, any reference to an approved social worker shall be construed as including a reference—

(a) in Scotland, to any mental health officer within the meaning of the Mental Health (Scotland) Act 1960;

(b) in Northern Ireland, to any social worker within the meaning of the Mental Health Act (Northern Ireland) 1961.

(4) This section does not apply to any person who is subject to guardianship.

DEFINITION
   "Approved social worker": s.145(1).

GENERAL NOTE
   This section permits patients from England or Wales who are absent without leave from hospital or who have escaped from custody, to be taken into custody in, and returned to England and Wales from Scotland, Northern Ireland, the Channel Islands or the Isle of Man.

Patients absent from hospitals in the Channel Islands or Isle of Man

89.—(1) Any person who under any provision corresponding to section 18 above or 138 below may be taken into custody in any of the Channel Islands or the Isle of Man may be taken into custody in, and returned to the island in question from, England and Wales by an approved social worker or a constable.

(2) This section does not apply to any person who is subject to guardianship.

DEFINITION
   "Approved social worker": s.145(1).

GENERAL NOTE
   The purpose of this section is to ensure that a detained patient who absconds to England or Wales from the Channel Islands or the Isle of Man can be apprehended and returned to the island in question. Patients who abscond in the opposite direction are liable to be detained and returned under s.88, above.

   Returned: For the powers of a constable or approved social worker, see s.137, below.

General

Regulations for purposes of Part VI

90. Section 32 above shall have effect as if references in that section to Part II of this Act included references to this Part of this Act and to Part VI of the Mental Health (Scotland) Act 1960, so far as those Parts apply to patients removed to England and Wales thereunder.

DEFINITION
   "Patient": s.145(1).

General provisions as to patients removed from England and Wales

91.—(1) Subject to subsection (2) below, where a patient liable to be detained or subject to guardianship by virtue of an application, order or direction under Part II or III of this Act (other than section 35, 36 or 38 above) is removed from England and Wales in pursuance of arrangements under this Part of this Act, the application, order or direction shall cease to have effect when he is duly received into a hospital or other institution, or placed under guardianship, in pursuance of those arrangements.

(2) Where the Secretary of State exercises his powers under section 86(2) above in respect of a patient who is detained pursuant to a hospital order under section 37 above and in respect of whom a restriction order is in force, those orders shall continue in force so as to apply to the patient if he returns to England and Wales at any time before the end of the period for which those orders would have continued in force.

DEFINITIONS
  "Patient": s.145(1).
  "Hospital": ss.92(2), 145(1).
  "Hospital order": ss.37, 145(1).
  "Restriction order": ss.41, 145(1).

TRANSITIONAL PROVISION
  Sched. 5, para. 17.

GENERAL NOTE
  This section provides that in most situations when a patient is removed from England or Wales under a provision in this Part any application, order or direction made in respect of him will cease to have effect on his arrival at his destination.

Subs. (1)
  Sections 35, 36 *or* 38: Are concerned with remands to hospital for a report on an accused person's mental condition (s.35), remands to hospital for treatment (s.36) and interim hospital orders (s.38).

Interpretation of Part VI

92.—(1) References in this Part of this Act to a hospital, being a hospital in England and Wales, shall be construed as references to a hospital within the meaning of Part II of this Act.

(2) Where a patient is treated by virtue of this Part of this Act as if he had been removed to a hospital in England and Wales in pursuance of a direction under Part III of this Act, that direction shall be deemed to have been given on the date of his reception into the hospital.

(3) A patient removed to England and Wales under this Part of this Act or under Part VI of the Mental Health (Scotland) Act 1960 shall be treated for the purposes of this Act as suffering from such form of mental disorder as may be recorded in his case in pursuance of regulations made by virtue of section 90 above, and references in this Act to the form or forms of mental disorder specified in the relevant application, order or direction shall be construed as including references to the form or forms of mental disorder so recorded.

DEFINITIONS
  "Patient": s.145(1).
  "Mental disorder": ss.1, 145(1).

Subs. (1)
  Hospital: See s.35(2), above.

PART VII

MANAGEMENT OF PROPERTY AND AFFAIRS OF PATIENTS

GENERAL NOTE

This Part is concerned with the powers of the Court of Protection over the management of the property and affairs of persons incapable, by reason of mental disorder, of managing their own affairs. There is no requirement that the person in respect of whom an order under this Part is made should be liable to be detained or subject to guardianship under Pt. II of this Act, and there are no patients who become automatically subject to the powers of the Court of Protection.

The court has extensive powers and it "is not limited in its jurisdiction to dealing with the patient's property or financial affairs, nor limited to dealing with such other matters as may be within its jurisdiction in their property or financial aspects . . . it has exclusive jurisdiction over all the property and all the affairs of the patient in all their aspects; but not the management or care of the patient's person", *per* Ungoed-Thomas J., in *Re W. (E.E.M.)* [1971] Ch. 123, at p.143.

Proceedings in the Court of Protection are normally started by an originating application. The patient's nearest relative usually makes the application but some other person such as another relative, a social worker or a friend, can also apply. If there is no one available to make an application the court can direct one of its own officers or the Official Solicitor to apply. Although the help of a solicitor is recommended in complex cases or where large sums of money are involved it is possible for an application to be made directly through the court's personal application branch at 25 Store Street, London, WC1E 7BP.

Legal practitioners who come into contact with the court are referred to the standard legal text in this field: Heywood and Massey, *Court of Protection Practice*, 10th Ed. 1978 by E. R. Taylor. For a critical analysis of the court's practice and procedure, see, Larry Gostin, *The Court of Protection*, 1983.

Judicial authorities and Court of Protection

93.—(1) The Lord Chancellor shall from time to time nominate one or more judges of the Supreme Court (in this Act referred to as "nominated judges") to act for the purposes of this Part of this Act.

(2) There shall continue to be an office of the Supreme Court, called the Court of Protection, for the protection and management, as provided by this Part of this Act, of the property and affairs of persons under disability; and there shall continue to be a Master of the Court of Protection appointed by the Lord Chancellor under section 89 of the Supreme Court Act 1981.

(3) The Master of the Court of Protection shall take the oath of allegiance and judicial oath in the presence of the Lord Chancellor; and the Promissory Oaths Act 1868 shall have effect as if the officers named in the Second Part of the Schedule to that Act included the Master of the Court of Protection.

(4) The Lord Chancellor may nominate other officers of the Court of Protection (in this Part of this Act referred to as "nominated officers") to act for the purposes of this Part of this Act.

DEFINITION
"Property": s.112.

TRANSITIONAL PROVISION
Sched. 5, para. 26.

GENERAL NOTE
By virtue of s.12(1)(*b*) of the Administration of Justice Act 1960, the publication of information relating to proceedings heard in private is a contempt of court.

Subs. (1)
Nominated judge: Who will be a judge of the Chancery Division of the High Court.

Subs. (2)

Court of Protection: The use of the term "court" is rather misleading as most matters under this Part are dealt with by post by non-judicial officers of the Court. Very little work is, in practice, referred to a judge.

Exercise of the judge's functions: "the patient"

94.—(1) The functions expressed to be conferred by this Part of this Act on the judge shall be exercisable by the Lord Chancellor or by any nominated judge, and shall also be exercisable by the Master of the Court of Protection or by any nominated officer, but—

(*a*) in the case of the Master or any nominated officer, subject to any express provision to the contrary in this Part of this Act or any rules made under this Part of this Act,

(*b*) in the case of any nominated officer, subject to any directions of the Master and so far only as may be provided by the instrument by which he is nominated;

and references in this Part of this Act to the judge shall be construed accordingly.

(2) The functions of the judge under this Part of this Act shall be exercisable where, after considering medical evidence, he is satisfied that a person is incapable, by reason of mental disorder, of managing and administering his property and affairs; and a person as to whom the judge is so satisfied is referred to in this Part of this Act as a patient.

DEFINITIONS

"Nominated judge": s.112.
"Nominated officer": s.112.
"Mental disorder": ss.1, 145(1).
"Property": s.112.

Subs. (2)

After considering medical evidence: There is no requirement that the medical evidence has to be provided by a doctor who has specialist knowledge of mental disorder. As most cases are dealt with by post there is little opportunity available to the Court to test the validity of the medical evidence. Medical evidence from one doctor would be sufficient.

Satisfied: The fact that some other person or body has been satisfied as to the patients mental disorder does not affect the requirement that the Court must consider the medical evidence, unless the person concerned is already subject to the jurisdiction of the Court (*Re S.(F.G.)* [1973] 1 W.L.R. 179).

Mental disorder: The fact that a person is suffering from mental disorder is not of itself evidence of incapacity. Note that there is no requirement that the person should be receiving in-patient hospital treatment for mental disorder.

Property and affairs: This phrase was given a wide interpretation by Ungoed-Thomas J. in *Re W. (E.E.M.) supra,* where it was held that the Court had jurisdiction to conduct divorce proceedings on behalf of the patient; see the General Note to this Part.

Patient: The Court has an emergency jurisdiction pending the determination of mental capacity; see s.98, below.

General functions of the judge with respect to property and affairs of patient

95.—(1) The judge may, with respect to the property and affairs of a patient, do or secure the doing of all such things as appear necessary or expedient—

(*a*) for the maintenance or other benefit of the patient,

(*b*) for the maintenance or other benefit of members of the patient's family,

(*c*) for making provision for other persons or purposes for whom or which the patient might be expected to provide if he were not mentally disordered, or (*d*) otherwise for administering the patient's affairs.

(2) In the exercise of the powers conferred by this section regard shall be had first of all to the requirements of the patient, and the rules of law which restricted the enforcement by a creditor of rights against property under the control of the judge in lunacy shall apply to property under the control of the judge; but, subject to the foregoing provisions of this subsection, the judge shall, in administering a patient's affairs, have regard to the interests of creditors and also to the desirability of making provision for obligations of the patient notwithstanding that they may not be legally enforceable.

DEFINITIONS
"The judge": s.112.
"Property": s.112.
"Patient": s.112.
"Mental disorder": ss.1, 145(1).

GENERAL NOTE
The scope of this section was considered in *Re W. (E.E.M.)* [1971] Ch. 123 where Ungoed-Thomas J. held that "benefit" in paras. (*a*) and (*b*) "is of wide significance comprehending whatever would be beneficial in any respect, material or otherwise." His Lordship also held that the reference to "requirements" in subs. (2) "must similarly and correspondingly bear its wide prima facie meaning."

Subs. (1)
Para. (*c*): in *Re T.B.* [1967] Ch. 247, Ungoed-Thomas J. indicated, at p.253, that in applying this paragraph the court would act as a properly advised decent sane person in the patient's position would act.

Subs. (2)
Subject to being satisfied that adequate means are available for the patient's maintenance, the court will have regard to the just and proper claims of creditors (*Re Seager Hunt* [1906] 2 Ch. 295).

Powers of the judge as to patient's property and affairs

96.—(1) Without prejudice to the generality of section 95 above, the judge shall have power to make such orders and give such directions and authorities as he thinks fit for the purposes of that section and in particular may for those purposes make orders or give directions or authorities for—

(*a*) the control (with or without the transfer or vesting of property or the payment into or lodgment in the Supreme Court of money or securities) and management of any property of the patient;

(*b*) the sale, exchange, charging or other disposition of or dealing with any property of the patient;

(*c*) the acquisition of any property in the name or on behalf of the patient;

(*d*) the settlement of any property of the patient, or the gift of any property of the patient to any such persons or for any such purposes as are mentioned in paragraphs (*b*) and (*c*) of section 95(1) above;

(*e*) the execution for the patient of a will making any provision (whether by way of disposing of property or exercising a power or otherwise) which could be made by a will executed by the patient if he were not mentally disordered;

(*f*) the carrying on by a suitable person of any profession, trade or business of the patient;

(*g*) the dissolution of a partnership of which the patient is a member;

(*h*) the carrying out of any contract entered into by the patient;

(*i*) the conduct of legal proceedings in the name of the patient or on his behalf;

(*j*) the reimbursement out of the property of the patient, with or without interest, of money applied by any person either in payment of the patient's debts (whether legally enforceable or not) or for the maintenance or other benefit of the patient or members of his family or in making provision for other persons or purposes for whom or which he might be expected to provide if he were not mentally disordered;

(*k*) the exercise of any power (including a power to consent) vested in the patient, whether beneficially, or as guardian or trustee, or otherwise.

(2) If under subsection (1) above provision is made for the settlement of any property of a patient, or the exercise of a power vested in a patient of appointing trustees or retiring from a trust, the judge may also make as respects the property settled or trust property such consequential vesting or other orders as the case may require, including (in the case of the exercise of such a power) any order which could have been made in such a case under Part IV of the Trustee Act 1925.

(3) Where under this section a settlement has been made of any property of a patient, and the Lord Chancellor or a nominated judge is satisfied, at any time before the death of the patient, that any material fact was not disclosed when the settlement was made, or that there has been any substantial change in circumstances, he may by order vary the settlement in such manner as he thinks fit, and give any consequential directions.

(4) The power of the judge to make or give an order, direction or authority for the execution of a will for a patient—

(*a*) shall not be exercisable at any time when the patient is a minor, and

(*b*) shall not be exercised unless the judge has reason to believe that the patient is incapable of making a valid will for himself.

(5) The powers of a patient as patron of a benefice shall be exercisable by the Lord Chancellor only.

DEFINITIONS
   "The judge": s.112.
   "Property": s.112.
   "Patient": s.112.
   "Will": s.112.
   "Mental disorder": ss.1, 145(1).
   "Nominated judge": s.112.

Subs. (1)
   In particular: What follows is not an exhaustive list of powers. The Court has exclusive jurisdiction over all of the patient's property and affairs.

para. (*d*)
   Settlement of any property: In *Re. L. (W.J.G.)* [1966] Ch. 135, Cross J., considers, at pp.144, 145, the approach to be adopted by a judge in determining whether and how he should exercise his discretion in regard to the making of a settlement under this paragraph and s.95(1)(*c*), above.
   The gift of any property of the patient: The Court has to answer the following question when determining whether a patient should make a gift: is the proposed gift such a gift as the patient might be expected to provide if she had ceased to be mentally disordered and was removed from any influence (*Re. C.M.G.* [1970] 1 Ch. 574).

para. (*e*)
   Under the Court of Protection Rules 1982 the Court has a discretion as to which persons are to be made respondents to or given notice of an application for the execution of a will under this paragraph. In the normal case the Court would generally insist on the joinder of a person who was adversely affected by the relief sought, but in circumstances of urgency

the position may be different (*Re. Davey (decd.)* [1981] 1 W.L.R. 164). In *Re D. (J.)* [1982] 2 All E.R. 37, Megarry V.-C. identifies, at pp.42, 43, five considerations which the Court should have in mind when deciding on what provisions should be inserted in a will.

para. (i)
The conduct of legal proceedings: Gostin states that in practice the patient's receiver (see s.99) "must have authorisation from the Court before bringing or defending an action on behalf of the patient. A patient may not bring or make a claim in any High Court proceedings except through his next friend, and may not defend a claim or intervene in such proceedings except through his guardian *ad litem*" (*The Court of Protection*, 1983, pp.42, 43).

Subs. (3)
The provisions of this subsection do not prevent trustees of a settlement from distributing the capital of a trust property during the lifetime of the patient (*Re C.W.H.T.* [1978] Ch. 67).

Subs. (4)
A *minor:* Is a person who has not attained the age of eighteen (Family Law Reform Act 1969, s.1).

Supplementary provisions as to wills executed under s.96

97.—(1) Where under section 96(1) above the judge makes or gives an order, direction or authority requiring or authorising a person (in this section referred to as "the authorised person") to execute a will for a patient, any will executed in pursuance of that order, direction authority shall be expressed to be signed by the patient acting by the authorised person, and shall be—

(a) signed by the authorised person with the name of the patient, and with his own name, in the presence of two or more witnesses present at the same time, and

(b) attested and subscribed by those witnesses in the presence of the authorised person, and

(c) sealed with the official seal of the Court of Protection.

(2) The Wills Act 1837 shall have effect in relation to any such will as if it were signed by the patient by his own hand, except that in relation to any such will—

(a) section 9 of that Act (which makes provision as to the signing and attestation of wills) shall not apply, and

(b) in the subsequent provisions of that Act any reference to execution in the manner required by the previous provisions of that Act shall be construed as a reference to execution in the manner required by subsection (1) above.

(3) Subject to the following provisions of this section, any such will executed in accordance with subsection (1) above shall have the same effect for all purposes as if the patient were capable of making a valid will and the will had been executed by him in the manner required by the Wills Act 1837.

(4) So much of subsection (3) above as provides for such a will to have effect as if the patient were capable of making a valid will—

(a) shall not have effect in relation to such a will in so far as it disposes of any immovable property, other than immovable property in England or Wales, and

(b) where at the time when such a will is executed the patient is domiciled in Scotland or Northern Ireland or in a country or territory outside the United Kingdom, shall not have effect in relation to that will in so far as it relates to any other property or matter, except any property or matter in respect of which, under the law of his domicile, any question of his testamentary capacity would fall to be determined in accordance with the law of England and Wales.

DEFINITIONS
"The judge": s.112.
"Will": s.112.
"Patient": s.112.
"Property": s.112.

GENERAL NOTE
If the formalities set out in subs. (1) of this section are complied with by a Master of the Court of Protection the will must, by virtue of subs. (3), be treated as if it were duly made and the High Court has no jurisdiction to interfere with it (*Re Davey (decd.)* [1981] 1 W.L.R. 164).

Judge's powers in cases of emergency

98. Where it is represented to the judge, and he has reason to believe, that a person may be incapable, by reason of mental disorder, of managing and administering his property and affairs, and the judge is of the opinion that it is necessary to make immediate provision for any of the matters referred to in section 95 above, then pending the determination of the question whether that person is so incapable the judge may exercise in relation to the property and affairs of that person any of the powers conferred on him in relation to the property and affairs of a patient by this Part of this Act so far as is requisite for enabling that provision to be made.

DEFINITIONS
"The judge": s.112.
"Mental disorder": ss.1, 145(1).
"Property": s.112.

GENERAL NOTE
This section enables the Court to act in an emergency without making a formal determination of the patient's incapacity if it considers that it is necessary to make immediate provision.
A person: Not a "patient" as defined in s.94(2), above.
May be incapable: The Court is not obliged to hear medical evidence of incapacity.
Any of the powers: But not including those powers specified in the third column of Sched. 3, below (s.113).

Power to appoint receiver

99.—(1) The judge may by order appoint as receiver for a patient a person specified in the order or the holder for the time being of an office so specified.

(2) A person appointed as receiver for a patient shall do all such things in relation to the property and affairs of the patient as the judge, in the exercise of the powers conferred on him by sections 95 and 96 above, orders or directs him to do and may do any such thing in relation to the property and affairs of the patient as the judge, in the exercise of those powers, authorises him to do.

(3) A receiver appointed for any person shall be discharged by order of the judge on the judge being satisfied that that person has become capable of managing and administering his property and affairs, and may be discharged by order of the judge at any time if the judge considers it expedient to do so; and a receiver shall be discharged (without any order) on the death of the patient.

DEFINITIONS
   "The judge": s.112.
   "Patient": s.112.
   "Property": s.112.

TRANSITIONAL PROVISIONS
   Sched. 5, paras. 23, 44.

GENERAL NOTE
   This section empowers the Court to exercise its jurisdiction by appointing a receiver for the patient. The receiver acts under the direction of the Court and he will be discharged once the Court is satisfied that the patient is capable of managing his own affairs. A receiver will automatically be discharged on the death of the patient.
   Receivership is the normal method of protecting a patient's estate and using it for his benefit. However, if the patient's assets do not exceed £5,000, the Court may make an order in summary manner pursuant to Rule 6 of the Court of Protection Rules 1982 without appointing a receiver. This type of order, called a "short procedure" order, can also be made if the patient's assets exceed £5,000 but the Court considers the appointment of a receiver to be unnecessary.
   If the patient's sole asset consists of a pension or salary payable by a Government Department the Department concerned can administer the asset under s.142, below.

Subs. (1)
   Person: The court will usually appoint a near relative of the patient or a solicitor to be the receiver.
   Holder . . . of an office: Who could be the Director of Social Services of a local authority. The expenses of an officer of a social services authority who is appointed receiver can be paid by virtue of s.49 of the National Assistance Act 1948.

Subs. (3)
   Shall be discharged: On an application for the discharge of the receiver and the restoration of the patient to the management of his own affairs the rules of natural justice, but not the rules of evidence, apply (*Re W.L.W.* [1972] Ch. 456).
   Expedient: This means expedient for the patient (*Re N.* (deceased) [1977] 1 W.L.R. 676).

Vesting of stock in curator appointed outside England and Wales

   100.—(1) Where the judge is satisfied—
     (*a*) that under the law prevailing in a place outside England and Wales a person has been appointed to exercise powers with respect to the property or affairs of any other person on the ground (however formulated) that that other person is incapable, by reason of mental disorder, of managing and administering his property and affairs, and
     (*b*) that having regard to the nature of the appointment and to the circumstances of the case it is expedient that the judge should exercise his powers under this section,
the judge may direct any stock standing in the name of the said other person or the right to receive the dividends from the stock to be transferred into the name of the person so appointed or otherwise dealt with as requested by that person, and may give such directions as the judge thinks fit for dealing with accrued dividends from the stock.
   (2) In this section "stock" includes shares and also any fund, annuity or security transferable in the books kept by any body corporate or unincorporated company or society, or by an instrument of transfer either alone or accompanied by other formalities, and "dividends" shall be construed accordingly.

DEFINITIONS
   "The judge": s.112.
   "Property": s.112.
   "Mental disorder": ss.1, 145(1).

  The "purpose of this section is that the Court in this country should be able to recognise judicially the operation of foreign law, whereunder some form of curatorship has been constituted for a mental patient, without itself having to go into the question of mental status and capacity", Heywood and Massey, *Court of Protection Practice*, 10th Ed. 1978, p.41.

Preservation of interests in patient's property

101.—(1) Where any property of a person has been disposed of under this Part of this Act, and under his will or his intestacy, or by any gift perfected or nomination taking effect on his death, any other person would have taken an interest in the property but for the disposal—

  (*a*) he shall take the same interest, if and so far as circumstances allow, in any property belonging to the estate of the deceased which represents the property disposed of; and

  (*b*) if the property disposed of was real property any property representing it shall so long as it remains part of his estate be treated as if it were real property.

(2) The judge, in ordering, directing or authorising under this Part of this Act any disposal of property which apart from this section would result in the conversion of personal property into real property, may direct that the property representing the property disposed of shall, so long as it remains the property of the patient or forms part of his estate, be treated as if it were personal property.

(3) References in subsections (1) and (2) above to the disposal of property are references to—

  (*a*) the sale, exchange, charging or other dealing (otherwise than by will) with property other than money,

  (*b*) the removal of property from one place to another,

  (*c*) the application of money in acquiring property, or

  (*d*) the transfer of money from one account to another;

and references to property representing property disposed of shall be construed accordingly and as including the result of successive disposals.

(4) The judge may give such directions as appear to him necessary or expedient for the purpose of facilitating the operation of subsection (1) above, including the carrying of money to a separate account and the transfer of property other than money.

(5) Where the judge has ordered, directed or authorised the expenditure of money for the carrying out of permanent improvements on, or otherwise for the permanent benefit of, any property of the patient, he may order that the whole or any part of the money expended or to be expended shall be a charge upon the property, whether without interest or with interest at a specified rate; and an order under this subsection may provide for excluding or restricting the operation of subsection (1) above.

(6) A charge under subsection (5) above may be made in favour of such person as may be just, and in particular, where the money charged is paid out of the patient's general estate, may be made in favour of a person as trustee for the patient; but no charge under that subsection shall confer any right of sale or foreclosure during the lifetime of the patient.

DEFINITIONS
  "Property": s.112.
  "Will": s.112.
  "The judge": s.112.
  "Patient": s.112.

TRANSITIONAL PROVISION
  Sched. 5, para. 45.

GENERAL NOTE
This section, which is concerned with the effect of dispositions made under this Part on the law of succession, is considered in *Heywood and Massey*, at pp.122 to 125.

Lord Chancellor's Visitors

102.—(1) There shall continue to be the following panels of Lord Chancellor's Visitors of patients constituted in accordance with this section, namely—
  (*a*) a panel of Medical Visitors;
  (*b*) a panel of Legal Visitors; and
  (*c*) a panel of General Visitors (being Visitors who are not required by this section to possess either a medical or legal qualification for appointment).
(2) Each panel shall consist of persons appointed to it by the Lord Chancellor, the appointment of each person being for such term and subject to such conditions as the Lord Chancellor may determine.
(3) A person shall not be qualified to be appointed—
  (*a*) to the panel of Medical Visitors unless he is a registered medical practitioner who appears to the Lord Chancellor to have special knowlege and experience of cases of mental disorder;
  (*b*) to the panel of Legal Visitors unless he is a barrister or solicitor of not less than 10 years' standing.
(4) If the Lord Chancellor so determines in the case of any Visitor appointed under this section, he shall be paid out of money provided by Parliament such remuneration and allowances as the Lord Chancellor may, with the concurrence of the Treasury, determine.

DEFINITION
  "Patient": s.112.

GENERAL NOTE
This section provides for the appointment and payment of Medical, Legal and General Visitors. The functions of Visitors are set out in s.103, below.

Subs. (1)
  General Visitors. According to Larry Gostin these are civil servants employed in the Lord Chancellor's Department; see Gostin, *The Court of Protection*, 1983, p.17.

Functions of Visitors

103.—(1) Patients shall be visited by Lord Chancellor's Visitors in such circumstances, and in such manner, as may be prescribed by directions of a standing nature given by the Master of the Court of Protection with the concurrence of the Lord Chancellor.
(2) Where it appears to the judge in the case of any patient that a visit by a Lord Chancellor's Visitor is necessary for the purpose of investigating any particular matter or matters relating to the capacity of the patient to manage and administer his property and affairs, or otherwise relating to the exercise in relation to him of the functions of the judge under this Part of this Act, the judge may order that the patient shall be visited for that purpose.
(3) Every visit falling to be made under subsection (1) or (2) above shall be made by a General Visitor unless, in a case where it appears to the judge that it is in the circumstances essential for the visit to be made by a Visitor with medical or legal qualifications, the judge directs that the visit shall be made by a Medical or a Legal Visitor.
(4) A Visitor making a visit under this section shall make such report on the visit as the judge may direct.

(5) A Visitor making a visit under this section may interview the patient in private.

(6) A Medical Visitor making a visit under this section may carry out in private a medical examination of the patient and may require the production of and inspect any medical records relating to the patient.

(7) The Master of the Court of Protection may visit any patient for the purpose mentioned in subsection (2) above and may interview the patient in private.

(8) A report made by a Visitor under this section, and information contained in such a report, shall not be disclosed except to the judge and any person authorised by the judge to receive the disclosure.

(9) If any person discloses any report or information in contravention of subsection (8) above, he shall be guilty of an offence and liable on summary conviction to imprisonment for a term not exceeding three months or to a fine not exceeding level 3 on the standard scale or both.

(10) In this section references to patients include references to persons alleged to be incapable, by reason of mental disorder, of managing and administering their property and affairs.

DEFINITIONS
"The judge": s.112.
"Property": s.112.
"Standard scale": s.145(1).
"Mental disorder": ss.1, 145(1).

GENERAL NOTE
"The most important part of [the Visitors'] duty is to assist the Court in determining what is the mental capacity of the person in question, whether in regard to an application for the appointment of a receiver or the discharge of a receiver on recovery, but many other matters arise in regard to which they visit the patient, under the directions of the Court, and report, *e.g.* testementary capacity, suitability of accommodation, care and attention and ascertaining the patient's views in regard to any matter", *Heywood and Massey*, p.21.

Subs. (1)
Patient: See subs. (10).

Subs. (5)
Making a visit: The obstruction of a Visitor constitutes an offence under section 129, below. It is also a contempt of court to interfere with the discharge of a Visitor's duties (*Re Anon* (1881) 18 Ch.D. 26, *per* James L.J. at p.27).

Subs. (8)
Report: When a patient is applying for the discharge of his receiver, the judge, save in exceptional circumstances, should exercise his discretion so as to allow the disclosure of the Visitor's report, and where disclosure is so ordered the patient should be able to test the report by putting questions to the Visitor (*Re W.L.W.* [1972] Ch. 456).

General powers of the judge with respect to proceedings

104.—(1) For the purposes of any proceedings before him with respect to persons suffering or alleged to be suffering from mental disorder, the judge shall have the same powers as are vested in the High Court in respect of securing the attendance of witnesses and the production of documents.

(2) Subject to the provisions of this section, any act or omission in the course of such proceedings which, if occurring in the course of proceedings in the High Court would have been a contempt of the Court, shall be punishable by the judge in any manner in which it could have been punished by the High Court.

(3) Subsection (2) above shall not authorise the Master, or any other officer of the Court of Protection to exercise any power of attachment or committal, but the Master or officer may certify any such act or omission to the Lord Chancellor or a nominated judge, and the Lord Chancellor or judge may upon such certification inquire into the alleged act or omission and take any such action in relation to it as he could have taken if the proceedings had been before him.

(4) Subsections (1) to (4) of section 36 of the Supreme Court Act 1981 (which provides a special procedure for the issue of writs of subpoena ad testificandum and duces tecum so as to be enforceable thoughout the United Kingdom) shall apply in relation to proceedings under this Part of this Act with the substitution for references to the High Court of references to the judge and for references to such writs of references to such document as may be prescribed by rules under this Part of this Act for issue by the judge for securing the attendance of witnesses or the production of documents.

DEFINITIONS
   "Mental disorder": ss.1, 145(1).
   "The judge": s.112.
   "Nominated judge": s.112.

GENERAL NOTE
   This section provides the Court of Protection judge with the same powers as are vested in the High Court to secure the attendance of witnesses and the production of documents.

Subs. (1)
   Attendance of witnesses: Rule 53 of the Court of Protection Rules 1982 provides for the issue of a witness summons.

Appeals

105.—(1) Subject to and in accordance with rules under this Part of this Act, an appeal shall lie to a nominated judge from any decision of the Master of the Court of Protection or any nominated officer.

(2) The Court of Appeal shall continue to have the same jurisdiction as to appeals from any decision of the Lord Chancellor or from any decision of a nominated judge, whether given in the exercise of his original jurisdiction or on the hearing of an appeal under subsection (1) above, as they had immediately before the coming into operation of Part VIII of the Mental Health Act 1959 as to appeals from orders in lunacy made by the Lord Chancellor or any other person having jurisdiction in lunacy.

DEFINITIONS
   "Nominated judge": s.112.
   "Nominated officer": s.112.

Subs. (1)
   Rules: See rules 59 and 60 of the Court of Protection Rules 1982.
   Appeal: On an appeal under this subsection the nominated judge has a complete discretion to consider the matter and he is in no way fettered by any decision of the Master or nominated officer (*Re D. (J.)* [1982] 2 All E.R. 37).

Rules of procedure

106.—(1) Proceedings before the judge with respect to persons suffering or alleged to be suffering from mental disorder (in this section referred to as "proceedings") shall be conducted in accordance with the provisions of rules made under this Part of this Act.

(2) Rules under this Part of this Act may make provision as to—
   (*a*) the carrying out of preliminary or incidental inquiries;

(*b*) the persons by whom and manner in which proceedings may be instituted and carried on;

(*c*) the persons who are to be entitled to be notified of, to attend, or to take part in proceedings;

(*d*) the evidence which may be authorised or required to be given in proceedings and the manner (whether on oath or otherwise and whether orally or in writing) in which it is to be given;

(*e*) the administration of oaths and taking of affidavits for the purposes of proceedings; and

(*f*) the enforcement of orders made and directions given in proceedings.

(3) Without prejudice to the provisions of section 104(1) above, rules under this Part of this Act may make provision for authorising or requiring the attendance and examination of persons suffering or alleged to be suffering from mental disorder, the furnishing of information and the production of documents.

(4) Rules under this Part of this Act may make provision as to the termination of proceedings, whether on the death or recovery of the person to whom the proceedings relate or otherwise, and for the exercise, pending the termination of the proceedings, of powers exercisable under this Part of this Act in relation to the property or affairs of a patient.

(5) Rules under this Part of this Act made with the consent of the Treasury may—

(*a*) make provision as to the scale of costs, fees and percentages payable in relation to proceedings, and as to the manner in which and funds out of which such costs, fees and percentages are to be paid;

(*b*) contain provision for charging any percentage upon the estate of the person to whom the proceedings relate and for the payment of costs, fees and percentages within such time after the death of the person to whom the proceedings relate or the termination of the proceedings as may be provided by the rules; and

(*c*) provide for the remission of fees and percentages.

(6) A charge upon the estate of a person created by virtue of subsection (5) above shall not cause any interest of that person in any property to fail or determine or to be prevented from recommencing.

(7) Rules under this Part of this Act may authorise the making of orders for the payment of costs to or by persons attending, as well as persons taking part in, proceedings.

DEFINITIONS
"The judge": s.112.
"Mental disorder": ss.1, 145(1).
"Property": s.112.
"Patient": s.112.

GENERAL NOTE
The Court of Protection Rules 1982 (S.I. 1982 No. 322) were made under the 1959 Act. By virtue of s.17(2)(*b*) of the Interpretation Act 1978 they are to be treated as if they were made under this Act.

Security and accounts

107.—(1) Rules under this Part of this Act may make provision as to the giving of security by a receiver and as to the enforcement and discharge of the security.

(2) It shall be the duty of a receiver to render accounts in accordance with the requirements of rules under this Part of this Act, as well after his discharge as during his receivership; and rules under this Part of this Act

may make provision for the rendering of accounts by persons other than receivers who are ordered, directed or authorised under this Part of this Act to carry out any transaction.

GENERAL NOTE
Subs. (1)
   Rules: See the Court of Protection Rules 1982, rules 61 to 65.

Subs. (2)
   Rules: See *ibid.,* rules 66 to 71.

General provisions as to rules under Part VII

108.—(1) Any power to make rules conferred by this Part of this Act shall be exercisable by the Lord Chancellor.

(2) Rules under this Part of this Act may contain such incidental and supplemental provisions as appear requisite for the purposes of the rules.

GENERAL NOTE
   See the General Note to s.106, above.

Effect and proof of orders, etc.

109.—(1) Section 204 of the Law of Property Act 1925 (by which orders of the High Court are made conclusive in favour of purchasers) shall apply in relation to orders made and directions and authorities given by the judge as it applies in relation to orders of the High Court.

(2) Office copies of orders made, directions or authorities given or other instruments issued by the judge and sealed with the official seal of the Court of Protection shall be admissible in all legal proceedings as evidence of the originals without any further proof.

DEFINITION
   "The judge": s.112.

GENERAL NOTE
   This section was considered by the Court of Appeal in *Pritchard* v. *Briggs* [1980] Ch. 338.

Reciprocal arrangements in relation to Scotland and Northern Ireland as to exercise of powers

110.—(1) This Part of this Act shall apply in relation to the property and affairs in Scotland or Northern Ireland of a patient in relation to whom powers have been exercised under this Part of this Act, or a person as to whom powers are exercisable and have been exercised under section 98 above as it applies in relation to his property and affairs in England and Wales unless a curator bonis, tutor, judicial factor, committee, receiver or guardian has been appointed for him in Scotland or, as the case may be, Northern Ireland.

(2) Where under the law in force in Scotland or Northern Ireland with respect to the property and affairs of persons suffering from mental disorder a curator bonis, tutor, judical factor, committee, receiver or guardian has been appointed for any person, the provisions of that law shall apply in relation to that person's property and affairs in England and Wales unless he is a patient in relation to whom powers have been exercised under this Part of this Act, or a person as to whom powers are exercisable and have been exercised under section 98 above.

(3) Nothing in this section shall affect any power to execute a will under section 96(1)(*e*) above or the effect of any will executed in the exercise of such a power.

(4) In this section references to property do not include references to land or interests in land but this subsection shall not prevent the receipt of rent or other income arising from land or interests in land.

DEFINITIONS
   "Patient": s.112.
   "Mental disorder": ss.1, 145(1).
   "Will": s.112.

Subs. (1)
   Property: See s.112, below, and subs. (4).

Construction of references in other Acts to judge or authority having jurisdiction under Part VII

111.—(1) The functions expressed to be conferred by any enactment not contained in this Part of this Act on the judge having jurisdiction under this Part of this Act shall be exercisable by the Lord Chancellor or by a nominated judge.

(2) Subject to subsection (3) below, the functions expressed to be conferred by any such enactment on the authority having jurisdiction under this Part of this Act shall, subject to any express provision to the contrary, be exercisable by the Lord Chancellor, a nominated judge, the Master of the Court of Protection or a nominated officer.

(3) The exercise of the functions referred to in subsection (2) above by a nominated officer shall be subject to any directions of the Master and they shall be exercisable so far only as may be provided by the instrument by which the officer is nominated.

(4) Subject to the foregoing provisions of this section—
   (*a*) references in any enactment not contained in this Part of this Act to the judge having jurisdiction under this Part of this Act shall be construed as references to the Lord Chancellor or a nominated judge, and
   (*b*) references in any such enactment to the authority having jurisdiction under this Part of this Act shall be construed as references to the Lord Chancellor, a nominated judge, the Master of the Court of Protection or a nominated officer.

DEFINITIONS
   "The judge": s.112.
   "Nominated judge": s.112.
   "Nominated officer": s.112.

Interpretation of Part VII

112. In this Part of this Act, unless the context otherwise requires—
   "nominated judge" means a judge nominated in pursuance of subsection (1) of section 93 above;
   "nominated officer" means an officer nominated in pursuance of subsection (4) of that section;
   "patient" has the meaning assigned to it by section 94 above;
   "property" includes any thing in action, and any interest in real or personal property;
   "the judge" shall be construed in accordance with section 94 above;
   "will" includes a codicil.

Disapplication of certain enactments in relation to persons within the jurisdiction of the judge

113. The provisions of the Acts described in Schedule 3 to this Act which are specified in the third column of that Schedule, so far as they make special provision for persons suffering from mental disorder, shall not have effect in relation to patients and to persons as to whom powers are exercisable and have been exercised under section 98 above.

DEFINITIONS
    "Mental disorder": ss.1, 145(1).
    "Patient": s.112.

PART VIII

MISCELLANEOUS FUNCTIONS OF LOCAL AUTHORITIES AND THE SECRETARY OF STATE

Approved social workers

Appointment of approved social workers

114.—(1) A local social services authority shall appoint a sufficient number of approved social workers for the purpose of discharging the functions conferred on them by this Act.

(2) No person shall be appointed by a local social services authority as an approved social worker unless he is approved by the authority as having appropriate competence in dealing with persons who are suffering from mental disorder.

(3) In approving a person for appointment as an approved social worker a local social services authority shall have regard to such matters as the Secretary of State may direct.

DEFINITIONS
    "Local social services authority": s.145(1).
    "Approved social worker": s.145(1).
    "Mental disorder": s.145(1).

TRANSITIONAL PROVISION
    Sched. 5, para. 4.

GENERAL NOTE
    This section requires local authorities to appoint a sufficient number of approved social workers to carry out the functions given to them by this Act. Approved social workers will replace the mental welfare officers who were appointed under the 1959 Act, on October 28, 1984. Anything done prior to October 28, 1984, by a mental welfare officer is not affected by this changeover and any work that is in the process of being done on that date may be continued by an approved social worker (who could be the same person). Until October 28, 1984, any reference in this Act to an approved social worker should be taken as a reference to a mental welfare officer; see Sched. 5, para. 4.

Subs. (1)
    Appoint: An approved social worker should be provided with documentary evidence of his appointment as some sections of this Act require him to produce such documentation (see, for example, s.115). The document, which should be authenticated by a member or officer of the appointing local authority, could read as follows: "[Name of approved social worker] has been appointed by the [name of local authority] to act as an approved social worker under the Mental Health Act 1983 (Mental Health Act 1983, s.114)". It might be advisable to reproduce the provisions of s.115 of this Act, which provides an approved social worker with a power of entry and inspection, on the document.
    Sufficient number: Guidance on the criteria to be adopted in ascertaining the number of approved social workers that need to be appointed is given in para. 8 of "Draft Guidelines for Approval of Social Workers under the Proposed Mental Health (Amendment) Act" published by the D.H.S.S. in December 1981: "Decline in the use of compulsory powers is a factor to be taken into account in deciding how many social workers an authority will need to train and approve under the amended legislation, but it should be balanced by a proper

assessment of the work to be undertaken and an appreciation of the role envisaged for them. Local social services authorities should establish criteria for deciding how many will be required to meet the demands in their area and generally speaking a count of the number of crises referred to the department is likely to be a better indicator than the recorded number of compulsory admissions to hospitals."

Functions: The relevant sections are 4, 10, 11, 13, 14, 18, 29, 30, 40, 87, 89, 115, 135, 136 and 138.

Subs. (2)

Appointed: When carrying out his functions under this Act the approved social worker acts in a personal capacity. He should therefore exercise his own judgment and not act at the behest of his superiors, or anyone else. At the House of Lords Committee stage an attempt was made to amend this section so as to preclude a hospital social worker from acting as an approved social worker in cases where the patient would be admitted to the hospital where the social worker was employed. Lord Elton, in resisting the amendment, said: "There may be cases where social workers based in a hospital and undertaking [approved social worker] duties find it difficult to act independently in making applications to that hospital, and that may well arise most often where the doctor with whom the social worker is working has made one of the medical recommendations . . . It is our view that this sort of case should be a matter of good practice rather than legislation." (H.L. Vol. 426, col. 1167). During the course of his speech Lord Elton referred to advice that the D.H.S.S. had given to Directors of Social Services, in a letter dated April 16, 1974, on the appointment of hospital social workers to act as mental welfare officers in which it was stated that it should be made clear to each hospital social worker who is so appointed that if in any case he feels that he cannot act or be seen to act independently he should get advice from his superior officer as to whether another person should be appointed to act in his stead.

Approved by the authority: The fact that a social worker has been "approved by the authority" does not necessarily mean that he will be *appointed* under subs. (1). Paras. 8 to 10 of D.H.S.S. Circular No. LAC (87) 7 (Welsh Office Circular 36/83) deal with approval arrangements:

"8. The procedures for formal approval and the role of elected members are matters for local decision. However, responsibility for the organisation and functioning of whatever machinery for approval and re-approval is decided upon should be held by a senior officer in the social services department.

9. Where an approved social worker moves from one authority to another the new authority should inquire of the old as to satisfactory performance of duties.

10. An employing authority has the right to withdraw its approval from any social worker no longer needed or suited to carry out the required duties."

Subs. (3)

Such matters as the Secretary of State may direct: Paras. 4 to 6 of D.H.S.S. Circular No. LAC (83) 7 (Welsh Office Circular No. 36/83) contain the Secretary of State's directions under this provision:

"4. The Secretary of State directs that any person to be approved from October 28, 1984, to carry out statutory duties under the Mental Health Act 1983 shall have received appropriate training and shall have succeeded in a system of assessment organised in relation to the Act by the Central Council for Education and Training in Social Work. This direction does not imply that any person who has received such training and has succeeded in such an assessment should automatically become an approved social worker. Approval to carry out the duties rests with the employing social services authority.

5. The Secretary of State directs that the period for which approval by a local authority can be given under para. 4 above shall not exceed five years. Social workers may be re-approved at the end of the five year period after appropriate re-appraisal by the local authority. Social workers moving from one employing authority to another must be re-approved by the new authority, which must be satisfied that such persons have met whatever requirements CCETSW specifies.

6. The Secretary of State directs that, except for mental welfare officers in post on October 28, 1982 (the date the Mental Health (Amendment) Act was passed), all candidates for assessment by CCETSW and for approval by social services authorities shall hold the Certificate of Qualification in Social Work or a qualification recognised as comparable by CCETSW."

Powers of entry and inspection

115. An approved social worker of a local social services authority may at all reasonable times after producing, if asked to do so, some duly authenticated document showing that he is such a social worker, enter and inspect any premises (not being a hospital) in the area of that authority in which a mentally disordered patient is living, if he has reasonable cause to believe that the patient is not under proper care.

DEFINITIONS
 "Approved social worker": s.145(1).
 "Local social services authority": s.145(1).
 "Mental disorder": ss.1, 145(1).
 "Patient": s.145(1).

GENERAL NOTE
 This section provides approved social workers with a power to enter and inspect premises where a mentally disordered patient is living. The power does not apply to hospitals and it can only be exercised within the area of the approved social worker's employing authority.
 All reasonable times: The reasonableness of the time will presumably depend upon the urgency of the situation.
 Enter and inspect: This section does not empower the approved social worker to force entry on to the premises. If entry is refused the approved social worker should point out to the person concerned that a refusal to allow the inspection to take place would constitute an offence under s.129, below. If this information fails to impress the obstructor and entry is still denied, the approved social worker should consider whether the facts of the case would justify him making an application to a justice of the peace under s.135, below, for a warrant authorising a policeman to enter the premises by force.
 Although it has been suggested that the long-recognised common law power to apprehend dangerous insane persons carries with it a power to force entry where necessary, it is submitted that, in the absence of express statutory authority, this power should not be relied on and the procedure set out in s.135 be followed if force is required (c.f. D. Lanham *Arresting and Insane*, [1974] Crim.L.R. 515).
 Further powers of inspection of mental nursing homes and residential homes for mentally disordered persons are contained in section 9 of the Nursing Homes Act 1975, and s.6 of the Residential Homes Act 1980, respectively.

Visiting patients

Welfare of certain hospital patients

116.—(1) Where a patient to whom this section applies is admitted to a hospital or nursing home in England and Wales (whether for treatment for mental disorder or for any other reason) then, without prejudice to their duties in relation to the patient apart from the provisions of this section, the authority shall arrange for visits to be made to him on behalf of the authority, and shall take such other steps in relation to the patient while in the hospital or nursing home as would be expected to be taken by his parents.
 (2) This section applies to—
  (*a*) a child or young person in respect of whom the rights and powers of a parent are vested in a local authority by virtue of—
   (i) section 3 of the Child Care Act 1980 (which relates to the assumption by a local authority of parental rights and duties in relation to a child in their care),
   (ii) section 10 of that Act (which relates to the powers and duties of local authorities with respect to persons committed to their care under the Children and Young Persons Act 1969), or
   (iii) section 17 of the Social Work (Scotland) Act 1968 (which makes corresponding provision for Scotland);

(*b*) a person who is subject to the guardianship of a local social services authority under the provisions of this Act or the Mental Health (Scotland) Act 1960; or

(*c*) a person the functions of whose nearest relative under this Act or under the Mental Health (Scotland) Act 1960 are for the time being transferred to a local social services authority.

DEFINITIONS
"Patient": s.145(1).
"Hospital": s.145(1).
"Mental disorder": ss.1, 145(1).
"Local social services authority": s.145(1).
"Nearest relative": ss.26(3), 145(1).

GENERAL NOTE
This section obliges local authorities to arrange for visits to be made to certain patients in hospitals and mental nursing homes. It also requires local authorities to take such other steps in relation to the patients as would be expected to be taken by the patients' parents. There is no requirement that the patients concerned need to be receiving treatment for mental disorder.

Subs. (1)
Such other steps: For example, discussing the patient's condition with the hospital doctors and providing the patient with toys or reading matter.

After-care

After-care

117.—(1) This section applies to persons who are detained under section 3 above, or admitted to a hospital in pursuance of a hospital order made under section 37 above, or transferred to a hospital in pursuance of a transfer direction made under section 47 or 48 above, and then cease to be detained and leave hospital.

(2) It shall be the duty of the District Health Authority and of the local social services authority to provide, in co-operation with relevant voluntary agencies, after-care services for any person to whom this section applies until such time as the District Health Authority and the local social services authority are satisfied that the person concerned is no longer in need of such services.

(3) In this section "the District Health Authority" means the District Health Authority for the district, and "the local social services authority" means the local social services authority for the area in which the person concerned is resident or to which he is sent on discharge by the hospital in which he was detained.

DEFINITIONS
"Hospital": s.145(1).
"Hospital order": ss.37, 145(1).
"Transfer direction": ss.47, 145(1).
"Local social services authority" s.145(1), subs. (3).

GENERAL NOTE
This section imposes a duty to provide after-care services for certain categories of mentally disordered patients who have ceased to be detained and leave hospital. The Government argued that the inclusion of this section into the 1982 Act was unnecessary because a statutory duty already existed for local authorities to provide after-care facilities for mentally disordered patients. This duty is contained in para. 2(1) of Sched. 8 to the National Health Service Act 1977 which states: "A local social services authority may, with the Secretary of State's approval, and to such extent as he may direct shall, make arrangements for the purpose of the prevention of illness and for the care of persons suffering from illness and for the after-care of persons who have been so suffering." Approval for the provision by local

authorities of after-care facilities for people who are or have been suffering from mental disorder was given by the Secretary of State in D.H.S.S. Circular No. 19/75 and in para. 4 of that circular the Secretary of State directed local authorities to provide "centres (including training centres and day centres) or other facilities (including domiciliary facilities), whether in premises managed by the [local authority] or otherwise, for training or occupation of persons suffering from or who have been suffering from mental disorder." By virtue of s.22(1) of the 1977 Act a local authority acting under powers contained in Sched. 8 is required to co-operate with the health authority "in order to advance the health and welfare of the people of England and Wales".

The Government's argument that this section duplicates the provisions of the 1977 Act is not entirely correct because while the 1977 Act directs local authorities to provide for the after-care of the *generality* of mentally disordered persons, this section places a duty on local authorities and District Health Authorities to consider the after-care needs of each *individual* to whom the section applies.

Subs. (1)

Cease to be detained: This section does not apply to patients who have been granted leave of absence from hospital under s.17, above, as such patients remain liable to be detained during their leave.

Subs. (2)

Duty: In *Southwark L.B.C.* v. *Williams* [1971] Ch. 734, Lord Denning referred, at p.743, to the principle that "where an Act creates an obligation, and enforces that obligation in a specified manner, we take it to be a general rule that performance cannot be enforced in any other manner." This principle was applied in *Wyatt* v. *Hillingdon L.B.C.* 76 L.G.R. 727. As section 124 of this Act provides for the Secretary of State to exercise default powers when a local social services authority fails to carry out its functions, and as the Secretary of State is unlikely ever to invoke such powers, an aggrieved person would have great difficulty in enforcing the duty imposed by this section.

After-care services: These are not defined. They could include social work support in helping the ex-patient with problems of employment, accommodation or family relationships, the provision of domiciliary services, and the use of day centre or residential facilities.

Any person: The local authority and District Health Authority must assess the particular after-care needs of each person to whom this section applies.

Satisfied: Presumably a local authority and District Health Authority can only be satisfied that the person concerned is no longer in need of after-care services if they have monitored that person's progress in the community since discharge.

Functions of the Secretary of State

Code of practice

118.—(1) The Secretary of State shall prepare, and from time to time revise, a code of practice—

  (*a*) for the guidance of registered medical practitioners, managers and staff of hospitals and mental nursing homes and approved social workers in relation to the admission of patients to hospitals and mental nursing homes under this Act; and

  (*b*) for the guidance of registered medical practitioners and members of other professions in relation to the medical treatment of patients suffering from mental disorder.

(2) The code shall, in particular, specify forms of medical treatment in addition to any specified by regulations made for the purposes of section 57 above which in the opinion of the Secretary of State give rise to special concern and which should accordingly not be given by a registered medical practitioner unless the patient has consented to the treatment (or to a plan of treatment including that treatment) and a certificate in writing as to the matters mentioned in subsection (2)(*a*) and (*b*) of that section has been given by another registered medical practitioner, being a practitioner appointed for the purposes of this section by the Secretary of State.

(3) Before preparing the code or making any alteration in it the Secretary of State shall consult such bodies as appear to him to be concerned.

(4) The Secretary of State shall lay copies of the code and of any alteration in the code before Parliament; and if either House of Parliament passes a resolution requiring the code or any alteration in it to be withdrawn the Secretary of State shall withdraw the code or alteration and, where he withdraws the code, shall prepare a code in substitution for the one which is withdrawn.

(5) No resolution shall be passed by either House of Parliament under subsection (4) above in respect of a code or alteration after the expiration of the period of 40 days beginning with the day on which a copy of the code or alteration was laid before that House; but for the purposes of this subsection no account shall be taken of any time during which Parliament is dissolved or prorogued or during which both Houses are adjourned for more than four days.

(6) The Secretary of State shall publish the code as for the time being in force.

DEFINITIONS
"The managers": s.145(1).
"Hospital": s.145(1).
"Mental nursing home": s.145(1).
"Approved social worker": s.145(1).
"Patient": s.145(1).
"Medical treatment": s.145(1).
"Mental disorder": ss.1, 145(1).

GENERAL NOTE
This section imposes a duty on the Secretary of State to prepare, publish and from time to time revise, a Code of Practice for the guidance of those concerned in the admission and treatment of mentally disordered patients. The Code will not be mandatory in that professionals carrying out functions under this Act are not legally obliged to follow the advice contained in it. However, a failure to have regard to the Code could be used in court proceedings as evidence of negligence.

Subs. (1)
Secretary of State: The Secretary of State will direct the Mental Health Act Commission to submit proposals for the Code (Cmnd. 8405, para. 38).
Patients suffering from mental disorder: The guidance in the Code will not be confined to the treatment of *detained* patients.

Subs. (2)
Practitioner appointed . . . by the Secretary of State: The appointment will be made by the Mental Health Act Commission acting on the Secretary of State's behalf (s.121(2)(*a*)). For the purposes of exercising his functions under this section, the medical practitioner has the powers set out in s.119(2), below.

Practitioners approved for Part IV and s.118

119.—(1) The Secretary of State may make such provision as he may with the approval of the Treasury determine for the payment of remuneration, allowances, pensions or gratuities to or in respect of registered medical practitioners appointed by him for the purposes of Part IV of this Act and section 118 above and to or in respect of other persons appointed for the purposes of section 57(2)(*a*) above.

(2) A registered medical practitioner or other person appointed by the Secretary of State for the purposes of the provisions mentioned in subsection (1) above may, for the purpose of exercising his functions under those provisions, at any reasonable time—

    (*a*) visit and interview and, in the case of a registered medical practitioner, examine in private any patient detained in a mental nursing home; and (*b*) require the production of and inspect any records relating to the treatment of the patient in that home.

DEFINITIONS
"Patient": s.145(1).
"Nursing home": s.145(1).

GENERAL NOTE
This section provides for the payment of medical practitioners appointed by the Secretary of State to carry out certain functions under this Act, and for them to have access to detained patients and their records.

Subs. (2)
Anyone who obstructs a person in the exercise of his functions under this section commits an offence under s.129, below.

General protection of detained patients

120.—(1) The Secretary of State shall keep under review the exercise of the powers and the discharge of the duties conferred or imposed by this Act so far as relating to the detention of patients or to patients liable to be detained under this Act and shall make arrangements for persons authorised by him in that behalf—
(*a*) to visit and interview in private patients detained under this Act in hospitals and mental nursing homes; and
(*b*) to investigate—
   (i) any complaint made by a person in respect of a matter that occurred while he was detained under this Act in a hospital or mental nursing home and which he considers has not been satisfactorily dealt with by the managers of that hospital or mental nursing home; and
   (ii) any other complaint as to the exercise of the powers or the discharge of the duties conferred or imposed by this Act in respect of a person who is or has been so detained.
(2) The arrangements made under this section in respect of the investigation of complaints may exclude matters from investigation in specified circumstances and shall not require any person exercising functions under the arrangements to undertake or continue with any investigation where he does not consider it appropriate to do so.
(3) Where any such complaint as is mentioned in subsection (1)(*b*)(ii) above is made by a Member of Parliament and investigated under the arrangements made under this section the results of the investigation shall be reported to him.
(4) For the purpose of any such review as is mentioned in subsection (1) above or of carrying out his functions under arrangements made under this section any person authorised in that behalf by the Secretary of State may at any reasonable time—
(*a*) visit and interview and, if he is a registered medical practitioner, examine in private any patient in a mental nursing home; and
(*b*) require the production of and inspect any records relating to the detention or treatment of any person who is or has been detained in a mental nursing home.
(5) The matters in respect of which regulations may be made under section 6 of the Nursing Homes Act 1975 shall include the keeping of records relating to the detention and treatment of persons detained under this Act in a mental nursing home.
(6) The Secretary of State may make such provision as he may with the approval of the Treasury determine for the payment of remuneration, allowances, pensions or gratuities to or in respect of persons exercising

functions in relation to any such review as is mentioned in subsection (1) above or functions under arrangements made under this section.

(7) The powers and duties referred to in subsection (1) above do not include any power or duty conferred or imposed by Part VII of this Act.

DEFINITIONS
  "Patients": s.145(1).
  "Hospital": s.145(1).
  "Mental nursing home": s.145(1).
  "The managers": s.145(1).

GENERAL NOTE
  This section places duties relating to the general protection of detained patients on the Secretary of State. By virtue of s.121(2)(*b*), below, the Secretary of State will direct the Mental Health Act Commission to carry out these duties on his behalf. The duties are: (1) to keep under review the exercise of the powers conferred by this Act which relate to detained patients; (2) to make arrangements for authorised persons to visit and interview patients detained in hospital and mental nursing homes; and, (3) to make arrangements for authorised persons to investigate complaints.

Subs. (1)
  Keep under review: In carrying out their review the Commission will not be concerned with the question of whether an individual should continue to be detained, which is the function of the Mental Health Review Tribunal. Neither will it inspect and report on the general services that are available in psychiatric hospitals, which is the function of the Health Advisory Service and the Development Team for the Mentally Handicapped. The Commission does not have the power to enforce its recommendations.
  Powers and . . . duties: Excluding the powers or duties conferred or imposed by Part VII of this Act (subs. (7)).

  para. (b).
  That occurred: The Commission can investigate a complaint made by an ex-patient as long as the complaint relates to a period when the patient was detained under this Act.
  He considers: If the person authorised by the Commission concludes that the patient's complaint has been satisfactorily dealt with by the managers, he need not undertake an investigation; see subs. (2).
  Any other complaint: Which does not have to be made by the patient himself. If the complaint is made by a Member of Parliament; see subs. (3).
  Who is . . . detained: The Commission does not have the power to discharge the patient.

Subs. (4)
  Anyone who obstructs an authorised person in the exercise of his functions under this section commits an offence under s.129, below.

Mental Health Act Commission

121.—(1) Without prejudice to section 126(3) of the National Health Service Act 1977 (power to vary or revoke orders or directions) there shall continue to be a special health authority known as the Mental Health Act Commission established under section 11 of that Act.

(2) Without prejudice to the generality of his powers under section 13 of that Act, the Secretary of State shall direct the Commission to perform on his behalf—

  (*a*) the function of appointing registered medical practitioners for the purposes of Part IV of this Act and section 118 above and of appointing other persons for the purposes of section 57(2)(*a*) above; and

  (*b*) the functions of the Secretary of State under sections 61 and 120(1) and (4) above.

(3) The registered medical practitioners and other persons appointed for the purposes mentioned in subsection (2)(*a*) above may include members of the Commission.

(4) The Secretary of State may, at the request of or after consultation with the Commission and after consulting such other bodies as appear to him to be concerned, direct the Commission to keep under review the care and treatment, or any aspect of the care and treatment, in hospitals and mental nursing homes of patients who are not liable to be detained under this Act.

(5) For the purpose of any such review as is mentioned in subsection (4) above any person authorised in that behalf by the Commission may at any reasonable time—
  (*a*) visit and interview and, if he is a registered medical practitioner, examine in private any patient in a mental nursing home; and
  (*b*) require the production of and inspect any records relating to the treatment of any person who is or has been a patient in a mental nursing home.

(6) The Secretary of State may make such provision as he may with the approval of the Treasury determine for the payment of remuneration, allowances, pensions or gratuities to or in respect of persons exercising functions in relation to any such review as is mentioned in subsection (4) above.

(7) The Commission shall review any decision to withhold a postal packet (or anything contained in it) under subsection (1)(*b*) or (2) of section 134 below if an application in that behalf is made—
  (*a*) in a case under subsection (1)(*b*), by the patient; or
  (*b*) in a case under subsection (2), either by the patient or by the person by whom the postal packet was sent;
and any such application shall be made within six months of the receipt by the applicant of the notice referred to in subsection (6) of that section.

(8) On an application under subsection (7) above the Commission may direct that the postal packet which is the subject of the application (or anything contained in it) shall not be withheld and the managers in question shall comply with any such direction.

(9) The Secretary of State may by regulations make provision with respect to the making and determination of applications under subsection (7) above, including provision for the production to the Commission of any postal packet which is the subject of such an application.

(10) The Commission shall in the second year after its establishment and subsequently in every second year publish a report on its activities; and copies of every such report shall be sent by the Commission to the Secretary of State who shall lay a copy before each House of Parliament.

(11) Paragraph 9 of Schedule 5 to the said Act of 1977 (pay and allowances for chairmen and members of health authorities) shall have effect in relation to the Mental Health Act Commission as if references in sub-paragraphs (1) and (2) to the chairman included references to any member and as if sub-paragraphs (4) and (5) were omitted.

DEFINITIONS
  "Hospital": s.145(1).
  "Mental nursing home": s.145(1).
  "Patient": s.145(1).

TRANSITIONAL PROVISION
  Sched. 5, para. 5.

GENERAL NOTE
  This Act provides for the continuance (or establishment: Sched. 5, para. 5) of a special health authority known as the Mental Health Act Commission. The Commission will carry out certain functions on the Secretary of State's behalf (subs. (2)) and will review the decision to withhold a postal packet if an application is made to it to do so (subs. (7)). The Government intend that there will be about 70 members of the Commission who will be

lawyers, doctors, nurses, psychologists, social workers and laymen. The Commissioners, who will work part-time, will probably visit each of the 300 or so local hospitals and mental nursing homes in England and Wales once or twice a year. Visits to the four special hospitals will take place approximately once a month. "In their visits the Commission members will make themselves available to detained patients who wish to see them, will ensure that staff are helping patients to understand their legal position and their rights. They will look at patients' records of admission and renewal of detention and at records relating to treatment. They will also ensure that detained patients are satisfied with the handling of any complaints they may make" (Cmnd. 8405, para. 32). Commissioners do not have to give notice of their intention to visit a hospital or mental nursing home.

The functions that the Commission will perform on the Secretary of State's behalf are: (1) appointing medical practitioners and other persons for the purposes of proving a second opinion and verifying consent under the consent to treatment provisions contained in Part IV of this Act; (2) to receive and examine reports on treatment given under the consent to treatment provisions; and, (3) to keep this Act under review and to visit patients and investigate complaints.

The Commission can also be directed by the Secretary of State to keep under review the care and treatment of informal patients in hospitals and mental nursing homes (subs. (4)).

Subs. (2)
Generality of his powers. S.13 of the National Health Service Act 1977 authorises the Secretary of State to direct a special health authority to exercise on his behalf such of his functions relating to the health service as are specified in the directions.

Subs. (4)
May: The Government has announced that it does not intend to invoke this power straight away "since the Commission's first priority must be the responsibilities for detained patients", *per* Lord Trefgarne, H.L. Vol. 435, col. 541.

Subs. (5): Anyone who obstructs a person authorised by the Commission to carry out the review mentioned in subs. (4) commits an offence under s.129, below.

Provision of pocket money for in-patients in hospital

122.—(1) The Secretary of State may pay to persons who are receiving treatment as in-patients (whether liable to be detained or not) in special hospitals or other hospitals, being hospitals wholly or mainly used for the treatment of persons suffering from mental disorder, such amounts as he thinks fit in respect of their occasional personal expenses where it appears to him that they would otherwise be without resources to meet those expenses.

(2) For the purposes of the National Health Service Act 1977, the making of payments under this section to persons for whom hospital services are provided under that Act shall be treated as included among those services.

DEFINITIONS
"Patient": s.145(1).
"Special hospital": s.145(1).
"Hospital": s.145(1).
"Mental disorder": ss.1, 145(1).

GENERAL NOTE
This section enables a patient in a psychiatric hospital to receive "pocket money" to cover his personal expenses, if he is without other resources. The policy of the Department of Health and Social Security regarding the payment of supplementary benefit to such patients is to pay an allowance to patients who were admitted to psychiatric hospitals after November 17, 1975 (Supplementary Benefit Handbook, 1982 edn., para. 6.28). Patients who receive an allowance from the D.H.S.S. have "other resources" and are therefore not eligible for payments under this section. Health authorities remain responsible for making payments under this section to patients who were admitted to psychiatric hospitals before November 17, 1975.

Social services authorities can provide money to cover the occasional personal expenses of children under 16 who are, or have been, suffering from mental disorder if they are being cared for in residential accommodation provided under the National Health Service Act 1977; see Sched. 8, para. 2 of that Act.

Transfers to and from special hospitals

123.—(1) Without prejudice to any other provisions of this Act with respect to the transfer of patients, any patient who is for the time being liable to be detained in a special hospital under this Act (other than under section 35, 36 or 38 above) may, upon the directions of the Secretary of State, at any time be removed into any other special hospital.

(2) Without prejudice to any such provision, the Secretary of State may give directions for the transfer of any patient who is for the time being liable to be so detained into a hospital which is not a special hospital.

(3) Subsections (2) and (4) of section 19 above shall apply in relation to the transfer or removal of a patient under this section as they apply in relation to the transfer or removal of a patient from one hospital to another under that section.

DEFINITIONS
  "Patient": s.145(1).
  "Special hospital": s.145(1).
  "Hospital": s.145(1).

GENERAL NOTE
  This section enables the Secretary of State to direct the transfer of a patient from one special hospital to another (subs. (1)) and to direct the transfer of a patient from a special hospital to a hospital which is not a special hospital (subs. (2)).

Subs. (1)
  Other provisions: See s.19, above.
  Removed: For general provisions relating to the conveyance of patients, see s.137, below.

Default powers of Secretary of State

124.—(1) Where the Secretary of State is of the opinion, on complaint or otherwise, that a local social services authority have failed to carry out functions conferred or imposed on the authority by or under this Act or have in carrying out those functions failed to comply with any regulations relating to those functions, he may after such inquiry as he thinks fit make an order declaring the authority to be in default.

(2) Subsections (3) to (5) of section 85 of the National Health Service Act 1977 (which relates to orders declaring, among others, a local social services authority to be in default under that Act) shall apply in relation to an order under this section as they apply in relation to an order under that section.

DEFINITION
  "Local social services authority": s.145(1).

GENERAL NOTE
  This section enables the Secretary of State to make an order declaring a local social services authority which has failed to carry out functions conferred or imposed on it by this Act to be in default. The order will direct the authority to discharge its functions and if it fails to comply the Secretary of State may make an order transferring to himself such of the functions of the authority as he thinks fit (National Health Service Act 1977, s.85(3)). It is unlikely that the Secretary of State will ever use his powers under this Act to declare a local authority to be in default.
  The approach that the courts take to the enforcement of Act containing default powers is considered in the note to s.117(2), above.

Inquiries

125.—(1) The Secretary of State may cause an inquiry to be held in any case where he thinks it advisable to do so in connection with any matter arising under this Act.

(2) Subsections (2) or (5) of section 250 of the Local Government Act 1972 shall apply to any inquiry held under this Act, except that no local authority shall be ordered to pay costs under subsection (4) of that section in the case of any inquiry unless the authority is a party to the inquiry.

GENERAL NOTE

The Tribunals and Inquiries Act 1971 applies to an inquiry held under the section to the extent provided for in the Tribunals and Inquiries (Discretionary Inquiries) Order 1975 (S.I. 1975 No. 1379) art. 3, Sched., Pt. I, para. 39.

PART IX

OFFENCES

GENERAL NOTE

S.128 of the 1959 Act is not repealed by this Act. That section makes it an offence, (1) for a man on the staff of, or employed by, a hospital or mental nursing home to have extra-marital sexual intercourse with a woman who is receiving treatment for mental disorder in that hospital or home either as an out-patient or an in-patient, and (2) for a man to have extramarital sexual intercourse with a woman who is subject to his guardianship or is otherwise in his custody or care. No offence is committed under s.128 if the man did not know, and had no reason to suspect, that the woman was a mentally disordered patient.

Forgery, false statements, etc.

126.—(1) Any person who without lawful authority or excuse has in his custody or under his control any document to which this subsection applies, which is, and which he knows or believes to be, false within the meaning of Part I of the Forgery and Counterfeiting Act 1981, shall be guilty of an offence.

(2) Any person who without lawful authority or excuse makes or has in his custody or under his control, any document so closely resembling a document to which subsection (1) above applies as to be calculated to deceive shall be guilty of an offence.

(3) The documents to which subsection (1) above applies are any documents purporting to be—
  (a) an application under Part II of this Act;
  (b) a medical recommendation or report under this Act; and
  (c) any other document required or authorised to be made for any of the purposes of this Act.

(4) Any person who—
  (a) wilfully makes a false entry or statement in any application, recommendation, report, record or other document required or authorised to be made for any of the purposes of this Act; or
  (b) with intent to deceive, makes use of any such entry or statement which he knows to be false,
shall be guilty of an offence.

(5) Any person guilty of an offence under this section shall be liable—
  (a) on summary conviction, to imprisonment for a term not exceeding six months or to a fine not exceeding the statutory maximum, or to both;
  (b) on conviction on indictment, to imprisonment for a term not exceeding two years or to a fine of any amount, or to both.

DEFINITION
"Statutory maximum": s.145(2).

TRANSITION PROVISION
Sched. 5, para. 28.

GENERAL NOTE
Under this section it is an offence to either forge or make false statements in applications, medical recommendations or other documents made under this Act.

Subs. (1)
Any person: Or corporation (Interpretation Act s.5, Sched. 1).
False: Is defined in s.9 of the Forgery and Counterfeiting Act 1981.
Offence: Proceedings can be instituted by a local social services authority (s.130).

Subs. (2)
To deceive. "To deceive is . . . to induce a man to believe a thing to be true which is false, and which the person practising the deceit knows or believes to be false", *per* Buckley J., in *Re London and Globe Finance Corporation Ltd.* [1903] 1 Ch. 728, 732. In *Weltham* v. *D.P.P.* [1961] A.C. 103 Lord Radcliffe extended the scope of Buckley J.'s obiter remarks to include the inducing of a man to believe a thing to be false which is true.

Subs. (4)
False: An entry or statement may be false on account of what it omits, even though the statement or entry itself is literally true (*R.* v. *Lord Kylsant* [1932] 1 K.B. 442.

Ill-treatment of patients

127.—(1) It shall be an offence for any person who is an officer on the staff of or otherwise employed in, or who is one of the managers of, a hospital or mental nursing home—
 (*a*) to ill-treat or wilfully to neglect a patient for the time being receiving treatment for mental disorder as an in-patient in that hospital or home; or
 (*b*) to ill-treat or wilfully to neglect, on the premises of which the hospital or home forms part, a patient for the time being receiving such treatment there as an out-patient.
(2) It shall be an offence for any individual to ill-treat or wilfully to neglect a mentally disordered patient who is for the time being subject to his guardianship under this Act or otherwise in his custody or care (whether by virtue of any legal or moral obligation or otherwise).
(3) Any person guilty of an offence under this section shall be liable—
 (*a*) on summary conviction, to imprisonment for a term not exceeding six months or to a fine not exceeding the statutory maximum, or to both;
 (*b*) on conviction on indictment, to imprisonment for a term not exceeding two years or to a fine of any amount, or to both.
(4) No proceedings shall be instituted for an offence under this section except by or with the consent of the Director of Public Prosecutions.

DEFINITIONS
"The managers": s.145(1).
"Hospital": s.145(1).
"Mental nursing home": s.145(1).
"Patient": s.145(1).
"Mental disorder": ss.1, 145(1).
"Statutory maximum": s.145(2).

GENERAL NOTE
Under this section it is an offence for a person to ill-treat a patient who is either an in-patient or out-patient, subject to guardianship or otherwise in that persons custody or care.

Subs. (1)

Offence: Proceedings under this section can either be instituted by the Director of Public Prosecutions, or by a local social services authority with the Director's consent (s.130 and Subs. (4)).

Officer on the staff of the hospital: See the note on s.17(3), above.

Ill-treat: A single act, such as slapping the patient's face on one occasion, could constitute ill-treatment under this section (*R.* v. *Holmes* [1979] Crim.L.R. 52, Bodmin Crown Court).

Wilfully: The offender must have known that the patient was in a state of neglect. See further *R.* v. *Sheppard* [1981] A.C. 394 where the House of Lords considered the offence of wilfully neglecting a child under s.1 of the Children and Young Persons Act 1933.

Neglect: Is an objective state which is not defined in this Act. A failure to provide adequate medical aid to a patient would probably constitute neglect under this section; *cf.* s.1 of the 1933 Act, noted above.

Subs. (2)

Otherwise in his custody or care: The custodians or carers could include social workers, teachers, relatives or friends.

Assisting patients to absent themselves without leave, etc.

128.—(1) Where any person induces or knowingly assists another person who is liable to be detained in a hospital within the meaning of Part II of this Act or is subject to guardianship under this Act to absent himself without leave he shall be guilty of an offence.

(2) Where any person induces or knowingly assists another person who is in legal custody by virtue of section 137 below to escape from such custody he shall be guilty of an offence.

(3) Where any person knowingly harbours a patient who is absent without leave or is otherwise at large and liable to be retaken under this Act or gives him any assistance with intent to prevent, hinder or interfere with his being taken into custody or returned to the hospital or other place where he ought to be he shall be guilty of an offence.

(4) Any person guilty of an offence under this section shall be liable—

    (*a*) on summary conviction, to imprisonment for a term not exceeding six months or to a fine not exceeding the statutory maximum, or to both;

    (*b*) on conviction on indictment, to imprisonment for a term not exceeding two years or to a fine of any amount, or to both.

DEFINITIONS

"Hospital": s.145(1).
"Absent without leave": ss.18(6), 145(1).
"Patient": s.145(1).
"Hospital": s.145(1).

GENERAL NOTE

Under this section it is an offence to induce or to help a patient escape from custody or to absent himself from hospital without leave, or to harbour or prevent the recapture or return to hospital of such patients. Proceedings under this section can be instituted by local social services authorities (s.130).

Subs. (4)

Statutory maximum: For the purposes of this provision "statutory maximum" is defined in s.74 of the Criminal Justice Act 1982 as amended by s.145(2), below.

Obstruction

129.—(1) Any person who without reasonable cause—

    (*a*) refuses to allow the inspection of any premises; or

    (*b*) refuses to allow the visiting, interviewing or examination of any person by a person authorised in that behalf by or under this Act; or

(c) refuses to produce for the inspection of any person so authorised any document or record the production of which is duly
required by him; or

(d) otherwise obstructs any such person in the exercise of his
functions,

shall be guilty of an offence.

(2) Without prejudice to the generality of subsection (1) above, any
person who insists on being present when required to withdraw by a
person authorised by or under this Act to interview or examine a person
in private shall be guilty of an offence.

(3) Any person guilty of an offence under this section shall be liable on
summary conviction to imprisonment for a term not exceeding three
months or to a fine not exceeding level 4 on the standard scale or to both.

DEFINITION
"Standard scale": s.145(1).

GENERAL NOTE
This section specifies when a person commits the offence of obstruction under this Act.

Subs. (1)
Any person: Or corporation (Interpretation Act 1978, s.5, Sched. 1).
Obstructs: Cases on the offence of obstructing a constable in the execution of his duty
suggest that an offence under this section: (1) need not involve physical violence (*Hinchcliffe*
v. *Sheldon* [1955] 1 W.L.R. 1207); (2) is not committed on a mere refusal to answer
questions (*Rice* v. *Connolly* [1966] 2 Q.B. 414); and (3) might be committed if a verbal
warning of an impending inspection was given (*Green* v. *Moore* [1982] 2 W.L.R. 671). In
Swallow v. *London County Council* [1916] 1 K.B. 224, a case on the Weights and Measure
Act 1889, it was held that, in the absence of a legal duty to act, standing by and doing
nothing did not amount to an obstruction.
Offence: Proceedings can be instituted by a local social services authority (s.130).

Subs. (2)
In private: An approved social worker is not authorised to interview a patient in private
before making an application under Pt. II of this Act (*cf.* s.13(2)).

Prosecutions by local authorities

130. A local social services authority may institute proceedings for any
offence under this Part of this Act, but without prejudice to any provision
of this Part of this Act requiring the consent of the Director of Public
Prosecutions for the institution of such proceedings.

DEFINITION
"Local social services authority": s.145(1).

GENERAL NOTE
This section empowers a local social services authority to institute proceedings for an
offence alleged to have been committed under this Part.
Consent of the Director of Public Prosecutions: Is required by section 127, above.

PART X

MISCELLANEOUS AND SUPPLEMENTARY

Miscellaneous provisions

Informal admission of patients

131.—(1) Nothing in this Act shall be construed as preventing a patient
who requires treatment for mental disorder from being admitted to any

hospital or mental nursing home in pursuance of arrangements made in that behalf and without any application, order or direction rendering him liable to be detained under this Act, or from remaining in any hospital or mental nursing home in pursuance of such arrangements after he has ceased to be so liable to be detained.

(2) In the case of a minor who has attained the age of 16 years and is capable of expressing his own wishes, any such arrangements as are mentioned in subsection (1) above may be made, carried out and determined notwithstanding any right of custody or control vested by law in his parent or guardian.

DEFINITION
"Patient": s.145(1).
"Mental disorder": ss.1, 145(1).
"Hospital": s.145(1).
"Mental nursing home": s.145(1).

GENERAL NOTE
This section provides that a patient can either enter hospital for treatment on an informal basis, or remain in hospital on an informal basis once the authority for his original detention has come to an end. There are no special formalities which need to be observed for an informal patient to be admitted to a psychiatric hospital. Subject to s.5, above, informal patients can leave hospital when they like. They are not subject to the consent to treatment provisions contained in Pt. IV of this Act and are not entitled to compulsory after care services (*cf.* s.117).

There is no legally established mechanism for reviewing either the reasons for an informal patient's admission to hospital or the justification for his continued hospitalisation. Once an informal patient has been admitted to hospital no person or body is placed under any legal obligation to inform him of his legal status and the fact that he is free to leave hospital whenever he wishes (*cf.* s.132). At some date in the future the Mental Health Act Commission will have responsibility for keeping under review the care and treatment of informal patients (s.121(4)).

At the present time about 90 per cent. of those admitted to psychiatric hospitals and 95 per cent. of those resident there at any one time are informal patients.

Subs. (2)
This subsection provides that if a child is under 16, his parents or guardian can arrange for his informal admission. A child between 16 and 18 who is capable of expressing his own wishes can make up his own mind about admission. An interested party, such as a social worker, who considers that the informal admission of a child might not be in the child's best interests, could consider making the child a ward of court.

Attained the age: At the commencement of his sixteenth birthday (Family Law Reform Act 1969, s.9(1)).

Duty of managers of hospitals to give information to detained patients

132.—(1) The managers of a hospital or mental nursing home in which a patient is detained under this Act shall take such steps as are practicable to ensure that the patient understands—

    (a) under which of the provisions of this Act he is for the time being detained and the effect of that provision; and

    (b) what rights of applying to a Mental Health Review Tribunal are available to him in respect of his detention under that provision;

and those steps shall be taken as soon as practicable after the commencement of the patient's detention under the provision in question.

(2) The managers of a hospital or mental nursing home in which a patient is detained as aforesaid shall also take such steps as are practicable to ensure that the patient understands the effect, so far as relevant in his case, of sections 23, 25, 56 to 64, 66(1)(g), 118 and 120 above and section 134 below; and those steps shall be taken as soon as practicable after the commencement of the patient's detention in the hospital or nursing home.

(3) The steps to be taken under subsections (1) and (2) above shall include giving the requisite information both orally and in writing.

(4) The managers of a hospital or mental nursing home in which a patient is detained as aforesaid shall, except where the patient otherwise requests, take such steps as are practicable to furnish the person (if any) appearing to them to be his nearest relative with a copy of any information given to him in writing under subsections (1) and (2) above; and those steps shall be taken when the information is given to the patient or within a reasonable time thereafter.

DEFINITIONS
"The managers": s.145(1).
"Hospital": s.145(1).
"Mental nursing home": s.145(1).
"Nearest relative": ss.26(3), 145(1).

TRANSITIONAL PROVISION
Sched. 5, para. 19.

GENERAL NOTE
This section requires the managers of a hospital or mental nursing home to inform a detained patient of his legal position and rights. Unless the patient requests otherwise, the information must also be given to the patient's nearest relative.

Subs. (1)
Such steps as are practicable: Including giving the requisite information both orally and in writing (subs. (3)).
For the time being detained: This section requires the patient be informed when the section under which he is detained changes.
As soon as practicable: Having regard to the patient's state of mind and his ability to understand the information. If the patient is detained for six hours under the nurses holding power or if he is detained under one of the 72 hour orders, an attempt would have to be made to give him the required information within those periods even though he might not be capable of understanding it.

Subs. (2)
S.23, 25 and 66(1)(*a*) are concerned with the powers of the responsible medical officer, the hospital managers and the nearest relative to discharge the patient, ss.56 to 64 contain the consent to treatment provisions, s.118 provides for the publishing of a Code of Practice, s.120 is concerned with the Mental Health Act Commission's functions relating to the general protection of detained patients and s.134 deals with the withholding of detained patient's correspondence.

Subs. (3)
Orally and in writing: These are not alternatives.

Subs. (4)
Patient otherwise requests: It is submitted that the patient should be informed of the provisions of this subsection at the same time as he is given the information required by subss. (1) and (2).
Appearing to them: The hospital managers must take reasonable steps to ascertain the identity of the patient's nearest relative.
Nearest relative: Or acting nearest relative if an appointment has been made under s.29, above.

Duty of managers of hospitals to inform nearest relatives of discharge

133.—(1) Where a patient liable to be detained under this Act in a hospital or mental nursing home is to be discharged otherwise than by virtue of an order for discharge made by his nearest relative, the managers of the hospital or mental nursing home shall, subject to subsection (2) below, take such steps as are practicable to inform the person (if any) appearing to them to be the nearest relative of the patient; and that information shall, if practicable, be given at least seven days before the date of discharge.

(2) Subsection (1) above shall not apply if the patient or his nearest relative has requested that information about the patient's discharge should not be given under this section.

"Patient": s.145(1).
"Hospital": s.145(1).
"Mental nursing home": s.145(1).
"Nearest relative": ss.26(3), 145(1).
"The managers": s.145(1).

GENERAL NOTE
   This section places a duty on the managers of hospitals or mental nursing homes to inform the nearest relative of a detained patient that he is about to be discharged. The duty does not arise if either the patient or his nearest relative has requested that this information should not be given.
   Order for discharge made by his nearest relative: Under s.23, above.
   Appearing to them: Nearest relative: See the notes on s.132(4), above.
   Seven days: The duty under this section arises even though the patient is to be discharged immediately after the expiration of one of the short-term orders.

Correspondence of patients

   134.—(1) A postal packet addressed to any person by a patient detained in a hospital under this Act and delivered by the patient for dispatch may be withheld from the Post Office—
   (*a*) if that person has requested that communications addressed to him by the patient should be withheld; or
   (*b*) subject to subsection (3) below, if the hospital is a special hospital and the managers of the hospital consider that the postal packet is likely—
        (i) to cause distress to the person to whom it is addressed or to any other person (not being a person on the staff of the hospital); or
        (ii) to cause danger to any person;
and any request for the purposes of paragraph (*a*) above shall be made by a notice in writing given to the managers of the hospital, the registered medical practitioner in charge of the treatment of the patient or the Secretary of State.
   (2) Subject to subsection (3) below, a postal packet addressed to a patient detained in a special hospital under this Act may be withheld from the patient if, in the opinion of the managers of the hospital, it is necessary to do so in the interests of the safety of the patient or for the protection of other persons.
   (3) Subsections (1)(*b*) and (2) above do not apply to any postal packet addressed by a patient to, or sent to a patient by or on behalf of—
   (*a*) any Minister of the Crown or Member of either House of Parliament;
   (*b*) the Master or any other officer of the Court of Protection or any of the Lord Chancellor's Visitors;
   (*c*) the Parliamentary Commissioner for Administration, the Health Service Commissioner for England, the Health Service Commissioner for Wales or a Local Commissioner within the meaning of Part III of the Local Government Act 1974;
   (*d*) a Mental Health Review Tribunal;
   (*e*) a health authority within the meaning of the National Health Service Act 1977, a local social services authority, a Community

Health Council or a probation and after-care committee appointed under paragraph 2 of Schedule 3 to the Powers of Criminal Courts Act 1973;

(*f*) the managers of the hospital in which the patient is detained;

(*g*) any legally qualified person instructed by the patient to act as his legal adviser; or

(*h*) the European Commission of Human Rights or the European Court of Human Rights.

(4) The managers of a hospital may inspect and open any postal packet for the purposes of determining—

> (*a*) whether it is one to which subsection (1) or (2) applies, and
>
> (*b*) in the case of a postal packet to which subsection (1) or (2) above applies, whether or not it should be withheld under that subsection;

and the power to withhold a postal packet under either of those subsections includes power to withhold anything contained in it.

(5) Where a postal packet or anything contained in it is withheld under subsection (1) or (2) above the managers of the hospital shall record that fact in writing.

(6) Where a postal packet or anything contained in it is withheld under subsection (1)(*b*) or (2) above the managers of the hospital shall within seven days give notice of that fact to the patient and, in the case of a packet withheld under subsection (2) above, to the person (if known) by whom the postal packet was sent; and any such notice shall be given in writing and shall contain a statement of the effect of section 121(7) and (8) above.

(7) The functions of the managers of a hospital under this section shall be discharged on their behalf by a person on the staff of the hospital appointed by them for that purpose and different persons may be appointed to discharge different functions.

(8) The Secretary of State may make regulations with respect to the exercise of the powers conferred by this section.

(9) In this section "hospital" has the same meaning as in Part II of this Act, "postal packet" has the same meaning as in the Post Office Act 1953 and the provisions of this section shall have effect notwithstanding anything in section 56 of that Act.

DEFINITIONS
  "Patient": s.145(1).
  "Hospital": ss.34(2), 145(1).
  "Special hospital": s.145(1).
  "The managers": s.145(1).
  "Local social services authority": s.145(1).

GENERAL NOTE

This section provides authority for the inspection and withholding of a detained patient's out-going and in-coming mail. There is no power to withhold or inspect the mail of an informal patient. Note, however, that if either a detained or an informal patient is sent articles of potential danger, such as weapons, explosives or matches, through the mail, s.3(1) of the Criminal Law Act 1967 provides authority for hospital staff to take reasonable measures to prevent the patient from receiving or keeping the article in his possession (see further, Consultative Document, para. 10.28).

Subs. (1)

This subsection authorises a person appointed by the hospital managers (subss. (4), (7)) to withold a detained patient's out-going mail from the Post Office if the addressee has requested that the communications addressed to him by the patient should be withheld. The out-going mail of patients detained in a special hospital can also be withheld if it is felt that the communication is likely to cause distress or danger to any person. There is no provision equivalent to that which was contained in s.36 of the 1959 Act which authorised the withholding of out-going mail which would "be likely to prejudice the interests of the patient." A patient whose mail is withheld under para. (*b*) can appeal to the Mental Health Act Commission (s.121(7)).

Postal packet: Is defined in subs. (9).

Detained: This section does not apply to voluntary patients or to patients who are subject to guardianship.

Withheld: There is no authority for the hospital managers to censor correspondence, *i.e.* to strike out certain passages in a letter. However, there is power to withhold something contained in a postal packet; see subs. (4).

Managers of the hospital: Their functions shall be discharged by a member of the hospital staff (subs. (7)).

Subs. (2)

This subsection authorises the withholding of the in-coming mail of a patient detained in a special hospital if it is considered that such action is necessary in the interests of the safety of the patient or for the protection of other persons. Either the patient or the sender can appeal to the Mental Health Act Commission against a decision to withhold mail (s.121(7)). Note that there is no power to withhold in-coming mail on the ground that it would cause distress to the patient.

The managers: See subs. (7).

Subs. (3)

This subsection excludes the provisions of subss. (1)(*b*) and (2) in respect of certain bodies and individuals. Any person listed in this subsection can, under subs. 1(*a*), request that communications addressed to him by the patient be withheld.

Subs. (4)

The managers: See subs. (7).

Open: It will not be necessary to open the mail of patients who are not detained in special hospitals, as the requirements of subs. (1)(*a*) can be met by looking at the addresses on patients' out-going mail.

Subs. (9)

Postal packet: This is defined in s.87(1) of the Post Office Act 1953 as "a letter, postcard, reply postcard, newspaper, printed packet, sample packet, or parcel, and every packet or article transmissible by post, and includes a telegram." S.56 of the 1953 Act is concerned with the criminal diversion of letters from addressees.

Warrant to search for and remove patients

135.—(1) If it appears to a justice of the peace, on information on oath laid by an approved social worker, that there is reasonable cause to suspect that a person believed to be suffering from mental disorder—

(*a*) has been, or is being, ill-treated, neglected or kept otherwise than under proper control, in any place within the jurisdiction of the justice, or

(*b*) being unable to care for himself, is living alone in any such place, the justice may issue a warrant authorising any constable named in the warrant to enter, if need be by force, any premises specified in the warrant in which that person is believed to be, and, if thought fit, to remove him to a place of safety with a view to the making of an application in respect of him under Part II of this Act, or of other arrangements for his treatment or care.

(2) If it appears to a justice of the peace, on information on oath laid by any constable or other person who is authorised by or under this Act or under section 83 of the Mental Health (Scotland) Act 1960 to take a patient to any place, or to take into custody or retake a patient who is liable under this Act or under the said section 83 to be so taken or retaken—

(*a*) that there is reasonable cause to believe that the patient is to be found on premises within the jurisdiction of the justice; and

(b) that admission to the premises has been refused or that a refusal of such admission is apprehended,

the justice may issue a warrant authorising any constable named in the warrant to enter the premises, if need be by force, and remove the patient.

(3) A patient who is removed to a place of safety in the execution of a warrant issued under this section may be detained there for a period not exceeding 72 hours.

(4) In the execution of a warrant issued under subsection (1) above, the constable to whom it is addressed shall be accompanied by an approved social worker and by a registered medical practitioner, and in the execution of a warrant issued under subsection (2) above the constable to whom it is addressed may be accompanied—

(a) by a registered medical practitioner;

(b) by any person authorised by or under this Act or under section 83 of the Mental Health (Scotland) Act 1960 to take or retake the patient.

(5) It shall not be necessary in any information or warrant under subsection (1) above to name the patient concerned.

(6) In this section "place of safety" means residential accommodation provided by a local social services authority under Part III of the National Assistance Act 1948 or under paragraph 2 of Schedule 8 to the National Health Service Act 1977, a hospital as defined by this Act, a police station, a mental nursing home or residential home for mentally disordered persons or any other suitable place the occupier of which is willing temporarily to receive the patient.

DEFINITIONS
"Approved social worker": s.145(1).
"Mental disorder": ss.1, 145(1).
"Patient": s.145(1).
"Local social services authority": s.145(1).
"Hospital": ss.34(2), 145(1).
"Mental nursing home": s.145(1).

GENERAL NOTE
This section provides for a magistrate to issue a warrant authorising a policeman to enter private premises, using force if necessary, for the purpose of removing a mentally disordered person to a place of safety for up to 72 hours so that his condition can be assessed. Warrants under this section are rarely issued (Cmnd. 7320, para. 2.20).

Subs. (1)
Approved social worker: Only an approved social worker can apply for a warrant to be issued under this subsection.
A person: This procedure can be invoked even though the name of the mentally disordered person is not known (subs. (5)).
Living alone: The suggestion by the Royal College of Psychiatrists that this section should also provide for a situation where two mentally disordered people were living together and were unable to care for themselves has not been adopted (Cmnd. 7320, para. 2.21).
Constable: Who must be accompanied by an approved social worker and a doctor (subs. (4)).
If thought fit: The doctor would be able to advise the policeman on whether the person should be removed to a place of safety.

Subs. (2)
This subsection provides for the issue of a warrant to a policeman to enter premises, using force if necessary, for the purposes of taking or retaking a patient into custody.
Any constable: Who may be accompanied by a doctor or any other person, such as an approved social worker, who is authorised to take or retake the patient (subs. (4)).

Subs. (3)

Removed: For general provisions relating to the conveyance of patients from one place to another, see section 137, below.

Place of safety: Is defined in subs. (6). It is submitted that detention in a police station should be avoided wherever possible.

72 hours: If the person escapes from the place of safety he cannot be retaken after the 72 hours have expired (s.138(3)).

Subs. (6)

Any other suitable place: Which could be the home of a relative or friend.

Mentally disordered persons found in public places

136.—(1) If a constable finds in a place to which the public have access a person who appears to him to be suffering from mental disorder and to be in immediate need of care or control, the constable may, if he thinks it necessary to do so in the interests of that person or for the protection of other persons, remove that person to a place of safety within the meaning of section 135 above.

(2) A person removed to a place of safety under this section may be detained there for a period not exceeding 72 hours for the purpose of enabling him to be examined by a registered medical practitioner and to be interviewed by an approved social worker and of making any necessary arrangements for his treatment or care.

DEFINITIONS

"Mental disorder": ss.1, 145(1).

"Approved social worker": s.145(1).

GENERAL NOTE

This section empowers a policeman to remove a person from a public place to a place of safety if he considers that the person is suffering from mental disorder and is in immediate need of care or control. The person can be detained in a place of safety for up to 72 hours so that he can be examined by a doctor and interviewed by an approved social worker in order that suitable arrangements can be made for his treatment or care. This power is usually invoked "where a person's abnormal behaviour is causing nuisance or offence" (Cmnd. 7320, para. 2.22).

Subs. (1)

Appears to him: Although some concern has been expressed about the ability of the police to recognise persons who are mentally disordered, research studies suggest that "the police are able to diagnose psychiatric patients and [are] efficient sources of referrals", P. Bean, *Compulsory Admissions to Mental Hospitals*, 1980, p. 73.

Remove: A person does not have to commit an offence before the police can use their power to remove. However, in most cases the behaviour of the person removed would have justified him being charged with an offence against public order.

Subs. (2)

Place of safety: The police are advised by the "Home Office Consolidated Circular to the Police on Crime and Kindred Matters" that a person who is removed under this section should normally be taken direct to a hospital, or, if this is not practicable, that the assistance of a social worker should immediately be sought; see the Butler Report, para. 9.3 and Appendix 7. A hospital is not legally obliged to admit a patient who has been removed under this section.

May be detained: Not necessarily by the police.

72 hours: The power to detain the person under this section will lapse as soon as he has been examined and interviewed and suitable arrangements have been made for his treatment or care. If a person escapes from the place of safety he cannot be retaken after the 72 hours have expired (s.138(3)).

Approved social worker: The role of the approved social worker "includes contacting the detained person's relatives, and ascertaining whether there is a history of psychiatric treatment. Should admission to hospital prove necessary this information may indicate which hospital would be most suitable; but he should always consider whether any course other than admission to hospital is appropriate. Knowing the range of resources which is available he is in a position to assess all the circumstances and is responsible for making sure whether treatment in hospital is the only solution" (Butler Report, para. 9.1).

Provisions as to custody, conveyance and detention

137.—(1) Any person required or authorised by or by virtue of this Act to be conveyed to any place or to be kept in custody or detained in a place of safety or at any place to which he is taken under section 42(6) above shall, while being so conveyed, detained or kept, as the case may be, be deemed to be in legal custody.

(2) A constable or any other person required or authorised by or by virtue of this Act to take any person into custody, or to convey or detain any person shall, for the purposes of taking him into custody or conveying or detaining him, have all the powers, authorities, protection and privileges which a constable has within the area for which he acts as constable.

(3) In this section "convey" includes any other expression denoting removal from one place to another.

GENERAL NOTE

This section specifies the circumstances when a person is deemed to be in legal custody and provides that a person who is required or authorised to detain or convey a person who is in legal custody shall have the powers of a constable when so acting. A person who escapes from legal custody can be retaken under s.138 below.

Subs. (2)

Powers . . . which a constable has: Which include the power to arrest a person who is wilfully obstructing a constable in the execution of his duty (Police Act 1964, s.51(3)). Reasonable force can be used in effecting an arrest (Criminal Law Act 1967, s.3). See further, L. H. Leigh, *Police Powers in England and Wales*, 1975.

Retaking of patients escaping from custody

138.—(1) If any person who is in legal custody by virtue of section 137 above escapes, he may, subject to the provisions of this section, be retaken—

(a) in any case, by the person who had his custody immediately before the escape, or by any constable or approved social worker;
(b) if at the time of the escape he was liable to be detained in a hospital within the meaning of Part II of this Act, or subject to guardianship under this Act, by any other person who could take him into custody under section 18 above if he had absented himself without leave.

(2) A person to whom paragraph (*b*) of subsection (1) above applies shall not be retaken under this section after the expiration of the period within which he could be retaken under section 18 above if he had absented himself without leave on the day of the escape unless he is subject to a restriction order under Part III of this Act or an order or direction having the same effect as such an order; and subsection (4) of the said section 18 shall apply with the necessary modifications accordingly.

(3) A person who escapes while being taken to or detained in a place of safety under section 135 or 136 above shall not be retaken under this section after the expiration of the period of 72 hours beginning with the time when he escapes or the period during which he is liable to be so detained, whichever expires first.

(4) This section, so far as it relates to the escape of a person liable to be detained in a hospital within the meaning of Part II of this Act, shall apply in relation to a person who escapes—

(a) while being taken to or from such a hospital in pursuance of regulations under section 19 above, or of any order, direction or authorisation under Part III or VI of this Act (other than under section 35, 36, 38, 53, 83 or 85) or under section 123 above; or

(b) while being taken to or detained in a place of safety in pursuance of an order under Part III of this Act (other than under section 35, 36 or 38 above) pending his admission to such a hospital,

as if he were liable to be detained in that hospital and, if he had not previously been received in that hospital, as if he had been so received.

(5) In computing for the purposes of the power to give directions under section 37(4) above and for the purposes of sections 37(5) and 40(1) above the period of 28 days mentioned in those sections, no account shall be taken of any time during which the patient is at large and liable to be retaken by virtue of this section.

(6) Section 21 above shall, with any necessary modifications, apply in relation to a patient who is at large and liable to be retaken by virtue of this section as it applies in relation to a patient who is absent without leave and references in that section to section 18 above shall be construed accordingly.

DEFINITIONS
"Approved social worker": s.145(1).
"Absent without leave": ss.18(6), 145(1).
"Restriction order": ss.41, 145(1).
"Patient": s.145(1).

GENERAL NOTE
This section provides for the retaking of people who have escaped from legal custody. A person who assists another person who is in legal custody to escape commits an offence under s.128(2), above.

Subs. (1)
Hospital within the meaning of Pt. II: See section 34(2), above.

Protection for acts done in pursuance of this Act

139.—(1) No person shall be liable, whether on the ground of want of jurisdiction or on any other ground, to any civil or criminal proceedings to which he would have been liable apart from this section in respect of any act purporting to be done in pursuance of this Act or any regulations or rules made under this Act, or in, or in pursuance of anything done in, the discharge of functions conferred by any other enactment on the authority having jurisdiction under Part VII of this Act, unless the act was done in bad faith or without reasonable care.

(2) No civil proceedings shall be brought against any person in any court in respect of any such act without the leave of the High Court; and no criminal proceedings shall be brought against any person in any court in respect of any such act except by or with the consent of the Director of Public Prosecutions.

(3) This section does not apply to proceedings for an offence under this Act, being proceedings which, under any other provision of this Act, can be instituted only by or with the consent of the Director of Public Prosecutions.

(4) This section does not apply to proceedings against the Secretary of State or against a health authority within the meaning of the National Health Service Act 1977.

(5) In relation to Northern Ireland the reference in this section to the Director of Public Prosecutions shall be construed as a reference to the Director of Public Prosecutions for Northern Ireland.

TRANSITIONAL PROVISION
Sched. 5, para. 28.

GENERAL NOTE

This section provides: (1) that, apart from proceedings against a health authority or the Secretary of State and proceedings under s.127, above, no civil or criminal proceedings can be brought against any person in any court in respect of an act purporting to be done under this Act without the leave of the High Court or the Director of Public Prosecutions; and (2) for such proceedings to succeed the court must be satisfied that the person proceeded against acted in bad faith or without reasonable care. It "is concerned only with the protection of individuals personally against legal proceedings for alleged wrongs. The section does not, therefore, affect the right of a patient or his friends to apply to the High Court at any time for discharge by means of a writ of *habeas corpus*, so that the lawfulness of his detention can be tested" (Consultative Document, para. 9.3).

Subs. (1)

Person: Or corporation (Interpretation Act 1978, s.5, Sched. 1).

Act done in pursuance of this Act: Nearly all acts done "in pursuance of this Act" will relate to detained patients. During the passage of the 1982 Act the Government resisted an amendment to exclude the provisions of this section for voluntary patients on the ground that this would remove the protection given to someone who purports to do something under the Act when he *believes* that the patient is a detained patient. The Minister for Health gave the following illustration in support of this argument: "An ambulance man . . . has a patient in his charge whom he believes is a detained patient because he is told so. Therefore, he is told that he should prevent the patient escaping. If the patient attempts to go off and he takes steps to stop him escaping, he might be liable to an action thereafter, but he would be protected if we retain [this section] with its present wording" (H.C., Vol. 29, col. 173). This interpretation has not yet been tested in the High Court but there is Crown Court authority for the contention that this section does not cover acts done in respect of informal patients; see *R.* v. *Runighian* [1977] Crim.L.R. 361.

In *Pountney* v. *Griffiths* [1976] A.C. 314, the House of Lords quashed the conviction of a nurse who had been charged with assaulting a patient when ushering the patient to his ward after a visit from the patient's family, on the ground that leave to prosecute had not been obtained under subsection (2) of this section. Their Lordships approved the finding of Lord Widgery C.J. in the Court of Appeal that, "when a male nurse is on duty and exercising his functions of controlling the patients in the hospital, acts done in pursuance of such control, are acts within the scope of [this section] and are thus protected by the section." Although this Act provides for the detention and treatment of patients, it nowhere explicitly refers to the control of patients. The House held that treatment necessarily involves the exercise of discipline and control, and that suitable arrangements for visits to patients by family and friends was an obvious part of the patient's treatment. If the assault had taken place when the nurse was not on duty, this section would not apply.

In the unreported case of *Ashingdane* v. *Secretary of State for Social Services*, February 18, 1980, the Court of Appeal held that the immunity conferred by this section is confined to an act done by a person to whom authority to do an act of that type is expressly or impliedly conferred by this Act or by regulations made under it. Applying this test the Court held that the decision of a nurses union not to allow patients who were subject to restriction orders to be transferred to a particular hospital was a policy decision which fell outside their express or implied authority and was not, therefore, covered by this section.

Acted in bad faith or without reasonable care: In *Richardson* v. *London County Council* [1957] 1 W.L.R. 751 it was held: (1) that whether a person has acted in bad faith or without reasonable care is a question of fact with the burden of proof lying with the applicant; and (2) that this section offers protection even though the person proceeded against acted either without jurisdiction or misconstrued this Act, as long as the misconstruction was one which this Act was reasonably capable of bearing. Although a mistake about the law can therefore provide a defence to an action, it is submitted that professional people who have functions placed upon them by this Act are under an obligation to acquire knowledge about the law they are operating.

Subs. (2)

Leave: The procedure for applications for leave of the High Court is contained in R.S.C., Ord. 32, r.9. Proceedings instituted without leave being obtained are a nullity (*Pountney* v. *Griffiths*, above). An appeal lies to the Court of Appeal against a judge's decision but either the leave of the judge or of the Court of Appeal is required before the appeal can be made (*Moore* v. *Commissioner of Metropolitan Police* [1968] 1 Q.B. 26).

Subs. (3)
  Consent of the Director of Public Prosecutions: Is required for proceedings under s.127, above.

Notification of hospitals having arrangements for reception of urgent cases

140. It shall be the duty of every Regional Health Authority and in Wales every District Health Authority to give notice to every local social services authority for an area wholly or partly comprised within the region or district, as the case may be, of the Authority specifying the hospital or hospitals administered by the Authority in which arrangements are from time to time in force for the reception, in case of special urgency, of patients requiring treatment for mental disorder.

DEFINITIONS
  "Local social services authority": s.145(1).
  "Hospital": s.145(1).
  "Patient": s.145(1).
  "Mental disorder": ss.1, 145(1).

GENERAL NOTE
  Reception: This section does not oblige the specified hospitals to admit patients.
  Requiring treatment: Either as informal or compulsory patients.

Members of Parliament suffering from mental illness

141.—(1) Where a member of the House of Commons is authorised to be detained on the ground (however formulated) that he is suffering from mental illness, it shall be the duty of the court, authority or person on whose order or application, and of any registered medical practitioner upon whose recommendation or certificate, the detention was authorised, and of the person in charge of the hospital or other place in which the member is authorised to be detained, to notify the Speaker of the House of Commons that the detention has been authorised.

(2) Where the Speaker receives a notification under subsection (1) above, or is notified by two members of the House of Commons that they are credibly informed that such an authorisation has been given, the Speaker shall cause the member to whom the notification relates to be visited and examined by two registered medical practitioners appointed in accordance with subsection (3) below.

(3) The registered medical practitioners to be appointed for the purposes of subsection (2) above shall be appointed by the President of the Royal College of Psychiatrists and shall be practitioners appearing to the President to have special experience in the diagnosis or treatment of mental disorders.

(4) The registered medical practitioners appointed in accordance with subsection (3) above shall report to the Speaker whether the member is suffering from mental illness and is authorised to be detained as such.

(5) If the report is to the effect that the member is suffering from mental illness and authorised to be detained as aforesaid, the Speaker shall at the expiration of six months from the date of the report, if the House is then sitting, and otherwise as soon as may be after the House next sits, again cause the member to be visited and examined by two such registered medical practitioners as aforesaid, and the registered medical practitioners shall report as aforesaid.

(6) If the second report is that the member is suffering from mental illness and authorised to be detained as mentioned in subsection (4) above, the Speaker shall forthwith lay both reports before the House of Commons, and thereupon the seat of the member shall become vacant.

(7) Any sums required for the payment of fees and expenses to registered medical practitioners acting in relation to a member of the House of Commons under this section shall be defrayed out of moneys provided by Parliament.

DEFINITIONS
  "Hospital": s.145(1).
  "Mental disorder": ss.1, 145(1).

GENERAL NOTE
  This section sets out the procedure for vacating the seat of a Member of Parliament who has been detained on the ground that he is suffering from mental illness.

Subs. (1)
  Mental illness: This section does not apply to an M.P. who is detained on the ground that he is suffering from any other form of mental disorder.

Pay, pensions, etc., of mentally disordered persons

142.—(1) Where a periodic payment falls to be made to any person by way of pay or pension or otherwise in connection with the service or employment of that or any other person, and the payment falls to be made directly out of moneys provided by Parliament or the Consolidated Fund, or other moneys administered by or under the control or supervision of a government department, the authority by whom the sum in question is payable, if satisfied after considering medical evidence that the person to whom it is payable (referred to in this section as "the patient") is incapable by reason of mental disorder of managing and administering his property and affairs, may, instead of paying the sum to the patient, apply it in accordance with subsection (2) below.

(2) The authority may pay the sum or such part of it as they think fit to the institution or person having the care of the patient, to be applied for his benefit and may pay the remainder (if any) or such part of the remainder as they think fit—

  (*a*) to or for the benefit of persons who appear to the authority to be members of the patient's family or other persons for whom the patient might be expected to provide if he were not mentally disordered, or

  (*b*) in reimbursement, with or without interest, of money applied by any person either in payment of the patient's debts (whether legally enforceable or not) or for the maintenance or other benefit of the patient or such persons as are mentioned in paragraph (*a*) above.

(3) In this section "government department" does not include a Northern Ireland department.

DEFINITION
  "Mental disorder": ss.1, 145(1).

GENERAL NOTE
  Under this section provision is made in the case of any pay, pension or similar payment payable by Parliament or the Government, for direct payment to the institution or person having the care of the patient. Any sums which remain can be paid to members of the patient's family, or to other persons for whom the patient might be expected to provide were he not mentally disordered, or to reimburse people who have paid his debts or helped to maintain him or his family.

Supplemental

General provisions as to regulations, orders and rules

143.—(1) Any power of the Secretary of State or the Lord Chancellor to make regulations, orders or rules under this Act shall be exercisable by statutory instrument.

(2) Any Order in Council under this Act and any statutory instrument containing regulations or rules made under this Act shall be subject to annulment in pursuance of a resolution of either House of Parliament.

(3) No order shall be made under section 68(4) or 71(3) above unless a draft of it has been approved by a resolution of each House of Parliament.

Power to amend local Acts

144. Her Majesty may by Order in Council repeal or amend any local enactment so far as appears to Her Majesty to be necessary in consequence of this Act.

Interpretation

145.—(1) In this Act, unless the context otherwise requires—
"absent without leave" has the meaning given to it by section 18 above and related expressions shall be construed accordingly;
"application for admission for assessment" has the meaning given in section 2 above;
"application for admission for treatment" has the meaning given in section 3 above;
"approved social worker" means an officer of a local social services authority appointed to act as an approved social worker for the purposes of this Act;
"hospital" means—
> (*a*) any health service hospital within the meaning of the National Health Service Act 1977; and
> (*b*) any accommodation provided by a local authority and used as a hospital or on behalf of the Secretary of State under that Act;

and "hospital within the meaning of Part II of this Act" has the meaning given in section 34 above;
"hospital order" and "guardianship order" have the meanings respectively given in section 37 above;
"interim hospital order" has the meaning given in section 38 above;
"local social services authority" means a council which is a local authority for the purpose of the Local Authority Social Services Act 1970;
"the managers" means—
> (*a*) in relation to a hospital vested in the Secretary of State for the purposes of his functions under the National Health Service Act 1977, and in relation to any accommodation provided by a local authority and used as a hospital by or on behalf of the Secretary of State under that Act, the District Health Authority or special health authority responsible for the administration of the hospital;
> (*b*) in relation to a special hospital, the Secretary of State;
> (*c*) in relation to a mental nursing home registered in pursuance of the Nursing Homes Act 1975, the person or persons registered in respect of the home;

and in this definition "hospital" means a hospital within the meaning of Part II of this Act;
"medical treatment" includes nursing, and also includes care, habilitation and rehabilitation under medical supervision;
"mental disorder", "severe mental impairment", "mental impairment" and "psychopathic disorder" have the meanings given in section 1 above;

"mental nursing home" has the same meaning as in the Nursing
    Homes Act 1975;
"nearest relative", in relation to a patient, has the meaning given in
    Part II of this Act;
"patient" (except in Part VII of this Act) means a person suffering
    or appearing to be suffering from mental disorder;
"restriction direction" has the meaning given to it by section 49
    above;
"restriction order" has the meaning given to it by section 41 above;
"special hospital" has the same meaning as in the National Health
    Service Act 1977;
"standard scale" has the meaning given in section 75 of the Criminal
    Justice Act 1982;
"transfer direction" has the meaning given to it by section 47 above.

(2) "Statutory maximum" has the meaning given in section 74 of the
Criminal Justice Act 1982 and for the purposes of section 128(4)(*a*)
above—

(*a*) subsection (1) of section 74 shall have effect as if after the words
    "England and Wales" there were inserted the words "or Northern
    Ireland"; and
(*b*) section 32 of the Magistrates' Courts Act 1980 shall extend to
    Northern Ireland.

(3) In relation to a person who is liable to be detained or subject to
guardianship by virtue of an order or direction under Part III of this Act
(other than under section 35, 36, or 38), any reference in this Act to any
enactment contained in Part II of this Act or in section 66 or 67 above
shall be construed as a reference to that enactment as it applies to that
person by virtue of Part III of this Act.

TRANSITIONAL PROVISION
    Sched. 5, para. 4(1)(*b*).

GENERAL NOTE
Subs. (1).
    Approved social worker: See the transitional provision, noted above.
    Hospital: This definition includes hospitals which do not specialise in mental disorder and
excludes prison hospitals and private hospitals.
    Local social services authority: Is a non-metropolitan county council, a metropolitan
district council, a London borough council or the Common Council of the City of London
(Local Authority Social Services Act 1970, s.1).
    The managers: A person who runs a mental nursing home must be registered under s.3
of the Nursing Homes Act 1975.
    Medical treatment: The definition of this term is wide enough to cover all measures
employed in the management of a patient. "Habilitation" is defined in the *Shorter Oxford
English Dictionary* as "the action of enabling or endowing with ability or fitness, capacitation,
qualification." An illustration of the distinction between habilitation and rehabilitation was
given by Mr. Terry Davis at the Special Standing Committee: " 'Habilitation' would cover
those cases in which someone, probably a child, was so severely mentally impaired that he
had never learnt certain social skills such as being able to eat or communicate in some way.
The remedying of that impairment cannot be called 'rehabilitation' because that person
never had those skills, so one has to use the word 'habilitation' in its technical sense."
(Sitting of June 22, 1982).
    Mental nursing home: Is defined in s.2 of the Nursing Homes Act 1975 as any premises
used, or intended to be used, for the reception of, and the provision of nursing or other
medical treatment (including care and training under supervision) for, one or more mentally
disordered patients, whether exclusively or in common with others. The definition excludes
hospitals or any other premises managed by a Government department or provided by a
local authority.
    Nearest relative: Is defined in s.26, above.

Patient: The voting rights of voluntary patients are contained in the Representation of the People Act 1983. Patients who are detained in a hospital or a mental nursing home under this Act are not entitled to have their names placed on the Register of Electors.

Special hospital: This is defined in s.4 of the National Health Service Act 1977 as an establishment for "persons subject to detention under the Mental Health Act 1983 who in the Secretary of State's opinion require treatment under conditions of special security on account of their dangerous, violent or criminal propensities." The four special hospitals at Broadmoor, Park Lane, Moss Side and Rampton are managed directly by the Department of Health and Social Security who apply fairly stringent criteria for admission. "The Department attach due weight to the consideration that admission to a special hospital entails subjecting patients to very close supervision and restriction of movement and taking them far from their homes and families" (Butler Report, para. 2·18). Although a patient who has been sent to a special hospital must have been detained under this Act, there is no requirement that the detention must have been ordered by a court.

Application to Scotland

146. Sections 42(6), 80, 88 (and so far as applied by that section sections 18, 22 and 138), 104(4), 110 (and so much of Part VII of this Act as is applied in relation to Scotland by that section), 116, 122, 128 (except so far as it relates to patients subject to guardianship), 137, 139(1), 141, 142, 143 (so far as applicable to any Order in Council extending to Scotland) and 144 above shall extend to Scotland together with any amendment or repeal by this Act or any provision of Schedule 5 to this Act relating to any enactment which so extends; but, except as aforesaid and except so far as it relates to the interpretation or commencement of the said provisions, this Act shall not extend to Scotland.

DEFINITION
"Patient": s.145(1).

GENERAL NOTE
This section provides for a limited application of this Act to Scotland.

Application to Northern Ireland

147. Sections 81, 82, 86, 87, 88 (and so far as applied by that section sections 18, 22, and 138), 104(4), 110 (and so much of Part VII as is applied in relation to Northern Ireland by that section), section 128 (except so far as it relates to patients subject to guardianship), 137, 139, 141, 142, 143 (so far as applicable to any Order in Council extending to Northern Ireland) and 144 above shall extend to Northern Ireland together with any amendment or repeal by this Act of or any provision of Schedule 5 to this Act relating to any enactment which so extends; but except as aforesaid and except so far as it relates to the interpretation or commencement of the said provisions, this Act shall not extend to Northern Ireland.

DEFINITION
"Patient": s.145(1).

GENERAL NOTE
This section provides for a limited application of this Act to Northern Ireland.

Consequential and transitional provisions and repeals

148.—(1) Schedule 4 (consequential amendments) and Schedule 5 (transitional and saving provisions) to this Act shall have effect but without prejudice to the operation of sections 15 to 17 of the Interpretation Act 1978 (which relate to the effect of repeals).

(2) Where any amendment in Schedule 4 to this Act affects an enactment amended by the Mental Health (Amendment) Act 1982 the amendment in Schedule 4 shall come into force immediately after the provision of the Act of 1982 amending that enactment.

(3) The enactments specified in Schedule 6 to this Act are hereby repealed to the extent mentioned in the third column of that Schedule.

Short title, commencement and application to Scilly Isles

149.—(1) This Act may be cited as the Mental Health Act 1983.

(2) Subject to subsection (3) below and Schedule 5 to this Act, this Act shall come into force on 30th September 1983.

(3) Sections 35, 36, 38 and 40(3) above shall come into force on such day (not being earlier than the said 30th September) as may be appointed by the Secretary of State and a different day may be appointed for each of those sections or for different purposes of any of those sections.

(4) Section 130(4) of the National Health Service Act 1977 (which provides for the extension of that Act to the Isles of Scilly) shall have effect as if the references to that Act included references to this Act.

SCHEDULES

SCHEDULE 1

APPLICATION OF CERTAIN PROVISIONS TO PATIENTS SUBJECT TO HOSPITAL AND GUARDIANSHIP ORDERS

PART I

PATIENTS NOT SUBJECT TO SPECIAL RESTRICTIONS

1. Sections 9, 10, 17, 21, 24(3) and (4), 26 to 28, 31, 32, 34, 67 and 76 shall apply in relation to the patient without modification.

2. Sections 16, 18, 19, 20, 22, 23 and 66 shall apply in relation to the patient with the modifications specified in paragraphs 3 to 9 below.

3. In section 16(1) for references to an application for admission or a guardianship application there shall be submitted references to the order or direction under Part III of this Act by virtue of which the patient is liable to be detained or subject to guardianship.

4. In section 18 subsection (5) shall be omitted.

5. In section 19(2) for the words from "as follows" to the end of the subsection there shall be substituted the words "as if the order or direction under Part III of this Act by virtue of which he was liable to be detained or subject to guardianship before being transferred were an order or direction for his admission or removal to the hospital to which he is transferred, or placing him under the guardianship of the authority or person into whose guardianship he is transferred, as the case may be".

6. In section 20—
   (a) in subsection (1) for the words from "day on which he was" to "as the case may be" there shall be substituted the words "date of the relevant order or direction under Part III of this Act"; and
   (b) in subsection (9) for the words "the application for admission for treatment or, as the case may be, in the guardianship application, that application" there shall be substituted the words "the relevant order or direction under Part III of this Act, that order or direction".

7. In section 22 for references to an application for admission or a guardianship application there shall be substituted references to the order or direction under Part III of this Act by virtue of which the patient is liable to be detained or subject to guardianship.

8. In section 23(2)—
   (a) in paragraph (a) the words "for assessment or" shall be omitted; and
   (b) in paragraphs (a) and (b) the references to the nearest relative shall be omitted.

9. In section 66—
   (a) in subsection (1), paragraphs (a), (b), (c), (g) and (h), the words in parenthesis in paragraph (i) and paragraph (ii) shall be omitted; and
   (b) in subsection (2), paragraphs (a), (b), (c) and (g) shall be omitted and in

paragraph (*d*) for the words "cases mentioned in paragraphs (*d*) and (*g*)" there shall be substituted the words "case mentioned in paragraph (*d*)".

PART II

PATIENTS SUBJECT TO SPECIAL RESTRICTIONS

1. Sections 24(3) and (4), 32 and 76 shall apply in relation to the patient without modification.

2. Sections 17 to 19, 22, 23 and 34 shall apply in relation to the patient with the modifications specified in paragraphs 3 to 8 below.

3. In section 17—
   - (*a*) in subsection (1) after the word "may" there shall be inserted the words "with the consent of the Secretary of State";
   - (*b*) In subsection (4) after the words "the responsible medical officer" and after the words "that officer" there shall be inserted the words "or the Secretary of State"; and
   - (*c*) in subsection (5) after the word "recalled" there shall be inserted the words "by the responsible medical officer", and for the words from "he has ceased" to the end of the subsection there shall be substituted the words "the expiration of the period of six months beginning with the first day of his absence on leave".

4. In section 18 there shall be omitted—
   - (*a*) in subsection (1) the words "subject to the provisions of this section"; and
   - (*b*) subsections (3), (4) and (5).

5. In section 19—
   - (*a*) in subsection (1) after the word "may" in paragraph (*a*) there shall be inserted the words "with the consent of the Secretary of State", and the words from "or into" to the end of the subsection shall be omitted; and
   - (*b*) in subsection (2) for the words from "as follows" to the end of the subsection there shall be substituted the words "as if the order or direction under Part III of this Act by virtue of which he was liable to be detained before being transferred were an order or direction for his admission or removal to the hospital to which he is transferred".

6. In section 22 subsection (1) and paragraph (*a*) of subsection (2) shall not apply.

7. In section 23—
   - (*a*) in subsection (1) references to guardianship shall be omitted and after the word "made" there shall be inserted the words "with the consent of the Secretary of State and"
   - (*b*) in subsection (2)—
     - (i) in paragraph (*a*) the words "for assessment or" and "or by the nearest relative of the patient" shall be omitted; and
     - (ii) paragraph (*b*) shall be omitted.

8. In section 34, in subsection (1) the definition of "the nominated medical attendant" and subsection (3) shall be omitted.

DEFINITIONS
"Hospital order": ss.37, 145(1).
"Guardianship order":
"Patient": s.145(1).

Section 65(2)   SCHEDULE 2

MENTAL HEALTH REVIEW TRIBUNALS

1. Each of the Mental Health Review Tribunals shall consist of—
   - (*a*) a number of persons (referred to in this Schedule as "the legal members") appointed by the Lord Chancellor and having such legal experience as the Lord Chancellor considers suitable;
   - (*b*) a number of persons (referred to in this Schedule as "the medical members") being registered medical practitioners appointed by the Lord Chancellor after consultation with the Secretary of State; and

(c) a number of persons appointed by the Lord Chancellor after consultation with the Secretary of State and having such experience in administration, such knowledge of social services or such other qualifications or experience as the Lord Chancellor considers suitable.

2. The members of Mental Health Review Tribunals shall hold and vacate office under the terms of the instrument under which they are appointed, but may resign office by notice in writing to the Lord Chancellor; and any such member who ceases to hold office shall be eligible for re-appointment.

3. One of the legal members of each Mental Health Review Tribunal shall be appointed by the Lord Chancellor as chairman of the Tribunals.

4. Subject to rules made by the Lord Chancellor under section 78(2)(c) above, the members who are to constitute a Mental Health Review Tribunal for the purposes of any proceedings or class or group of proceedings under this Act shall be appointed by the chairman of the tribunal or, if for any reason he is unable to act, by another member of the tribunal appointed for the purpose by the chairman; and of the members so appointed—

(a) one or more shall be appointed from the legal members;

(b) one or more shall be appointed from the medical members; and

(c) one or more shall be appointed from the members who are neither legal nor medical members.

5. A member of a Mental Health Review Tribunal for any area may be appointed under paragraph 4 above as one of the persons to constitute a Mental Health Review Tribunal for any other area for the purposes of any proceedings or class or group of proceedings; and for the purposes of this Act, a person so appointed shall, in relation to the proceedings for which he was appointed be deemed to be a member of that other tribunal.

6. Subject to any rules made by the Lord Chancellor under section 78(4)(a) above, where the chairman of the tribunal is included among the persons appointed under paragraph 4 above, he shall be president of the tribunal; and in any other case the president of the tribunal shall be such one of the members so appointed (being one of the legal members) as the chairman may nominate.

Section 113   SCHEDULE 3

ENACTMENTS DISAPPLIED IN RESPECT OF PERSONS
WITHIN JURISDICTION UNDER PART VII

Session and Chapter	Short Title	Enactments
13 Geo. 3. c.81	The Inclosure Act 1773.	Sections 22 and 24.
7 Geo. 4. c.16.	The Chelsea and Kilmainham Hospitals Act 1826.	Sections 44 to 48.
2 & 3 Will. 4. c.80	The Ecclesiastical Corporations Act 1832.	Section 3.
1 & 2 Vict. c.106.	The Pluralities Act 1838.	Section 127.
4 & 5 Vict. c.38.	The School Sites Act 1841.	Section 5.
5 & 6 Vict. c.26.	The Ecclesiastical Houses of Residence Act 1842.	Section 12.
5 & 6 Vict. c.108.	The Ecclesiastical Leasing Act 1842.	Section 24.
8 & 9 Vict. c.16.	The Companies Clauses Consolidation Act 1845.	Section 79.
8 & 9 Vict. c.18.	The Lands Clauses Consolidation Act 1845.	Section 9.
8 & 9 Vict. c.118.	The Inclosure Act 1845.	Sections 20, 133, 134 and 137.
9 & 10 Vict. c.73.	The Tithe Act 1846.	Sections 5, 9 and 10.
17 & 18 Vict. c.112.	The Literary and Scientific Institutions Act 1854.	Section 5.
25 and 26 Vict. c.53.	The Land Registry Act 1826.	Section 116.
27 & 28 Vict. c.114.	The Improvement of Land Act 1864.	Section 24.
29 & 30 Vict. c.122.	The Metropolitan Commons Act 1866.	Section 28.
31 & 32 Vict. c.109.	The Compulsory Church Rate Abolition Act 1868.	Section 7.
36 & 37 Vict. c.50.	The Places of Worship Sites Act 1873.	Sections 1 and 3.
40 & 41 Vict. c.59.	The Colonial Stock Act 1877.	Section 6.
57 & 58 Vict. c.60.	The Merchant Shipping Act 1894.	In section 55, subsection (1).

Section 148   SCHEDULE 4

CONSEQUENTIAL AMENDMENTS

1. In the Fines and Recoveries Act 1833—
    (a) in section 33 for the words "the Mental Health Act 1959" and "Part VIII" there shall be substituted respectively the words "the Mental Health Act 1983" and "Part VII";
    (b) in sections 48 and 49 for the references to the judge having jurisdiction under Part VIII of the Mental Health Act 1959 there shall be substituted references to the judge having jurisdiction under Part VII of this Act.

2. In section 68 of the Improvement of Land Act 1864 for the words "Part VIII of the Mental Health Act 1959" there shall be substituted the words "Part VII of the Mental Health Act 1983".

3. In section 10(3) of the Colonial Prisoners Removal Act 1884 for the words "section seventy-one of the Mental Health Act 1959", "section seventy-two" and "section seventy-four" there shall be substituted respectively the words "section 46 of the Mental Health Act 1983", "section 47" and "section 49".

4. In the Trustee Act 1925—
> (*a*) in section 36(9) for the words "the Mental Health Act 1959" and "Part VIII of the Mental Health Act 1959" there shall be substituted respectively the words "the Mental Health Act 1983" and "Part VII of the Mental Health Act 1983";
>
> (*b*) in section 41(1) for the words "the Mental Health Act 1959" there shall be substituted the words "the Mental Health Act 1983";
>
> (*c*) in section 54—
>> (i) in subsection (1) for the words "Part VIII of the Mental Health Act 1959" there shall be substituted the words "Part VII of the Mental Health Act 1983"; and
>>
>> (ii) in subsection (3) for the words "section one hundred and one of the Mental Health Act 1959" and "exercisable and have been exercised under section one hundred and four" there shall be substituted respectively the words "section 94 of the Mental Health Act 1983" and "exercisable under section 98 of that Act and have been exercised under that section or section 104 of the Mental Health Act 1959";
>
> (*d*) in section 55 except so far as it applies to existing orders made before the commencement of this Act, for the words "Part VIII of the Mental Health Act 1959" there shall be substituted the words "Part VII of the Mental Health Act 1983".

5. In the Law of Property Act 1925—
> (*a*) in section 22(1) for the words "Part VIII of the Mental Health Act 1959" there shall be substituted the words "Part VII of the Mental Health Act 1983".
>
> (*b*) in section 205(1)(xiii) for the words "section four of the Mental Health Act 1959" and "Part VIII" there shall be substituted respectively the words "section 1 of the Mental Health Act 1983" and "Part VIII of the Mental Health Act 1959 or Part VII of the said Act of 1983".

6. In section 111 of the Land Registration Act 1925—
> (*a*) in subsection (5) for the words "the Mental Health Act 1959" and "Part VIII of the Mental Health Act 1959" there shall be substituted respectively the words "the Mental Health Act 1983" and "Part VII of the Mental Health Act 1983"; and
>
> (*b*) in subsection (6) for the words "Part VIII of the Mental Health Act 1959" there shall be substituted the words "Part VII of the Mental Health Act 1983".

7. In paragraph (ii) of the proviso to section 41(1) of the Administration of Estates Act 1925 for the words "the Mental Health Act 1959" there shall be substituted the words "the Mental Health Act 1983".

8. In sections 4(1) and 11(3)(*b*) of the Polish Resettlement Act 1947 for the words "the Mental Health Act 1959" there shall be substituted the words "the Mental Health Act 1983".

9. In section 1(4) of the U.S.A. Veterans' Pensions (Administration) Act 1949 after the words "curator bonis" there shall be inserted the words "or for whom a receiver has been appointed under section 105 of the Mental Health Act 1959 or section 99 of the Mental Health Act 1983".

10. In section 116(7) of the Army Act 1955 for the words "section 71 of the Mental Health Act 1959" and "within the meaning of the Mental Health Act 1959" there shall besubstituted respectively the words "section 46 of the Mental Health Act 1983" and "within the meaning of the Mental Health Act 1983".

11. In section 116(7) of the Air Force Act 1955 for the words "section 71 of the Mental Health Act 1959" and "within the meaning of the Mental Health Act 1959" there shall be substituted respectively the words "section 46 of the Mental Health Act 1983" and "within the meaning of the Mental Health Act 1983".

12. In section 38(4) of the Sexual Offences Act 1956 for the words "the Mental Health Act 1959" there shall be substituted the words "the Mental Health Act 1983".

13. In section 71(6) of the Naval Discipline Act 1957 for the words "section 71 of the Mental Health Act 1959" and "within the meaning of the Mental Health Act 1959" there shall be substituted respectively the words "section 46 of the Mental Health Act 1983" and "within the meaning of the Mental Health Act 1983".

14. In section 1 of the Variation of Trusts Act 1958—
> (*a*) in subsection (3) for the words "Part VIII of the Mental Health Act 1959" and

"the said Part VIII" there shall be substituted respectively the words "Part VII of the Mental Health Act 1983" and "the said Part VII"; and

(b) in subsection (6) for the words "Part VIII of the Mental Health Act 1959" there shall be substituted the words "Part VII of the Mental Health Act 1983".

15. In section 128(1)(b) of the Mental Health Act 1959 for the words "this Act" in both places where they occur there shall be substituted the words "the Mental Health Act 1983".

16. In the Mental Health (Scotland) Act 1960—

(a) in section 10(1)(b) and (c) for the words "the Mental Health Act 1959" there shall be substitued the words "the Mental Health Act 1983";

(b) in section 73(5) for the words "Part IV of the Mental Health Act 1959" there shall be substituted the words "Part II of the Mental Health Act 1983";

(c) in section 75 for the words "Part IV of the Mental Health Act 1959", "section forty-nine of the said Act of 1959", "Part IV of that Act", "Part IV of the said Act of 1959", and "section fifty-two" wherever they occur there shall be substituted respectively the words "Part II of the Mental Health Act 1983", "section 26 of the said Act of 1983", "Part II of that Act", "Part II of the said Act of 1983" and "section 29";

(d) in section 76—

(i) in subsection (1) for the words "the Mental Health Act 1959 as amended by this Act" and "Part IV of that Act" there shall be substituted respectively the words "the Mental Health Act 1983" and "Part II of that Act";

(ii) in subsection (2) for the words "sections forty-nine to fifty-one of the said Act of 1959" and "Part IV of that Act" there shall be substituted respectively the words "sections 26 to 28 of the said Act of 1983" and "Part II of that Act"; and

(iii) in subsection (3) after the words "the Mental Health Act 1959" there shall be inserted the words "or section 29 or 30 of the Mental Health Act 1983".

(e) in section 83(3)(a) for the words "mental welfare officer within the meaning of the Mental Health Act 1959" there shall be substituted the words "approved social worker within the meaning of the Mental Health Act 1983".

(f) in sections 85 and 87 for the words "the Mental Health Act 1959" there shall be substituted the words "the Mental Health Act 1983".

(g) in section 88(2) after "1959" there shall be inserted the words "or Part VI of the Mental Health Act 1983";

(h) in section 103(3) and (5) for the words "section ninety-three of the Mental Health Act 1959" there shall be substituted the words "section 88 of the Mental Health Act 1983";

(i) in section 107(2) for the words "section one hundred and forty-one of the Mental Health Act 1959" there shall be substituted the words "section 139 of the Mental Health Act 1983".

17. In section 5 of the Administration of Justice Act 1960—

(a) in subsection (4) for the words "Part V of the Mental Health Act 1959" and the words "the said Part V" there shall be substituted respectively the words "Part III of the Mental Health Act 1983 (other than under section 35, 36 or 38)" and "the said Part III"; and

(b) in subsection (4A) for the words "section 31 of the Mental Health (Amendment) Act 1982", "Part V of the said Act of 1959" and "the said section 31" there shall be substituted respectively "section 38 of the Mental Health Act 1983", "Part III of the said Act of 1983" and "the said section 38".

18. In the Criminal Procedure (Insanity) Act 1964—

(a) in section 8(2) for the words "the Mental Health Act 1959", "Part V" and "sections 139 to 141" there shall be substituted respectively the words "the Mental Health Act 1983", "Part III" and "sections 137 to 139";

(b) in Schedule 1—

(i) in paragraph 1(3) for the words "sections 60 and 65 of the Mental Health Act 1959" there shall be substituted the words "sections 37 and 41 of the Mental Health Act 1983";

(ii) in paragraph 2(1) for the words "the Mental Health Act 1959", "section 60" and "section 65" there shall be substituted respectively, "the Mental Health Act 1983", "section 37" and "section 41";

(iii) in paragraph 2(2) for the words "section 66 of the said Act of 1959" and "section 65" there shall be substituted respectively the words "section 42 of the said Act of 1983" and "section 41";

(iv) in paragraph 2(3) for the words "section 63(5) of the Mental Health Act 1959" and the words from "the proviso" to "the reference" there shall be substituted respectively the words "section 40(5) of the Mental Health Act 1983" and "the reference in the said section 40(5)";

19. In section 18 of the Administration of Justice Act 1965 for the words "Part VIII of the Mental Health Act 1959" there shall be substituted the words "Part VII of the Mental Health Act 1983".

20. In paragraph 1(2)(*b*) of Schedule 1 to the Compulsory Purchase Act 1965 at the end there shall be inserted the words "or section 98 of the Mental Health Act 1983".

21. In the Criminal Justice Act 1967—

(*a*) in section 72(1)(*b*) for the words "section 40 or 140 of the Mental Health Act 1959 or section 31(8) of the Mental Health (Amendment) Act 1982" there shall be substituted the words "section 18, 38(7) or 138 of the Mental Health Act 1983";

(*b*) in section 72(3) for the words "Section 139 of the Mental Health Act 1959" and "the said Act of 1959" there shall be substituted respectively the words "Section 137 of the Mental Health Act 1983" and "the said Act of 1983";

(*c*) in section 72(4) for the words "Part V of the Mental Health Act 1959", "section 31 of the Mental Health (Amendment) Act 1982" and "Part V of the said Act of 1959" there shall be substituted respectively the words "Part III of the Mental Health Act 1983", "section 38 of the said Act of 1983" and "Part III of the said Act of 1983".

22. In section 26(2) of the Leasehold Reform Act 1967 for the words "the Mental Health Act 1959", "appointed under Part VIII of that Act" and "having jurisdiction under Part VIII of that Act" there shall be substituted respectively the words "Mental Health Act 1983", "appointed under Part VII of the said Act of 1983 or Part VIII of the Mental Health Act 1959" and "having jurisdiction under Part VII of the said Act of 1983".

23. In the Criminal Appeal Act 1968—

(*a*) in section 6(4) for the words "section 72 of the Mental Health Act 1959" and "subsection (6)" there shall be substituted respectively the words "section 47 of the Mental Health Act 1983" and "subsection (5)";

(*b*) in section 8(3) after the words "Part V of the Mental Health Act 1959" there shall be inserted the words "or under Part III of the Mental Health Act 1983 (other than under section 35, 36 or 38 of that Act)";

(*c*) in section 8(3A)—

(i) for the words "section 30 of the Mental Health (Amendment) Act 1982" there shall be substituted the words "section 36 of the Mental Health Act 1983";

(ii) for the words "section 31 of that Act" there shall be substituted the words "section 38 of that Act"; and

(iii) for the words "Part V of the Mental Health Act 1959" there shall be substituted the words "Part III of that Act";

(*d*) in section 11—

(i) in subsection (5) for the words "the Mental Health (Amendment) Act 1982" there shall be substituted the words "the Mental Health Act 1983"; and

(ii) in subsection (6)(*b*) for the words "section 31(8) of the said Act of 1982" there shall be substituted the words "section 38(7) of the said Act of 1983".

(*e*) in section 14(5) for the words "section 72 of the Mental Health Act 1959" and "subsection (6)" there shall be substituted respectively the words "section 47 of the Mental Health Act 1983" and "subsection (5)";

(*f*) in section 16(3) for the words "the Mental Health Act 1959" and "Part V" there shall be substituted respectively the words "the Mental Health Act 1983" and "Part III";

(*g*) in section 37(4) for the words "Part V of the Mental Health Act 1959" and "the Mental Health Act 1959" there shall be substituted respectively the words "Part III of the Mental Health Act 1983 (otherwise than under section 35, 36 or 38 of that Act)" and "the Mental Health Act 1983";

(*h*) in section 37(4A) for the words "section 30 of the Mental Health (Amendment) Act 1982", "section 31" and "Part V of the said Act of 1959" wherever they occur there shall be substituted respectively the words "section 36 of the Mental Health Act 1983", "section 38" and "Part III of the said Act of 1983";

(*i*) in section 50(1), for the words from "Part V" to "1982" there shall be substituted the words "Part III of the Mental Health Act 1983, with or without a restriction order, and an interim hospital order under that Part";

(*j*) in section 51(2) for the words "section 147(1) of the Mental Health Act 1959" there shall be substituted the words "section 145(1) of the Mental Health Act 1983";

(*k*) in paragraph 1(3) of Schedule 1 for the words "the Mental Health Act 1959" there shall be substituted the words "the Mental Health Act 1983";

(*l*) in paragraph 2 of Schedule 1 for the words "the Mental Health Act 1959", "section 60" and "section 65" there shall be substituted respectively the words "the Mental Health Act 1983", "section 37" and "section 41";

(*m*) in paragraph 3 of Schedule 1 for the words "Part IV of the Mental Health Act 1959" and "the said Part IV" there shall be substituted respectively the words "Part II of the Mental Health Act 1983" and "the said Part II";

(*n*) in Schedule 3—

    (i) in the heading to the Schedule for the words "PART V OF MENTAL HEALTH ACT 1959" there shall be substituted the words "PART III OF MENTAL HEALTH ACT 1983"; and

    (ii) for paragraph 2 there shall be substituted—

        "Order for continued detention under Act of 1983

    2. Where an order is made by the Court of Appeal under section 16(3) of this Act for a person's continued detention under the Mental Health Act 1983, Part III of that Act (patients concerned in criminal proceedings or under sentence) shall apply to him as if he had been ordered under the said section 16(3) to be kept in custody pending trial and were detained in pursuance of a transfer direction together with a restriction direction.".

24. In the Courts-Martial (Appeals) Act 1968—

(*a*) in sections 20(4) and 43(4) for the words "Part V of the Mental Health Act 1959" there shall be substituted the words "Part III of the Mental Health Act 1983";

(*b*) in section 23, in subsection (1) for the words "section 71 of the Mental Health Act 1959" there shall be substituted the words "section 46 of the Mental Health Act 1983" and in subsection (2) for the words "the Mental Health Act 1959" there shall be substituted the words "the Mental Health Act 1983";

(*c*) in section 25(4) for the words "the Mental Health Act 1959" there shall be substituted the words "the Mental Health Act 1983".

25. In section 21(4) of the Family Law Reform Act 1969 for the words "the Mental Health Act 1959" there shall be substituted the words "the Mental Health Act 1983".

26. In the Children and Young Persons Act 1969—

(*a*) in section 1(3) for the words "Part V of the Mental Health Act 1959" there shall be substituted the words "Part III of the Mental Health Act 1983";

(*b*) in section 1(5) for the words "section 60 of the said Act of 1959" there shall be substituted the words "section 37 of the said Act of 1983";

(*c*) in section 2(10) for the words "section 31 of the Mental Health (Amendment) Act 1982" and "the said section 31" there shall be substituted respectively the words "section 38 of the Mental Health Act 1983" and "the said section 38".

(*d*) in section 12(4) for the words "section 28 of the Mental Health Act 1959", "Part V" and "the said Act of 1959" there shall be substituted respectively the words "section 12 of the Mental Health Act 1983", "Part III" and "the said Act of 1983";

(*e*) in paragraph 7(7) of Schedule 4 for the words from the beginning to "1959" there shall be substituted the words "A restriction direction which was given under section 49 of the Mental Health Act 1983".

27. In Schedule 1 to the Local Authorities Social Services Act 1970—

(*a*) in the entry relating to the Mental Health Act 1959, in the first column for the words "Parts II to VI and IX" there shall be substituted the words "sections 8 and 9" and for the entry in the second column there shall be substituted the words "Welfare and accommodation of mentally disordered persons.";

(*b*) there shall be inserted at the end—

    "Mental Health Act
    1983 (c.20)
    Parts II, III and VI   Welfare of the mentally disordered; guardian-

	ship of persons suffering from mental disorder including such persons removed to England and Wales from Scotland or Northern Ireland; exercise of functions of nearest relative of person so suffering.
Sections 66, 67, 69(1)	Exercise of functions of nearest relative in relation to applications and references to Mental Health Review Tribunals.
Section 114	Appointment of approved social workers.
Section 115	Entry and inspection.
Section 116	Welfare of certain hospital patients.
Section 117	After-care of detained patients.
Section 130	Prosecutions.";

(c) the entry relating to the Mental Health (Amendment) Act 1982 shall cease to have effect.

28. In section 57(1) of the Courts Act 1971 for the words "Part V of the Mental Health Act 1959" there shall be substituted the words "Part III of the Mental Health Act 1983".

29. In Schedule 1 to the Tribunals and Inquiries Act 1971, in the second column of the entry relating to the Mental Health Review Tribunals for the words following "Tribunals" there shall be substituted the words "constituted or having effect as if constituted under section 65 of the Mental Health Act 1983 (c.20)".

30. In section 30(2) of the Immigration Act 1971 for the words from the beginning to "1960)" there shall be substituted the words "Under section 82 of the Mental Health (Scotland) Act 1960" and the words from "and accordingly" onwards shall be omitted.

31. In section 20(2) of the Parliamentary and other Pensions Act 1972 for the words "Section 138 of the Mental Health Act 1959" there shall be substituted the words "Section 142 of the Mental Health Act 1983".

32. In section 118 of the Local Government Act 1972—
(a) in subsection (1) for the words "the Mental Health Act 1959" there shall be substituted the words "the Mental Health Act 1983"; and
(b) in subsection (4) for the words "Part VIII of the said Act of 1959" there shall be substituted the words "Part VII of the said Act of 1983".

33. In the Costs in Criminal Cases Act 1973—
(a) in section 3(7) for the words from "under Part V" to "1982" there shall be substituted the words "and an interim hospital order under Part III of the Mental Health Act 1983"; and
(b) in section 18(1)(c) for the words "Part V of the Mental Health Act 1959" there shall be substituted the words "Part III of the Mental Health Act 1983".

34. In section 12(d) of the Matrimonial Causes Act 1973 for the words "the Mental Health Act 1959" there shall be substituted the words "the Mental Health Act 1983".

35. In section 1 of the Guardianship Act 1973—
(a) in subsection (8), the words from "and" to the end of the subsection shall be omitted; and
(b) after subsection (8) there shall be inserted—
  "(9) Nothing in this section shall be taken to affect the provisions of the Mental Health Act 1983 as to the person who is 'the nearest relative' for the purposes of that Act.".

36. In section 3 of the Powers of Criminal Courts Act 1973—
(a) in subsection (1) for the words "section 28 of the Mental Health Act 1959" and "Part V of that Act" there shall be substituted respectively the words "section 12 of the Mental Health Act 1983" and "Part III of that Act";
(b) in subsection (2) for the words "hospital or mental nursing home within the meaning of the Mental Health Act 1959" and "that Act" there shall be substituted respectively the words "hospital within the meaning of the Mental Health Act 1983 or mental nursing home within the meaning of the Nursing Homes Act 1975" and "the National Health Service Act 1977"; and
(c) in subsection (7) for the words "Subsections (2) and (3) of section 62 of the Mental Health Act 1959" and "section 60(1)(a)" there shall be substituted respectively the words "Subsections (2) and (3) of section 54 of the Mental Health Act 1983" and "section 37(2)(a)".

37. In Group D in Schedule 1 to the Juries Act 1974 for the words "section 33 of the Mental Health Act 1959", "Part VIII of that Act" and "the said Act of 1959" there shall be substituted respectively the words "section 7 of the Mental Health Act 1983", "Part VII of that Act" and "the said Act of 1983".

38. In the Solicitors Act 1974—
    (*a*) in section 12(1)(*j*) for the words "section 101 of the Mental Health Act 1959" and "section 104 of that Act" there shall be substituted respectively the words "section 94 of the Mental Health Act 1983" and "section 104 of the Mental Health Act 1959 or section 98 of the said Act of 1983";
    (*b*) in section 62(4)(*c*) for the words "under Part VIII of the Mental Health Act 1959" there shall be substituted the words "appointed under Part VII of the Mental Health Act 1983";
    (*c*) in paragraph 1(1)(*f*) of Schedule 1 for the words "section 104 (emergency powers) or 105 (appointment of receiver) of the Mental Health Act 1959" there shall be substituted the words "section 104 of the Mental Health Act 1959 or section 98 of the Mental Health Act 1983 (emergency powers) or section 105 of the said Act of 1959 or section 99 of the said Act of 1983 (appointment of receiver)".

39. In section 5(7) of the Rehabilitation of Offenders Act 1974 for the words "Part V of the Mental Health Act 1959" there shall be substituted the words "Part III of the Mental Health Act 1983".

40. In paragraph 19(4) of Schedule 5 to the Finance Act 1975 for the words "the Mental Health Act 1959" there shall be substituted the words "the Mental Health Act 1983".

41. In the Criminal Procedure (Scotland) Act 1975—
    (*a*) in sections 13(1)(*b*) and 322(1)(*b*) for the words "section 40 or 140 of the Mental Health Act 1959, section 31(8) of the Mental Health (Amendment) Act 1982" there shall be substituted the words "section 18, 38(7) or 138 of the Mental Health Act 1983";
    (*b*) in sections 13(3) and 322(3) for the words "Section 139 of the Mental Health Act 1959" and "the said Act of 1959" there shall be substituted respectively "Section 137 of the Mental Health Act 1983" and "the said Act of 1983";
    (*c*) in sections 13(4) and 322(4) for the words "Part V of the Mental Health Act 1959", "section 31 of the Mental Health (Amendment) Act 1982" and "Part V of the said Act of 1959" there shall be substituted respectively the words "Part III of the Mental Health Act 1983", "section 38 of the said Act of 1983" and "Part III of the said Act of 1983".

42. In Part II of Schedule 1 to the House of Commons Disqualification Act 1975 in the entry relating to Mental Health Review Tribunals for the words "constituted under the Mental Health Act 1959" there shall be substituted the words "constituted or having effect as if constituted under the Mental Health Act 1983".

43. In the Nursing Homes Act 1975—
    (*a*) in sections 3(2)(*c*) and 10(2) for the words "the Mental Health Act 1959 or the Mental Health (Amendment) Act 1982" there shall be substituted the words "the Mental Health Act 1983";
    (*b*) in section 20(1) for the words "section 4 of the Mental Health Act 1959" there shall be substituted the words "section 1 of the Mental Health Act 1983";
    (*c*) in section 21 for the words "those sections" there shall be substituted the words "the sections of the Mental Health Act 1983 corresponding to those sections, namely sections 126, 139 and 125 respectively".

44. In section 98(4) of the Children Act 1975 for the words "or residential home within the meaning of Part III of the Mental Health Act 1959" there shall be substituted the words "residential home for mentally disordered persons within the meaning of the Nursing Homes Act 1975 or the Residential Homes Act 1980".

45. In section 32(6)(*c*) of the Adoption Act 1976 for the words "the Mental Health Act 1959 or the Mental Health (Amendment) Act 1982" there shall be substituted the words "the Mental Health Act 1983".

46. In section 3(6B) of the Bail Act 1976 for the words "section 28 of the Mental Health Act 1959" there shall be substituted the words "section 12 of the Mental Health Act 1983".

47. In the National Health Service Act 1977—
    (*a*) in section 4 for the words "the Mental Health Act 1959 or the Mental Health (Amendment) Act 1982" there shall be substituted the words "the Mental Health Act 1983";
    (*b*) in section 105(1) for the words "Part IV of the Mental Health Act 1959" there shall be substituted the words "Part II of the Mental Health Act 1983";
    (*c*) in section 105(3) the words "or the Mental Health Act 1959" shall be omitted;
    (*d*) in section 128(1), in the definition of "illness", for the words "the Mental Health Act 1959" there shall be substituted the words "the Mental Health Act 1983";

    (*e*) in paragraph 2 of Schedule 8—

        (i) for sub-paragraph (1)(*d*) there shall be substituted—

        "(*d*) for the exercise of the functions of the authority in respect of persons suffering from mental disorder who are received into guardianship under Part II or III of the Mental Health Act 1983 (whether the guardianship of the local social services authority or of other persons).";

        (ii) in sub-paragraph (2)(*b*)(i) for the words "the Mental Health Act 1959" there shall be substituted the words "the Mental Health Act 1983"; and

        (iii) in sub-paragraph (3) for the words "that Act of 1959" there shall be substituted the words "that Act of 1983";

    (*f*) in paragraph 13(1)(*b*) of Schedule 14 for the words "80 to 83, 86 to 91, 93 and 96" there shall be substituted "80 to 82, 96".

    48. In section 16A(1)(*b*)(ii) of the National Health Service (Scotland) Act 1978 for the words "section 10 of the Mental Health Act 1959" there shall be substituted the words "section 116 of the Mental Health Act 1983".

    49. In paragraph 5(2) of Schedule 1 to the Capital Gains Tax Act 1979 for the words "the Mental Health Act 1959" there shall be substituted the words "the Mental Health Act 1983".

    50. In the Child Care Act 1980—

    (*a*) in section 3(1)(*b*)(iii) for the words "the Mental Health Act 1959" there shall be substituted the words "the Mental Health Act 1983"; and

    (*b*) in section 79(5)(*c*) for the words "section 10 of that Act" and "subsection (1)(*a*)" there shall be substituted respectively the words "section 116 of the Mental Health Act 1983" and "subsection (2)(*a*)".

    51. In section 2(5) of the Foster Children Act 1980 for the words "the Mental Health Act 1959 or the Mental Health (Amendment) Act 1982" there shall be substituted the words "the Mental Health Act 1983".

    52. In the Residential Homes Act 1980—

    (*a*) in section 1(3)(*a*) for the words "section 147(1) of the Mental Health Act 1959" there shall be substituted the words "section 145(1) of the Mental Health Act 1983"; and

    (*b*) in section 10(1) for the words "the Mental Health Act 1959" there shall be substituted the words "the Mental Health Act 1983".

    53. In paragraph 2(*a*) of Schedule 2 to the Reserve Forces Act 1980 for the words "the Mental Health Act 1959" there shall be substituted the words "the Mental Health Act 1983".

    54. In section 31(2)(*c*) of the Transport Act 1980 for the words "Part VIII of the Mental Health Act 1959" there shall be substituted the words "Part VII of the Mental Health Act 1983".

    55. In section 38 of the Limitation Act 1980—

    (*a*) in subsection (3) for the words "Mental Health Act 1959" there shall be substituted the words "Mental Health Act 1983"; and

    (*b*) in subsection (4)—

        (i) in paragraph (*a*), for the words "the Mental Health Act 1959 or section 30 or 31 of the Mental Health (Amendment) Act 1982" there shall be substituted the words "the Mental Health Act 1983 (otherwise than by virtue of section 35 or 89)"; and

        (ii) for paragraph (*b*) there shall be substituted—

    "(*b*) while he is receiving treatment as an in-patient in any hospital within the meaning of the Mental Health Act 1983 or mental nursing home within the meaning of the Nursing Homes Act 1975 without being liable to be detained under the said Act of 1983 (otherwise than by virtue of section 35 or 89), being treatment which follows without any interval a period during which he was liable to be detained orsubject to guardianship under the Mental Health Act 1959, or the said Act of 1983 (otherwise than by virtue of section 35 or 89) or by virtue of any enactment repealed or excluded by the Mental Health Act 1959".

    56. In section 57(2)(*c*) of the Public Passenger Vehicles Act 1981 for the words "Part VIII of the Mental Health Act 1959" there shall be substituted the words "Part VII of the Mental Health Act 1983".

    57. In the Contempt of Court Act 1981—

    (*a*) in section 14(4) for the words "section 60 of the Mental Health Act 1959" and "section 31 of the Mental Health (Amendment) Act 1982" there shall be substituted respectively the words "section 37 of the Mental Health Act 1983" and "section 38 of that Act"; and (*b*) in section 14(4A) for the words "section 29 of the said Act of 1982" there shall be substituted the words "section 35 of the said Act of 1983".

    (*c*) in paragraph 10(*b*) of Schedule 1 for the words "paragraph (*b*) of subsection (2) of section 76 of the Mental Health Act 1959" there shall be substituted the words "section 51(5) of the Mental Health Act 1983".

58. In the Supreme Court Act 1981—

    (*a*) in section 48(6)(*a*) for the words "Part V of the Mental Health Act 1959" and "the Mental Health (Amendment) Act 1982" there shall be substituted respectively the words "Part III of the Mental Health Act 1983" and "that Act";

    (*b*) in section 48(7) for the words "the said Act of 1982" there shall be substituted the words "the said Act of 1983"; and

    (*c*) in section 48(8)(*b*) for the words "section 31(8) of the said Act of 1982" there shall be substituted the words "section 38(7) of the said Act of 1983".

59. In section 13(9) of the Armed Forces Act 1981 or the words "the Mental Health Act 1959" there shall be substituted the words "the Mental Health Act 1983".

60. In paragraph 9 of Schedule 1 to the British Nationality Act 1981—

    (*a*) in sub-paragraph (1)(*b*) for the words "Part V of the Mental Health Act 1959" there shall be substituted the words "Part III of the Mental Health Act 1983"; and

    (*b*) in sub-paragraph (2)(*b*) for the words "Part V of the Mental Health Act 1959" there shall be substituted the words "Part III of the Mental Health Act 1983".

61. In the Mental Health (Amendment) Act 1982—

    (*a*) in section 70(2)—

        (i) for the words "Section 62 and 64(2)" there shall be substituted the words "Section 62", and

        (ii) the words "sections 35(1) and (2) and 64(6) above extend to Northern Ireland" shall be omitted;

    (*b*) in section 70(3) for the words "Section 154(2) of the principal Act" there shall be substituted the words "Section 149(4) of the Mental Health Act 1983".

Section 148   SCHEDULE 5

TRANSITIONAL AND SAVING PROVISIONS

1. Where any period of time specified in an enactment repealed by this Act is current at the commencement of this Act, this Act shall have effect as if the corresponding provision of this Act had been in force when that period began to run.

2. Nothing in this Act shall affect the interpretation of any provision of the Mental Health Act 1959 which is not repealed by this Act and accordingly sections 1 and 145(1) of this Act shall apply to any such provision as if it were contained in this Act.

3. Where, apart from this paragraph, anything done under or for the purposes of any enactment which is repealed by this Act would cease to have effect by virtue of that repeal it shall have effect as if it had been done under or for the purposes of the corresponding provision of this Act.

4.—(1) Until the expiration of the period of two years beginning with the day on which the Mental Health (Amendment) Act 1982 was passed this Act shall have effect as if—

    (*a*) section 114 were omitted;

    (*b*) in section 145(1) the definition of an approved social worker were omitted and there were inserted in the appropriate place the following definition:—

        "'mental welfare officer' means an officer of a local social services authority appointed to act as mental welfare officer for the purposes of the Mental Health Act 1959 or this Act";

    (*c*) for paragraph 16(*e*) of Schedule 4 there were substituted—

        "(*e*) in section 83(3)(*a*) for the words 'the Mental Health Act 1959' there were substituted the words 'the Mental Health Act 1983'";

    (*d*) for paragraph 47(*e*)(i) of Schedule 4 there were substituted—

        "(i) in sub-paragraph (1)(*d*) for the words 'the Mental Health Act 1959' and 'Part IV or Part V' there were substituted respectively the words 'the Mental Health Act 1983' and 'Part II or III'"; and

    (*e*) for any reference to an approved social worker there were substituted a reference to a mental welfare officer.

(2) Any appointment of a person as a mental welfare officer for the purposes of the Mental Health Act 1959 or this Act shall terminate at the expiration of the period mentioned in sub-paragraph (1) above but without prejudice to anything previously done by that person

or to the continuation by an approved social worker of anything which is then in process of being done by that person.

5. If no order has been made under section 11 of the National Health Service Act 1977 before 30th September 1983 establishing the Mental Health Act Commission the following shall be substituted for subsection (1) of section 121 of this Act—

"(1) The Secretary of State shall under section 11 of the National Health Service Act 1977 establish a special health authority to be known as the Mental Health Act Commission.".

6. This Act shall apply in relation to any authority for the detention or guardianship of a person who was liable to be detained or subject to guardianship under the Mental Health Act 1959 immediately before 30th September 1983 as if the provisions of this Act which derive from provisions amended by section 1 or 2 of the Mental Health (Amendment) Act 1982 and the amendments in Schedule 3 to that Act which are consequential on those sections were included in this Act in the form the provisions from which they derive would take if those amendments were disregarded but this provision shall not apply to any renewal of that authority on or after that date.

7. This Act shall apply to any application made before 30th September 1983 as if the provisions of this Act which derive from provisions amended by sections 3 to 5 of the Mental Health (Amendment) Act 1982 and the amendments in Schedule 3 to that Act which are consequential on those sections were included in this Act in the form the provisions from which they derive would take if those amendments were disregarded.

8.—(1) Where on 30th September 1983 a person who has not attained the age of sixteen years is subject to guardianship by virtue of a guardianship application the authority for his guardianship shall terminate on that day.

(2) Section 8(1) of this Act has effect (instead of section 34(1) of the Mental Health Act 1959) in relation to a guardianship application made before the coming into force of this Act as well as in relation to one made later.

9.—(1) Section 20(1) of this Act shall have effect in relation to any application for admission for treatment and to any guardianship application made before 1st October 1983 with the substitution for the words "six months" of the words "one year".

(2) Section 20(2) of this Act shall have effect in relation to any authority renewed before 1st October 1983 with the substitution for the words "six months" of the words "one year" and for the words "one year" in both places they occur of the words "two years".

(3) Where an authority has been renewed on or before 30th September 1983 for a period of two years of which less than 16 months has expired on that date that period shall expire at the end of 18 months from the date on which it began.

10. Section 23(2)(*a*) of this Act shall have effect in relation to a patient liable to be detained in pursuance of an application under section 25 of the Mental Health Act 1959 made before 30th September 1983 as if the reference to the nearest relative of the patient were omitted.

11. Where at any time before 30th September 1983 an application to a Mental Health Review Tribunal has been made by a person who at that time was the patient's nearest relative and the application has not then been determined and by reason of the coming into force of section 26 of this Act that person ceased to be the patient's nearest relative on that date, that person shall nevertheless be treated for the purposes of the application as continuing to be his nearest relative.

12. A person—

    (*a*) who was admitted to hospital in pursuance of an application for admission for treatment; or

    (*b*) in respect of whom a guardianship application was accepted; or

    (*c*) in respect of whom a hospital order was made,

before 30th September 1983 may make an application to a tribunal under section 66 of this Act in the cases mentioned in subsection (1)(*b*) and (*c*) of that section and under section 69(1)(*b*) of this Act within the period of six months beginning with the day on which he attains the age of 16 years if that period is later than that which would otherwise apply to an application in his case.

13. Subsection (1) of section 68 of this Act does not apply to any patient admitted or transferred to hospital more than six months before 30th September 1983; and subsection (2) of that section applies only in relation to a renewal of authority for detention after that date.

14. Section 69(1)(*b*) of this Act shall have effect in relation to patients liable to be detained immediately before 30th September 1983 as if after the words "in respect of a patient" there were inserted the words "admitted to a hospital in pursuance of a hospital order or".

15. The provisions of this Act which derive from sections 24 to 27 of the Mental Health (Amendment) Act 1982 shall have effect in relation to a transfer direction given before 30th September 1983 as well as in relation to one given later, but where, apart from this paragraph, a transfer direction given before 30th September 1983 would by virtue of the words in section 50(3) of this Act which are derived from section 24(3) of the Mental Health (Amendment) Act 1982 have ceased to have effect before that date it shall cease to have effect on that date.

16. The words in section 42(1) of this Act which derive from the amendment of section 66(1) of the Mental Health Act 1959 by section 28(1) of the Mental Health (Amendment) Act 1982 and the provisions of this Act which derive from section 28(3) of and Schedule 1 to that Act have effect in relation to a restriction order or, as the case may be, a restriction direction made or given before 30th September 1983 as well as in relation to one made or given later, but—

    (a) any reference to a tribunal under section 66(6) of the said Act of 1959 in respect of a patient shall be treated for the purposes of subsections (1) and (2) of section 77 of this Act in their application to sections 70 and 75(2) of this Act as an application made by him; and

    (b) sections 71(5) and 75(1)(a) of this Act do not apply where the period in question has expired before 30th September 1983.

17. Section 91(2) of this Act shall not apply in relation to a patient removed from England and Wales before 30th September 1983.

18.—(1) Subsection (3) of section 58 of this Act shall not apply to any treatment given to a patient in the period of six months beginning with 30th September 1983 if—

    (a) the detention of the patient began before the beginning of that period; and

    (b) that subsection has not been complied with in respect of any treatment previously given to him in that period.

(2) The Secretary of State may by order reduce the length of the period mentioned in sub-paragraph (1) above.

19. In the case of a patient who is detained at the time when section 132 of this Act comes into force, the steps required by that section shall be taken as soon as practicable after that time.

20. The repeal by the Mental Health (Amendment) Act 1982 of section 77 of the Mental Health Act 1959 does not affect subsection (4) of that section in its application to a transfer direction given before 30th September 1983, but after the coming into force of this Act that subsection shall have effect for that purpose as if for the references to subsection (6) of section 60, Part IV of that Act and the provisions of that Act there were substituted respectively references to section 37(8), Part II and the provisions of this Act.

21. Section 46(3) of this Act shall apply to any direction to which section 71(4) of the Mental Health Act 1959 applied immediately before the commencement of this Act.

22. Notwithstanding the repeal by this Act of section 53(5) of the Mental Health Act 1959, the discharge or variation under that section of an order made under section 52 of that Act shall not affect the validity of anything previously done in pursuance of the order.

23. For any reference in any enactment, instrument, deed or other document to a receiver under Part VIII of the Mental Health Act 1959 there shall be substituted a reference to a receiver under Part VII of this Act.

24. Nothing in this Act shall affect the operation of the proviso to section 107(5) of the Mental Health Act 1959 in relation to a charge created before the commencement of this Act under that section.

25. Nothing in this Act shall affect the operation of subsection (6) of section 112 of the Mental Health Act 1959 in relation to a charge created before the commencement of this Act by virtue of subsection (5) of that section.

26. If the person who is the Master of the Court of Protection at the commencement of this Act has before that time duly taken the oaths required by section 115(1) of the Mental Health Act 1959 he shall not be obliged to take those oaths again by virtue of section 93(3) of this Act.

27. Nothing in this Act shall affect the operation of section 116 of the Mental Health Act 1959 in relation to orders made, directions or authorities given or other instruments issued before the commencement of this Act.

28. References to applications, recommendations, reports and other documents in section 126 of this Act shall include those to which section 125 of the Mental Health Act 1959 applied immediately before the commencement of this Act and references in section 139 of this Act to the acts to which that section applies shall include those to which section 141 of the said Act of 1959 applied at that time.

29. The repeal by the Mental Health Act 1959 of the Mental Treatment Act 1930 shall not

affect any amendment effected by section 20 of that Act in any enactment not repealed by the said Act of 1959.

30. The repeal by the Mental Health Act 1959 of the provisions of the Lunacy Act 1890 and of the Mental Deficiency Act 1913 relating to the superannuation of officers or employees shall not affect any arrangements for the payment of allowances or other benefits made in accordance with those provisions and in force on 1st November 1960.

31.—(1) Any patient who immediately before the commencement of this Act was liable to be detained in a hospital or subject to guardianship by virtue of paragraph 9 of Schedule 6 to the Mental Health Act 1959 shall unless previously discharged continue to be so liable for the remainder of the period of his treatment current on 1st November 1960.

(2) The patient may before the expiration of the period of treatment referred to in sub-paragraph (1) above apply to a Mental Health Review Tribunal.

32. Any patient who immediately before the commencement of this Act was liable to be detained or subject to guardianship by virtue of an authority which had been renewed under paragraph 11 of Schedule 6 to the Mental Health Act 1959 shall unless previously discharged continue to be so liable during the period for which that authority was so renewed.

33.—(1) This paragraph applies to patients who at the commencement of this Act are liable to be detained or subject to guardianship by virtue of paragraph 31 or 32 above.

(2) Authority for the detention or guardianship of the patient may on the expiration of the relevant period, unless the patient has previously been discharged, be renewed for a further period of two years.

(3) Sections 20(3) to (10) and 66(1)(*f*) of this Act shall apply in relation to the renewal of authority for the detention or guardianship of a patient under this paragraph as they apply in relation to the renewal of authority for the detention or guardianship of the patient under section 20(2).

(4) In this paragraph "the relevant period" means—

    (*a*) in relation to a patient liable to be detained or subject to guardianship by virtue of the said paragraph 31, the period of his treatment referred to in that paragraph;

    (*b*) in relation to a patient detained by virtue of the said paragraph 32, the period for which authority for the detention or guardianship of the patient has been renewed under paragraph 11 of Schedule 6 to the 1959 Act;

    (*c*) in relation to a patient the authority for whose detention or guardianship has previously been renewed under this paragraph, the latest period for which it has been so renewed.

34.—(1) Any patient who is liable to be detained in a hospital or subject to guardianship by virtue of paragraph 31 above shall (subject to the exceptions and modifications specified in the following provisions of this paragraph) be treated as if he had been admitted to the hospital in pursuance of an application for admission for treatment under Part II of this Act or had been received into guardianship in pursuance of a guardianship application under the said Part II and had been so admitted or received as a patient suffering from the form or forms of mental disorder recorded under paragraph 7 of Schedule 6 to the Mental Health Act 1959 or, if a different form or forms have been specified in a report under section 38 of that Act as applied by that paragraph, the form or forms so specified.

(2) Section 20 of this Act shall not apply in relation to the patient, but the provisions of paragraph 33 above shall apply instead.

(3) Any patient to whom paragraph 9(3) of Schedule 6 to the Mental Health Act 1959 applied at the commencement of this Act who fell within paragraph (*b*) of that paragraph shall cease to be liable to be detained on attaining the age of 25 years unless, during the period of two months ending on the date when he attains that age, the responsible medical officer records his opinion under the following provisions of this Schedule that the patient is unfit for discharge.

(4) If the patient was immediately before 1st November 1960 liable to be detained by virtue of section 6, 8(1) or 9 of the Mental Deficiency Act 1913, the power of discharging him under section 23 of this Act shall not be exercisable by his nearest relative, but his nearest relative may make one application in respect of him to a Mental Health Review Tribunal in any period of 12 months.

35.—(1) The responsible medical officer may record for the purposes of paragraph 34(3) above his opinion that a patient detained in a hospital is unfit for discharge if it appears to the responsible medical officer—

    (*a*) that if that patient were released from the hospital he would be likely to act in a manner dangerous to other persons or to himself, or would be likely to resort to criminal activities; or

    (*b*) that that patient is incapable of caring for himself and that there is no suitable hospital or other establishment into which he can be admitted and where he would be likely to remain voluntarily;

and where the responsible medical officer records his opinion as aforesaid he shall also record the grounds for his opinion.

(2) Where the responsible medical officer records his opinion under this paragraph in respect of a patient, the managers of the hospital or other persons in charge of the establishment where he is for the time being detained or liable to be detained shall cause the patient to be informed, and the patient may, at any time before the expiration of the period of 28 days beginning with the date on which he is so informed, apply to a Mental Health Review Tribunal.

(3) On any application under sub-paragraph (2) above the tribunal shall, if satisfied that none of the conditions set out in paragraphs (*a*) and (*b*) of sub-paragraph (1) above are fulfilled, direct that the patient be discharged, and subsection (1) of section 72 of this Act shall have effect in relation to the application as if paragraph (*b*) of that subsection were omitted.

36. Any person who immediately before the commencement of this Act was deemed to have been named as the guardian of any patient under paragraph 14 of Schedule 6 to the Mental Health Act 1959 shall be deemed for the purposes of this Act to have been named as the guardian of the patient in an application for his reception into guardianship under Part II of this Act accepted on that person's behalf by the relevant local authority.

37.—(1) This paragraph applies to patients who immediately before the commencement of this Act were transferred patients within the meaning of paragraph 15 of Schedule 6 to the Mental Health Act 1959.

(2) A transferred patient who immediately before the commencement of this Act was by virtue of sub-paragraph (2) of that paragraph treated for the purposes of that Act as if he were liable to be detained in a hospital in pursuance of a direction under section 71 of that Act shall be treated as if he were so liable in pursuance of a direction under section 46 of this Act.

(3) A transferred patient who immediately before the commencement of this Act was by virtue of sub-paragraph (3) of that paragraph treated for the purposes of that Act as if he were liable to be detained in a hospital by virtue of a transfer direction under section 72 of that Act and as if a direction restricting his discharge had been given under section 74 of that Act shall be treated as if he were so liable by virtue of a transfer direction under section 47 of this Act and as if a restriction direction had been given under section 49 of this Act.

(4) Section 84 of this Act shall apply to a transferred patient who was treated by virtue of sub-paragraph (5) of that paragraph immediately before the commencement of this Act as if he had been removed to a hospital under section 89 of that Act as if he had been so removed under the said section 84.

(5) Any person to whom sub-paragraph (6) of that paragraph applied immediately before the commencement of this Act shall be treated for the purposes of this Act as if he were liable to be detained in a hospital in pursuance of a transfer direction given under section 48 of this Act and as if a restriction direction had been given under section 49 of this Act, and he shall be so treated notwithstanding that he is not suffering from a form of mental disorder mentioned in the said section 48.

38. Any patient who immediately before the commencement of this Act was treated by virtue of sub-paragraph (1) of paragraph 16 of Schedule 6 to the Mental Health Act 1959 as if he had been conditionally discharged under section 66 of that Act shall be treated as if he had been conditionally discharged under section 42 of this Act and any such direction as is mentioned in paragraph (*b*) of that sub-paragraph shall be treated as if it had been given under the said section 42.

39. Upon a restriction direction in respect of a patient who immediately before the commencement of this Act was a transferred patient within the meaning of paragraph 15 of Schedule 6 to the Mental Health Act 1959 ceasing to have effect, the responsible medical officer shall record his opinion whether the patient is suffering from mental illness, severe mental impairment, psychopathic disorder or mental impairment, and references in this Act to the form or forms of mental disorder specified in the relevant application, order or direction shall be construed as including references to the form or forms of mental disorder recorded under this paragraph or under paragraph 17 of the said Schedule 6.

40. A person who immediately before the commencement of this Act was detained by virtue of paragraph 19 of Schedule 6 to the Mental Health Act 1959 may continue to be detained until the expiration of the period of his treatment current on 1st November 1960 or until he becomes liable to be detained or subject to guardianship under this Act, whichever occurs first, and may be so detained in any place in which he might have been detained under that paragraph.

41. Any opinion recorded by the responsible medical officer under the foregoing provisions of this Schedule shall be recorded in such form as may be prescribed by regulations made by the Secretary of State.

42.—(1) In the foregoing provisions of this Schedule—

(*a*) references to the period of treatment of a patient that was current on 1st November 1960 are to the period for which he would have been liable to be detained or subject to guardianship by virtue of any enactment repealed or excluded by the Mental Health Act 1959, or any enactment repealed or replaced by any such enactment as aforesaid, being a period which began but did not expire before that date; and

(*b*) "the responsible medical officer" means—

(i) in relation to a patient subject to guardianship, the medical officer authorised by the local social services authority to act (either generally or in any particular case or for any particular purpose) as the responsible medical officer;

(ii) in relation to any other class of patient, the registered medical practitioner in charge of the treatment of the patient.

(2) Subsection (2) of section 34 of this Act shall apply for the purposes of the foregoing provisions of this Schedule as it applies for the purposes of Part II of this Act.

(3) The sentence or other period of detention of a person who was liable to be detained or subject to guardianship immediately before 1st November 1960 by virtue of an order under section 9 of the Mental Deficiency Act 1913 shall be treated for the purposes of the foregoing provisions of this Schedule as expiring at the end of the period for which that person would have been liable to be detained in a prison or other institution if the order had not been made.

(4) For the purposes of the foregoing provisions of this Schedule, an order sending a person to an institution or placing a person under guardianship made before 9th March 1956 on a petition presented under the Mental Deficiency Act 1913 shall be deemed to be valid if it was so deemed immediately before the commencement of this Act by virtue of section 148(2) of the Mental Health Act 1959.

43.—(1) Any order or appointment made, direction or authority given, or thing done which by virtue of paragraph 25 of Schedule 6 to the Mental Health Act 1959 had effect immediately before the commencement of this Act as if made, given or done under any provision of Part VIII of that Act shall have effect as if made, given or done under Part VII of this Act.

(2) Where at the commencement of this Act Part VIII of the Mental Health Act 1959 applied in any person's case by virtue of paragraph 25 of Schedule 6 to that Act as if immediately after the commencement of that Act it had been determined that he was a patient within the meaning of the said Part VIII, Part VII of this Act shall apply in his case as if immediately after the commencement of this Act it had been determined that he was a patient within the meaning of the said Part VII.

44. Where a person who immediately before 1st November 1960 was the committee of the estate of a person of unsound mind so found by inquisition was immediately before the commencement of this Act deemed by virtue of paragraph 26 of Schedule 6 to the Mental Health Act 1959 to be a receiver appointed under section 105 of that Act for that person, he shall be deemed to be a receiver appointed under section 99 of this Act for that person and shall continue to have the same functions in relation to that person's property and affairs as were exercisable by him immediately before the commencement of that Act as committee of the estate and references in any document to the committee of the estate of that person shall be construed accordingly.

45. Section 101(1) of this Act shall apply in relation to any disposal of property (within the meaning of that section) of a person living on 1st November 1960, being a disposal effected under the Lunacy Act 1890 as it applies in relation to the disposal of property of a person effected under Part VII of this Act.

46. For the purposes of section 15 of the National Health Service Reorganisation Act 1973 (preservation of certain boards of governors) any provision of this Act which corresponds to a provision amended by that Act shall be treated as if it were such a provision and any reference in any order for the time being in force under that section to such a provision shall have effect as if it were a reference to the corresponding provision of this Act.

DEFINITIONS
"Local social services authority": s.145(1).
"Approved social worker": s.145(1).

"Application for admission for treatment": ss.3, 145(1).
"Patient": s.145(1).
"Nearest relative": ss.26(3), 145(1).
"Hospital order": ss.37, 145(1).
"Transfer direction": ss.47, 145(1).
"Restriction order": ss.41, 145(1).
"Restriction direction": ss.49, 145(1).
"Mental disorder": ss.1, 145(1).
"Hospital": s.145(1).
"The managers": s.145(1).
"Severe mental impairment": ss.1, 145(1).
"Psychopathic disorder": ss.1, 145(1).
"Mental impairment": ss.1, 145(1).

GENERAL NOTE
This Schedule makes provision to cover the transition from the 1959 Act, as amended by the 1982 Act, to this Act. It therefore affects patients detained on or before the commencement date of this Act (September 30, 1983) and anything which was in the process of being done at that date.

Section 134   SCHEDULE 6

REPEALS

Chapter	Short title	Extent of repeal
7 & 8 Eliz. 2. c.72.	The Mental Health Act 1959.	Sections 1 to 5. Section 10. Section 22. Sections 25 to 35. Sections 37 to 43. Sections 45 to 60. Sections 62 to 68. Sections 70 to 76. Sections 80 and 81. Section 85. Section 87. Sections 89 and 90. Sections 92 to 96. Sections 99 to 119. Sections 121 to 126. Sections 129 and 130. Sections 132 and 133. Sections 135 to 141. In section 144, in subsection (1), paragraph (*b*). Section 145(2) Sections 147 and 148. Section 149(3) to (5). In section 150, the words from "section ten" to "section one hundred and forty one" and from "section one hundred and forty six" to "Schedules". In section 152, the words from "sections eighty-five" to "Northern Ireland by that section", from "section one hundred and twenty-nine" to "Schedules" and the words "Part II of the Seventh Schedule; Part II of the Eighth Schedule". Section 153. Schedule 1.

Chapter	Short title	Extent of repeal
		Schedule 3.
		Schedule 5.
		Schedule 6, except paragraph 15(4).
		In Schedule 7, in Part I the entry relating to sections 48 and 49 of the Fines and Recoveries Act 1833 and in Part II the entries relating to the Polish Resettlement Act 1947 and the USA Veterans' Pensions (Administration) Act 1949.
1960 c.61.	The Mental Health (Scotland) Act 1960.	Section 74.
		In Schedule 4, all the entries relating to the Mental Health Act 1959 except those relating to section 9 and Schedule 7.
1961 (N.I.) c.15.	The Mental Health Act (Northern Ireland) 1961.	In Schedule 5, paragraphs 1 to 4.
1964 c.84.	The Criminal Procedure (Insanity) Act 1964.	Section 4(7).
1965 c.2.	The Administration of Justice Act 1965.	In Schedule 1, the entry relating to the Mental Health Act 1959.
1968 c.20.	The Courts-Martial (Appeals) Act 1968.	In Schedule 4, the entry relating to the Mental Health Act 1959.
1968 c.49.	The Social Work (Scotland) Act 1968.	In Schedule 8, paragraphs 48 and 49.
1969 c.46.	The Family Law Reform Act 1969.	In Schedule 1 the entries relating to the Mental Health Act 1959.
1969 c.54.	The Children and Young Persons Act 1969.	In Schedule 5, paragraphs 38 to 40.
1969 c.58.	The Administration of Justice Act 1969.	Sections 17 to 19.
1970 c.42.	The Local Authority Social Services Act 1970.	In Schedule 1, the entry relating to the Mental Health (Amendment) Act 1982.
1971 c.23	The Courts Act 1971.	In Schedule 8, paragraph 38.
		In Part I of Schedule 9, the entry relating to the Mental Health Act 1959.
1971 c.77.	The Immigration Act 1971.	In section 30(2), the words from "and accordingly" onwards.
1972 c.70.	The Local Government Act 1972.	In Schedule 23, in paragraph 9, in sub-paragraph (1) the words "35, 56(2)(*c*) and 56(3)", in sub-paragraph (2) the words "10(1), 22, 27(2), 33, 34, 38(3), 40 to 43, 47(2), 52, 53, 59, 60" and "132", sub-paragraphs (4), (5) and (6).
1973 c.29.	The Guardianship Act 1973.	In section 1(8), the words from "and" to the end of the subsection.
1975 c.37.	The Nursing Homes Act 1975.	In Schedule 1, paragraphs 1 to 4.
1977 c.45.	The Criminal Law Act 1977.	In Schedule 6, the entry relating to section 130(3) of the Mental Health Act 1959.
1977 c.49.	The National Health Service Act 1977.	In section 105(3), the words "or the Mental Health Act 1959".
		In Schedule 15, paragraphs 23, 26 to 28, 30, 31 and 33.
1978 c.29.	The National Health Service (Scotland) Act 1978.	In paragraph 10(*b*) of Schedule 15, the figure "102".
1980 c.5.	The Child Care Act 1980.	In Schedule 5, paragraphs 13 and 14.
1980 c.43.	The Magistrates' Courts Act 1980.	In Schedule 7, paragraphs 31 and 32.
1980 c.53.	The Health Services Act 1980.	In Schedule 1, paragraph 13.

Chapter	Short title	Extent of repeal
1981 c.45.	The Forgery and Counter-feiting Act 1981.	Section 11(1).
1981 c.54.	The Supreme Court Act 1981.	Section 144. In Schedule 5, paragraph 2 and 3 of the entry relating to the Mental Health Act 1959. In Schedule 6, paragraph 4.
1981 c.61.	The British Nationality Act 1981.	In section 39(7) the words "section 90 of the Mental Health Act 1959 and".
1982 c.51.	The Mental Health (Amendment) Act 1982.	Sections 1 to 33. Sections 35 to 61. In section 63, subsection (1) and in subsection (2) the words from the beginning to "Act and". Section 64(1), (2), (3), (5) and (6). Section 66. Section 68(2) and (3). Section 69(2), (3), and (4). In section 70(2), the words "sections 35(1) and (2) and 64(6) above extend to Northern Ireland". Schedule 1. In Schedule 3, in Part I paragraphs 1 to 26, in paragraph 35 sub-paragraph (*a*), paragraphs 40, 42, 45 and 46, in paragraph 50 sub-paragraph (*a*), in paragraph 51 sub-paragraph (*a*), paragraphs 52 to 55, 57 and 58 and Part II. In Schedule 5, paragraphs 2 to 15.